REINVENTING TECHNOLOGY, REDISCOVERING COMMUNITY

Critical Explorations of Computing as a Social Practice

edited by

Philip E. Agre
University of California, San Diego

Douglas Schuler
Computer Professionals for Social Responsibility
Seattle Community Network Association

Ablex Publishing Corporation
Greenwich, Connecticut
London, England

Printed in the United States of America

Library of Congress Cataloging-in-Publication Data

Reinventing technology, rediscovering community : critical
    explorations of computing as a social practice / edited by Philip E.
    Agre and Douglas Schuler.
        p.   cm.
    Includes bibliographical references and index.
    ISBN 1-56750-258-X (cloth). — ISBN 1-56750-259-8 (pbk.)
    1. Computers—Social aspects. I. Agre, Philip. II. Schuler,
Douglas.
QA76.9.C66R47   1996
303.48'34—dc20   96–36613
                                                                        CIP

Ablex Publishing Corporation
P.O. Box 5297
55 Old post Road #2
Greenwich, CT 06831

Published in the U.K. and Europe by:
JAI Press Ltd.
38 Tavistock Street
Covent Garden
London WC2E 7PB
England

Contents

Preface

The seventeen papers collected in this book explore how computing technology has affected important social relations. Most of these papers were originally presented at the Directions and Implications of Advanced Computing (DIAC) conferences, hosted biannually since 1987 by Computer Professionals for Social Responsibility. CPSR is a national public-interest organization of computer scientists and others who are concerned about the uses and abuses of computer technology in society.

We wish to thank the authors for their cooperation in the editorial process and all of those who have organized, participated in, or attended the DIAC conferences. We would also like to especially acknowledge the Ethics and Values Office of the National Science Foundation for their support. We hope that these chapters will contribute to an informed, inclusive, and ongoing dialogue on the role of computers in society.

—Phillip E. Agre, pagre@ucsd.edu
Douglas Schuler, douglas@scn.org
October 1996

1

Computing as a
Social Practice

Philip E. Agre
University of California, San Diego

The chapters in this volume represent a broad range of theoretical and practical work over the last decade on the relationship between computer technology and society. They report numerous exemplary interventions within the technology, institutions, and policies around computing. This Introduction will offer a general analysis of their shared premise, which is that computer professionals can work within society for responsible applications of computer technology.

The very concept of working for socially responsible computing implies several things. It implies, first, that a special kind of work actually is necessary. Computer people bring an ordinary degree of responsibility to the daily practice of their profession, of course, and outside social mechanisms such as laws and markets promote and regulate the use of computing in their own ways. Yet these factors together have not produced all the potential social benefits of applied computing, and they have not prevented certain institutional pathologies. Another implication is that computer professionals can, by departing from usual ways of doing things, actually ameliorate these problems. Doing so, whether as part of one's paid employment or on one's own time, amounts to a type of social activism whose relation to existing practices may not be simple.

One might approach the concept of socially responsible computing in a variety of ways, for example, through ethical philosophy (Johnson & Snapper, 1985), but my own analysis of them will be primarily sociological in nature. Some of the relevant questions include

- What, in social terms, *is* computing technology, and how does this technology condition the ways people use it in society?
- How does the historical development of the computer profession shape attitudes and approaches toward social activism in the present day?
- What are the possibilities and limits of activism for socially responsible computing, and how are these influenced by the technology itself and by the institutions that have defined it?

These are large questions, and it will not be possible to provide final answers to them. Nonetheless, a brief consideration of them may provide some orientation to a new generation of computer professionals who wish to connect theory with practice in actively shaping the future of computing.

It is not obvious to many people that social activism aimed at shaping the use of computing by society is even feasible. Many skeptics have asked, how is it even possible to predict the future of computing and its place in society? After all, the technology continues to change at a tremendous rate, and the interactions between emerging technologies and evolving social institutions are difficult to define after they have happened, much less years beforehand. Moreover, as Winner (1986) points out, scenarios that connect technical advances to anticipated political changes have frequently relied on facile equations between information, knowledge, power, and democracy. This is a serious objection, and it should provoke reflection on the nature and goals of social activism around computing. Yet the business of prediction seems less overwhelming when placed in the context of the many continuities across four decades of computing technologies. Some of these continuities are technical, for example the von Neumann register-transfer model of computer processing. Others pertain to the design process, for example the use of special languages to represent data flows in the dominant traditions of systems analysis. And others are institutional, such as the basic structures of society and the legal and economic underpinnings of the industries that employ computing technology. All of these things of course are capable of change, but their historical development and persistence seem amenable to investigation. Social activism that intervenes in the institutions of technology can be guided by explanations of such things, and can provide an occasion for testing and refining explanations of them as well.

Other arguments are more concrete. Social activism by computer people has had considerable influence, though the stories are not often told. Lee Felsenstein, for example, originated some of the basic concepts of both personal computers and community networking as part of a project to mechanize the maintenance of telephone-based bulletin boards by activists (Freiberger & Swaine 1984). In doing so he may not have predicted in detailed the profound changes in the computer industry that personal computing would later bring, but his philosophy of democratic computing has had a lasting influence nonetheless, and the Community Memory Project (see the chapter by Farrington & Pine) was an early model for an explosion of community networking activity in the last few years. Another example might be found in the participatory design movement, which originated in Scandinavia as a collaboration between unionists and academic computer scientists with an interest in democratic processes for developing technical systems (Bodker, 1991). It is not certain whether this movement will spread in the United States beyond universities and industrial research centers (Schuler & Namioka, 1993), but the difficulty of predicting technology is at most a minor determinant of the movement's success.

Even beyond these examples, though, the project of socially responsible computing is aligned with much larger trends in the use of computing in society. So long as computing was confined to laboratories or to the automation of existing work tasks, nobody had to give much consideration to the interactions between computing technology and social institutions. As Friedman (1989) points out, computer systems development researchers spent their first few decades working out basic algorithms, learning to define technical specifications for programs, and fashioning good user interfaces. Only now that those three problems have been provisionally solved has the even greater problem of integrating computers into the workings of organizations begun its difficult movement into the mainstream of information technology research (Kling, 1993). This latter-day emphasis on the human dimensions of computing draws on many sources, some of which have more fully articulated visions of socially responsible technology than others (Weizenbaum, 1976; Kling, 1980). Nevertheless, the broadening of vision that social activists have promoted—from a technology focus to a technology-and-society focus—has proven necessary across a broad range of institutions and professions, as the difficulties of integrating technology with the human problems of organization have become more obtrusive.

Despite their diversity, the chapters in this volume are united by their common pursuit of this broadened vision of technology as a social phenomenon. The authors' approaches can be neatly classified into the categories of criticism and construction. Critical chapters use theories from sociology, economics, law, and other fields to describe computing as it is now, in the fullness of the institutionally structured situations in which it is actually encountered. Constructive chapters report projects to create computer systems that operate on alternative premises, including the lessons learned in submitting these systems to use by people in complex human environments. The purpose of this Introduction, though, is not to encourage this distinction between critical and constructive styles of research, but rather to sketch a wide range of considerations that affect efforts to integrate these two styles. How can system designers take critical theories of computing into account in constructing and fielding real systems? And how can theorists paint conceptual pictures of computing in society that are responsive to the needs of practitioners while also challenging the implicit assumptions that the practices have inherited from technical tradition?

We are only beginning to appreciate the enormity of these questions. Analyses like those of Kling, for example, are exposing the many layers of unreflective habit that shape contemporary discourses on computing, including some discourses that are motivated by critical social projects. What is more, the widespread deployment of distributed computer technology is starting to challenge some of the most basic categories of social thought. For example, as Davis and Stack and Dandekar point out, it is not at all obvious what it means to speak of information as property. As a result, one of the basic concepts of common law is suddenly up for renegotiation. Concepts of community and knowledge are also challenged by the ideas and practices around computing. As these concepts expand their scope, do we necessarily lose our appreciation for the rich human phenomena to which they once exclusively applied? Clearly, the issues at stake are social and cultural as well as technical.

The remainder of this Introduction explores these issues in the following way in successive sections:

It sketches some of the large-scale economic issues that provide the background for work on socially responsible computing, starting with the notion that computerization is the occasion for another industrial revolution.

It recounts two historical traditions of social action in science and technology. Each of these traditions has had a considerable influence over attitudes toward social issues among scientists and technologists to the present day.

It describes certain aspects of the institutional organization of computer work, and particularly the predicament of the computer professional. These structural factors also play important roles in shaping computer professionals' understandings of the political issues that bear on their work.

It presents some of the critique of computer work that research has developed over the last decade. The orientation to technical problems, it has been claimed, constantly threatens to foreshorten computer professionals' awareness of the human environments in which their systems will be used.

It moves into these contexts of computer use, tracing the difficulties inherent in attempts to understand these contexts in ways that acknowledge the complexity and specificity of their technical and social aspects alike.

It builds on these analyses by describing the situation of the activist for socially responsible computing, who must simultaneously confront some deeply contested social boundaries and build the alliances that become possible as computing begins to affect the lives of numerous social groups. Yet, although the future remains as hard to predict as ever, the increasing pervasiveness of computing in society means that activism around technology increasingly becomes coextensive with social change work in general. No longer a specialized concern, computing becomes both an indispensable tool and a facet of every particular site of human practice.

THE ECONOMIC BACKGROUND

It is commonly asserted that computer technology is bringing a new industrial revolution or the rise of an information economy qualitatively different in its rules than before (Drucker, 1993). Although perhaps hyperbolic, these assertions do challenge us to articulate more precisely the nature of the structural changes that the application of information technology is making possible. Claims for a new industrial revolution are mistaken in at least one sense: except for the computer industry itself and certain parts of banking and finance, the United States is not witnessing anything like the tremendous growth of productivity that the rise of national distribution systems made possible in the late nineteenth century (Chandler, 1977; Strassman, 1990; Kling & Dunlop, 1993). Rapidly expanding use of computer technology has not led to spectacular improvements in the price or quality of food, clothing, housing, or transportation. Nonetheless, computing has become remarkably pervasive across functions and industries throughout the economy. Compared with a milling machine, which makes a readily measurable contribution to the efficiency of specific types of manufacturing, computers are extraordinarily plastic, capable of being fitted to the needs of an enormous range of productive activities. As a result, it is hard to make definite statements about the role that information technology is playing in the undeniably profound changes that are taking place in the global economy.

Davis and Stack begin their analysis of these questions by noting the special properties of information. Unlike sandwiches and steel, information that has been created and captured in some digital medium can be replicated in unlimited quantities for a negligible cost. This fact has a wide variety of implications, depending on what the information in question represents. Robot programming that captures the movements that human beings perform in building a car, for example, can easily be put to work in factories around the world. Likewise, information about new techniques of efficient production can just as easily be transferred to all of the other sites where it is applicable. Finally, software that might have been written by a large team at great expense can be distributed to ten users or ten million for only a small increment in cost, so that its market price bears little systematic relationship to its costs of production. As a result, participants in a market economy are never certain what to do with digitized information. As a result, Davis and Stack argue, information actually tends to subvert a market economy. At a minimum, as Dandekar points out, the subtleties of information call for a fundamental re-examination of the nature of property and ownership.

Davis and Stack join other scholars (e.g., Reich, 1991) in arguing that the pervasive application of computing is contributing to a stratification of the workforce, with a growing economic gap between those who manipulate information and those who manipulate physical materials or interact with people in routinized service encounters. Information technology contributes to this type of social division in several ways. By making it easy to move information instantaneously across large distances, for example, technology makes it easier for firms to relocate industrial activities that produce or consume information. Information technology is also contributing to greatly sophisticated logistical systems that permit activities to be coordinated globally while increasing centralized control of farflung operations. Each of these trends helps intensify wage competition among geographically dispersed groups of workers. Some types of information work, such as highly structured computer programming, are also subject to these changes. But many kinds of information work consist of unique and complex activities that are hard to routinize, and the people who have the skills to engage in this kind of work have successfully maintained their relatively prosperous position in the labor market.

The scope and magnitude of these phenomena pose considerable challenges to would-be activists for socially responsible computing. Yet the easy replication of digitized information is a powerful resource for social activism as well. If a computer program is useful to ordinary people, for example, then distributing it for free on global computer networks can affect many people's lives in a sort period with little effort. As Davis and Stack noted, many programmers have experimented with alternative means of distributing their work, for example, with remuneration depending on good faith and the ability to pay. Another common practice is to distribute a basic version of a program for free and to provide more advanced features and support services to customers who are willing to pay. Activists have also put tremendous effort into creating free and low-cost global computer networks, for example, the simple store-and-forward mechanisms employed by BITNET, Usenet, and Fidonet (Quarterman, 1990) and the local community networks described by Schuler, Resnick and King, and Farrington and Pine. In each case, the goal is to put the easy replicability of information to work for ordinary people by creating a cheap digital medium of communication.

SCIENTISTS, ENGINEERS, AND SOCIAL RESPONSIBILITY

Although the metaphysics of information in the global economy defines the background for any attempts at social activism, it does little to explain the actual history of activism within the computer profession. Computing is an engineering profession (Johnson, 1990), and certain historical continuities between computing and earlier engineering disciplines are readily apparent. As professions go, engineering stands out for its relatively low degree of autonomy, and the computer profession is particularly extreme in this regard. Physicians and attorneys, for example make their own rules and police their own ranks to a considerable extent, but the professional societies of engineering have done little to define the conditions of engineering work. Noble (1977) argues that the reasons for this can be found in the historical origins of the engineering professions in the early twentieth century. Influenced more by the values of their employers than by guild traditions like those of medicine and law, engineers were generally willing to apply to themselves the same instrumentalism that they brought to the technical problems of their daily work (cf. Meiksins, 1988). If computer professionals in particular have largely avoided the experience of systematic deskilling depicted by Kraft (1977), the reason, as Friedman (1989) makes clear in his critique, is not to be found in the strength of their professional organizations but in the disruptions brought by continual changes in the technology itself.

However, engineers have not lacked conceptions of society and their place in it. Quite the contrary, the founding of the American engineering professions during the Progressive Era was a deeply and self-consciously political process. Frederick Taylor, for example, viewed time studies of work as a program of social amelioration in the context of serious conflicts over the organization of work (Nelson & Taylor, 1980). If the engineer were to discover, by scientific means, the "one best way" to organize a given industrial process, he reasoned, then surely nothing would be left to fight about. Although Taylor himself was hardly regarded as a spokesman by the engineering profession as a whole (Noble, 1977), the engineer's position as an objective referee standing outside of social conflicts was an important theme in US culture throughout the first half of the century (Banta, 1993).

The foremost philosopher of this movement was Veblen (1921). In a period when the very practicability of capitalism was uncertain, Veblen contrasted two principles of economic organization: the "price system" run by financiers who did no real work and much damage, and the rational operation of industry by engineers. Although drawing upon—indeed, creating—popular caricatures about the rich and their speculation and consumption, Veblen was by no means a populist or socialist. His focus was on the productive infrastructure and his utopia was not based on property or class by on reason. This philosophy, which was by no means limited to Veblen himself (Layton, 1971), took a whole series of cultural forms, eventually including the strange Technocracy movement with its fetishistic symbolism of technical order (Ross, 1991). Social activists often wonder why it is so difficult to involve engineers in their campaigns; one reason is surely that engineering is *already* a utopian social project.

Although engineering no longer plays the same role in US culture that it played during the 1920s, the events of this period shaped engineering in many ways. In particular, engineering came to be understood within a series of binary oppositions: order versus chaos, reason versus emotion, mathematics versus language, technology versus society, and so forth. As a result, engineers have often viewed moral appeals to social responsibility as a disruptive force, alien to the nature of their work (Florman, 1978). In place of these ideals of individual choice and the tacit conventions of tradition, engineering has sought to institute a form of reasoning that is objective because it is external; the rationale behind a technical design can be laid out on paper and argued through in a public way, at least within the community of engineers and their expertise. This reasoning is instrumental; starting with a problem to be solved, it does not question the problem but simply seeks the demonstrably most efficient means of solving it. Its claims to social authority lie not in the choice of problems but in the methods for their solution.

A different tradition of social concern about technology grew out of World War II, most especially the development of the atomic bomb. Many of the bomb's inventors were disturbed by its use on civilian populations, and they set about articulating an ethical protest that had a broad influence throughout the cold war. By the 1980s this tradition led to a relatively small but highly visible movement of scientists and engineers who refused to work on projects related to the military, either in general or specifically weapons research.

This ethical movement understands its dilemma and its responsibilities in a specific way. Its focus is on dangerous technologies or on evil uses of technology, and its question is whether to participate in the development of such technologies and "where to draw the line." The technologies themselves are given, having been defined by others, and are beyond individual control. The primary focus is on individual choices rather than larger collective movements, on public statements rather than broad-based organizing, and on the refusal to do bad rather than the positive obligation to do good.

This type of ethical concern about technology has been applied widely and made into a framework for formulating social choices about technologies such as nuclear power. Marx's chapter is a good representative of this tradition. Although not specifically concerned with military technologies, his starting point is the framing of ethical choices about a given technology, and his aim is a rigorous and searching clarification of thinking, diagnosing fallacies and ensuring that the broadest range of considerations is taken into account. Similar ideas were influential in the founding in 1981 of Computer Professionals for Social Responsibility, whose first major campaigns concerned the use of computer technology in controversial military research and development projects such as the Strategic Computing Initiative and Strategic Defense Initiative.

Yet despite its honorable inheritance, the ethical choice framework fails to appeal to many computer professionals. The connections between individual professionals' work projects and the claims of evil consequences are often distant and diffused, and the negative notion of refraining from work does not appeal to practical-minded engineers nearly as much as a positive agenda might. Another, deeper factor is the conception of engineering reason as something apart from, or above, social conflicts. It is difficult to conceive of arguments for refraining from engineering when engineering is conceived in this way.

COMPUTER PROFESSIONALS

The ideology that computer professionals have inherited from the broader engineering profession, then, has both a majority and a minority tradition. The majority tradition views engineering not simply as socially neutral but as a positively millenarian creation of order from social chaos. The minority tradition views certain kinds of engineering work as complicit with evils that engineers cannot control. Neither of these traditions, however, suffices to describe the experience of contemporary computer professionals. This experience is profoundly shaped by the dynamics of the labor market.

The most important feature of the market for computer work is the continual, rapid change in the technology. Computer professionals do well financially in good times, but they are aware that their continued success depends on maintaining a range of up-to-date skills. Employers, by contrast, have an interest in hiring employees whose skills run deep in a particular area. This tension has pervasive consequences for the culture of the computer industry. Lacking a guild-like system of collective control over the market supply of technical skill, computer professionals must individually place continual "bets" on the direction that the industry is taking, choosing jobs and undertaking training courses that will position them adequately in the labor market of a few years hence. The size and complexity of the computer industry, as well as the microspecialization of computer skills in the marketplace, reinforces a sense of the industry as autonomous and uncontrollable when viewed from any given individual's perspective—something to be predicted and accommodated rather than collectively chosen.

An enormous and highly developed discourse spins around this endless project of prediction. Much of this discourse is esoteric in nature, as engineers debate which technical standard (e.g., for wireless data transmission) is "the way to go". On one level these debates are matters of pure engineering reason, as the tradeoffs inherent in different technical approaches are compared and weighed. On another, deeper level, however, often not sharply distinguished from the first, these debates are about the direction of something much larger—a market whose interacting elements include as much finance and marketing and law as technical rationality. In addition to their predictive function, these debates produce self-fulfilling prophecies, inasmuch as the success of a technical standard depends on the emergence of a critical mass of parties willing to adopt it (Davidow, 1986). Entrepreneurs, as one might expect, are masters of the discourse of market prediction, but it is also a well-cultivated necessity throughout the industry. As technical possibilities grow and multiply, this discourse begins to draw on a wide range of resources, particularly science fiction, and whole discursive worlds of psychological and sociological speculation develop. The process is remarkably volatile, and a technological and discursive fashion such as "virtual reality" can develop from novel coinage to enormous metaphorical elaboration to wholesale dismissal as yesterday's fad to modestly successful occupant of niche markets in a period of a few years. In the meantime, sizeable companies will rise and possibly fall, considerable investments will be made and perhaps liquidated, and numerous bets about tomorrow's marketable skills will be placed and won or lost.

In this context it is easy to understand Kling's observations concerning the proliferation of utopian writing about information technology. As business managers have been compelled to face the complexities of organizational computing, though, this hyperbole has become mixed in many ways with genuinely sophisticated ideas. This can be seen, for example, in the proliferation of books by management consultants about the novel organizational forms made possible be emerging technologies for distributed computing (Davis, 1987; Quinn, 1992; Walton, 1989). These books increasingly attend to the communicative dimension of system implementation, inasmuch as resistance by users is often a real threat to the systems' success (Agre, 1995). At the same time, the profound sense of technics-out-of-control (Winner, 1977) has also given rise within computer culture to a proliferation of dystopian narratives about electronic surveillance and other types of repression. It is striking, for example, that the full range of these narratives can routinely be found, all equally hyperbolic in their rhetoric despite their superficially opposite politics, in publications such a *Wired* magazine. The ideological libertarianism reflected in *Wired* is a recent development in the computer profession, but it is wholly understandable in the context of the profession's narratives of individualism, rational progress, technological determinism, and the autonomous development of the market.

Of course, the professional ideologies that have been shaped by the market for computer skills are not completely hegemonic. The Association for Computing Machinery, for example, has developed a Code of Ethics and Professional Conduct that encourages the socialization of computer professionals within various canons of professional responsibility (Anderson, Johnson, Gotterbarn, & Perolle, 1993). Moreover, numerous individuals have acquired computer skills because of the relative freedom that many kinds of computer work provide; contract programming pays the bills for independent projects by numerous artists, musicians, and political activists. The point, rather, is that the computer profession as such has not experienced itself as capable of collective choice or action. Instead, it has more commonly identified itself with an impersonal historical process that it cannot predict but that it nonetheless basically trusts.

COMPUTER WORK

In their work, then, computer people are specialists, building the particular types of hardware and software that lie within their domain of expertise. In order to apply their specialized expertise to real situations in the world, computer people need those situations to be packaged into discrete problems—problems that their particular techniques can be expected to solve. To be a computer person is to possess a certain repertoire of specialized hammers and to be constantly looking out for nails to hit with them. This does not reflect any narrowness of mind or other such deficiency; it simply reflects the institutional organization of the skills. The institutions of computer work are arranged to match computer professionals with problems they can solve, and much of the skill of computer science research is to discover or devise a series of problems that permit existing techniques to be extended, one step at a time, into new territory.

As a result of these phenomena, the specialization of computer work poses significant challenges to computer professionals who would wish to apply their skills in socially beneficial ways. Given the fragmentation of technical work and the distance between individual engineers and the consequences of their work, it is extremely difficult to translate a large social concern such as poverty or inequality or gender relations into a technical problem that demands one's own specific skills (cf. Ladd, 1982). Calls for social responsibility sound unreasonable or arbitrary to many computer people because they seem to bear no clear relationship to the definition of technical problems, or to the institutions that match problems to the people who can solve them. Moreover, when computer people do present examples of system design as social activism, such as several of the chapters in this book, the technologies involved often turn out to be relatively simple—far from the "cutting edge" where computer professionals must invest their effort in order for their skills to remain marketable. This is a significant obstacle to efforts to broaden the socially responsible computing movement. The most significant exception lies on the subfield of human–computer interaction, whose core value of usability is readily framed as both a social justice issue and an imperative of the mass market for personal computers (Adler & Winograd, 1992; Shneiderman, 1992; Nardi, 1993).

Other aspects of computing work have led to criticism by social scientists and activists. Most large computer systems are built by teams of these specialists, and computer people and their managers have developed numerous methods of coordinating all of this complex activity. These structured relationships among computer professionals are an important part of their daily work. However, computer professionals have another set of significant relationships as well—to the people who will use their systems. These relationships have been deeply influenced by the history of engineering. The task of a systems analyst, for example, is to investigate some existing work practices, for example in a billing office, and represent these practices in a way that can be replicated in the programming of a computer. The methods of systems analysis thus are continuous, historically, with other forms of work automation practiced by earlier generations of engineers. These methods differ, however, in that computer software can easily be replicated in computers and robots across the world. As Davis and Stack point out, this continuity may have profound effects on the economics of work.

Computer system design has certainly grown more complex and varied since the early days of systems analysis. The larger point, though, is that system design requires computer professionals to make representations of people's activities. These representations might be largely informal, for example when designers talk among themselves about what users are likely to do with a system. But even when informal methods are used, at some point it is necessary to make technical decisions and actually start building things. As a result, every system incorporates certain assumptions about the users and about the larger network of human activities within which the system will be used.

Critiques of computer work have often focused on these built-in assumptions. Gray, for example, identifies a long list of assumptions that were built into the US military's Aegis missile defense system. Although the system seems to have performed correctly according to its technical specification, nonetheless it can be viewed as incorporating ideas about battle situations that did not correspond to reality on the day that a US ship shot down a Iranian civilian airliner in the Persian Gulf. Sheridan and Zeltzer demonstrate the contrast between the transparent immersion promised by the metaphors of "virtual reality" and the many opaque features of actual systems. Suchman and Jordan take this critique further, arguing that systems analysts who study women's work often overlook much of its complexity since they restrict their observations to aspects of the work that can be readily articulated in formal terms, leaving out all of the tacit knowledge that local communities of workers have built up over time. This trend can lead to misguided decisions about which activities to automate (just because an activity goes smoothly doesn't mean it can be mechanized) and to poorly designed systems that do not stand up to the complexities and variations of the actual tasks. These authors all argue that problematic assumptions built into a system lead to trouble later on, and that detailed study of the trouble can lead to insights about the design processes and their limitations.

CONTEXTS OF USE

As these examples illustrate, the empirical study of actual contexts of computer use has played an important role in the development of theory and activism around socially responsible computing. These contexts of use can be analyzed on several levels. Bromley, for example, directs attention to the institutions that adopt computers. Observing a series of "stubborn tendencies" in the use of computers, he asks where these tendencies come from. They are probably not inherent in the machinery itself, as is evident from the innovative uses of computing reported in this book. Yet they are not wholly independent of the machinery itself, since computing machinery has been shaped in many ways by the special types of thinking and working of its creators. Rather than explain the stubborn tendencies of computer use in purely social or purely technical terms, Bromley offers ways of thinking about the historical role of institutions in shaping both the technology and the ways it is used. This approach is congruent with a broad tradition in the social studies of science (MacKenzie & Wajcman, 1985; Latour, 1987) which seeks to erase the distinction between "technology" and "society" and replace them both with useful hybrid concepts.

Kling offers another way of thinking about the social embedding of computer use, tracing the social "webs" that connect computer users with fellow users, managers, designers, maintainers, and many others. The design of any complex computer system will reflect an equally complex social process of alliance-building, frequently organized within a larger social movement for computerization. Both Bromley and Kling emphasize that this technosocial style of research goes significantly beyond the neat apposition between technical utopianism, with its visions of social good produced by new technologies, and technical dystopianism, with its equally simple visions of social evil produced by the same technologies. The point is not to split the difference but rather to erase the distinctions and replace them with concepts that are more responsive to the reality one discovers in actual, empirically studied contexts of computer use.

Empirical studies of actual contexts of computer use have also been central to computer professionals' attempts to redefine computing in socially responsible ways. This trend is illustrated by several of the chapters in this book—those concerned with communities and networking, whether in local community networks or in on-line network communities. Computer networking has been a natural technology for activists, inasmuch as it permits people to organize new kinds of relationships without the fixed structures and procedures that have been imposed by many computer systems developed for use in particular work sites. Beyond their concern with computer networking, however, the projects reported here also share a commitment to learning through use—permitting groups of users to explore the system's possibilities, watching what they do, and interacting with them. The results of these projects are both technical and social. They include insights about which mechanisms are most useful, but these insights are meaningless except in the larger social context: which policies, which conflict-resolution tactics, and which ways of involving the users in the whole process are most useful. Schuler's paper in particular attempts to summarize these insights in a way that can allow others to replicate the early successes. If it is difficult to articulate the specifically technical results of these projects then that is precisely the point.

The chapters that report these projects are helpful both in their anecdotes and in their ability to distill generalizations and advice from a mass of accumulated experience. But this experience has often been difficult to obtain. Computer professionals who wish to assist particular social groups, as for example, in the case of Resnick and King's work in an economically depressed Boston neighborhood, must overcome all of the barriers that have historically kept those groups away from a deeper involvement in technology. The Berkeley Community Memory Project, likewise, placed its terminals in public places where nontechnical people go, and this meant that they had to face numerous issues that do not arise when computer systems are deployed in controlled work environments. In each case, the systems' success depended on the designers' evolving knowledge of how the systems might fit into the larger fabric of the people's lives.

Experiments with on-line communities drew on a population of users who already had some involvement with computing, but they had to face an unprecedented complexity of interactions among the users as the collective life of the community unfolded. Concepts of identity, civility, and community were suddenly transformed beyond recognition—and not just in a theoretical way, but in a way that the system maintainers and the users themselves had to work with daily. System maintainers like Coate and Curtis have been, in many ways, rediscovering the basics of democracy as they negotiate the social contract that balances individual freedom and social harmony while confronting a whole range of social distinctions and divisions.

All of these studies point the way toward an enormous intellectual and practical challenge: reformulating ideas about the interactions between computing machinery and social processes in ways that depend on nontrivial ideas about both of them. Schuler, for example, argues that a community networking project requires attention both to computer architecture and to the social architecture around it. Likewise, Resnick and King present a rationale for their telephone-based bulletin-board system that is grounded in community activists' ideas about knowledge and community that predate computing.

How can this integration of social and technical ideas be extended, and how can they influence both social and technical practices? For example, if we believe that various communities differ significantly in their cultures and social structures, then it might follow that these communities require equally disparate types of computing machinery. How deep should these difference run? Do different communities need different interfaces, or different underlying system metaphors, or different operating systems, or different hardware architectures? The answers to these questions are important because they determine the extent to which hardware and software developed for one context can usefully be shared with people in other contexts. But the questions themselves cannot be explored abstractly. Instead, system designers need to retain a living sense of their technical options, including options not normally valued or explored.

ACTIVISM

As these considerations make clear, activists for socially responsible computing are forever traversing difficult borders. These borders are comprised precisely of the dichotomies that have defined engineering, and even though these dichotomies may not be tenable they are often well defended: emotional vindications of reason, chaos induced by attempts to impose order, solidarity in defense of individualism, and so forth. Durlach makes these barriers the object of his artistic investigations, and they have forced many others to engage in constant improvisations in their professional relationships. Other barriers are institutional: between universities and city streets, laboratories and work sites, technical and nontechnical disciplines, and so forth again. These institutional barriers present opportunities as well as hazards—the trouble they cause is real and not abstract, and effective means of bridging them will often have broader applications. The community-building projects reported in this volume, for example, have been extraordinarily influential, as their experiences have contributed to rapidly growing movements both in commercial systems and in systems built by other activists for other purposes.

Perhaps the most fundamental challenge for computer activism is the creation of broader coalitions with people outside the computer profession. These coalitions must seek issues that articulate common interests across a range of geographical or professional communities, and they must identify styles of collective action that bridge the gaps between technical complexities and people's lives. The atmosphere for this kind of coalition-building has improved considerably in the last several years, simply through the spread of computers. As Agre points out, the broad social distribution of computing technology immediately creates common interests, if only the interest in keeping the computers working. These common interests are expressed in various kinds of collective action. Some, like local computer societies and e-mail discussion groups, are relatively organized, whereas others are more informal. As computing technology becomes more deeply consequential for the organization of work in various professions, such as librarianship, education, nursing, social work, and law, other types of common interests arise as well.

It is commonly held that much of our society's life will be conducted someday soon through the mediation of computing and networking. If this is true then a fundamental common interest arises, which has often been formulated in terms of equity of access to technology. Although this formulation has important limitations, it has nonetheless served as the basis for impressive coalition-building. In the United States, the Communication Act of 1994, which failed in the final moments of the Senate's calendar despite broad bipartisan support, contained a number of provisions that had brought together a wide range of organizations. Many of these groups coordinated their political efforts on a national level through the Telecommunications Policy Roundtable (1994), and similar coordination groups have been formed in some local areas as well.

Other projects, too varied to enumerate here, are proceeding on other fronts. These include projects to build women's spaces on the Internet and other network venues, as well as efforts to explore and articulate a distinctive women's approach to network-based interactions (Shade, 1994). They also include remarkably successful movements to make public information available on the net. Research originating in Scandinavia, already mentioned, has sought to democratize the process of system design, discovering along the way the profound interconnection of issues that connects technology activism with other types of social action. The authors in this volume have contributed in a wide variety of substantive ways to projects like these. However, they have also contributed in less tangible ways by providing models of socially concerned critical and constructive research on the place of technology in society. A great deal remains to be done, but these projects represent a start.

ACKNOWLEDGMENTS

This Introduction has benefited from comments by Harold Driscoll, Alexander Glockner, Rob Kling, and Doug Schuler.

REFERENCES

Adler, P. S., & Winograd, T. A. (Eds.). (1992). *Usability: Turning technologies into tools.* New York: Oxford University Press.

Agre, P. E. (1995). Conceptions of the user in computer systems design, in Thomas, P. (Ed.), *Social and Interactional dimensions of human-computer interfaces.* Cambridge University Press.

Anderson, R. E., Johnson, D. G., Gotterbarn, D., & Perolle, J. (1993). Using the new ACM Code of Ethics in decision making. *Communications of the ACM 36*(2), 98–107.

Banta, M. (1993). *Taylored lives: Narrative productions in the age of Taylor, Veblen, and Ford.* Chicago: University of Chicago Press.

Bodker, S. (1991). *Through the interface: A human activity approach to user interface design.* Hillsdale, NJ: Erlbaum.

Chandler, A. D., Jr. (1977). *The visible hand: The managerial revolution in American business.* Cambridge: Harvard University Press.

Davidow, W. H. (1986). *Marketing high technology: An insider's view.* New York: Free Press.

Davis, S. M. (1987). *Future perfect.* Reading, MA: Addison-Wesley.

Derber, C. (1982). *Professionals as workers: Mental labor in advanced capitalism.* Boston: G. K. Hall.

Drucker, P. F. (1993). *Post-capitalist society.* New York: HarperBusiness.

Florman, S. C. (1971). Moral blueprints: On regulating the ethics of engineers. *Harper's 257*(10), 30–33.

Freiberger, P. & Swaine, M. (1984). *Fire in the valley: The making of the personal computer.* Berkeley: Osborne/McGraw-Hill.

Friedman, A. L. (1989). *Computer systems development: History, organization and implementation.* Chichester, UK: Wiley.

Johnson, D. G. (1990). The social responsibility of computer professionals. *The Journal of Computing and Society 1*(2), 107–118.

Johnson, D. G. & Snapper, J. W. (Eds.). (1995). *Ethical issues in the use of computers.* Belmont, CA: Wadsworth.

Kling, R. (1980). Social analyses of computing: Theoretical perspectives in recent empirical research. *Computing Surveys 12*(1), 61–110.

Kling, R. (1993). Organizational analysis in computer science. *The Information Society 9*(2), 71–87.

Kling, R. & Dunlop, C. (1993). Controversies about computerization and the character of white collar worklife. *The Information Society 9*(1), 1–30.

Kraft, P. (1977). *Programmers and managers: The routinization of computer programming in the United States.* New York: Springer-Verlag.

Ladd, J. (1982). Collective and individual moral responsibility in engineering: Some questions. *IEEE Technology and Society Magazine 1*(2), 3–10.

Latour, B. (1987). *Science in action: How to follow scientists and engineers through society.* Cambridge: Harvard University Press.

Layton, E. T., Jr. (1971). *The revolt of the engineers: Social responsibility and the American engineering profession.* Cleveland: Case Western University Press.

MacKenzie, D. & Wajcman, J. (Eds.). (1995). *The social shaping of technology: How the refrigerator got its hum.* Milton Keynes: Open University Press.

Meiksins, P. (1988). The "revolt of the engineers" reconsidered. *Technology and Culture 29*(2), 219–246.

Nardi, B. A. (1993). *A small matter of programming: Perspectives on end user computing.* Cambridge: MIT Press.

Nelson, D., & Taylor, F. W. (1980). *The rise of scientific management.* Madison: University of Wisconsin Press.

Noble, D. F. (1977). *America by design: Science, technology, and the rise of corporate capitalism.* New York: Knopf.

Quarterman, J. (1990). *The matrix: Computer networks and conferencing systems worldwide.* Bedford, NA: Digital Press.

Quinn, J. B. (1992). *Intelligent enterprise: A knowledge and service based paradigm for industry.* New York: Free Press.

Reich, R. B. (1991). *The work of nations: Preparing ourselves for 21st-century capitalism.* New York: Knopf.

Ross, A. (1991). Getting out of the Gernsback continuum, in *Strange weather: Culture, science, and technology in the age of limits.* London: Verso.

Schuler, D., & Namioka, A. (Eds.). (19913). *Participatory design: Principles and Practices.* Hillsdale, NJ: Erlbaum.

Shade, L. R. (1994). Gender issues in computer networking, (Adam, A., Emms, J., Green, E., & Owen, J., Eds.), in *Women, work and computerization: Breaking old boundaries, building new forms* (pp. 91–100). Amsterdam: Elsevier.

Shneiderman, B. (1992). *Designing the user interface: Strategies for effective human-computer interaction* (2nd ed.), Reading, MA: Addison-Wesley.

Strassman, P. A. (1990). *The business value of computers; An executive's guide.* New Canaan, CT: Information Economics Press.

Telecommunications Policy Roundtable (1994). Renewing the commitment to a public interest telecommunications policy. *Communications of the ACM 37*(1), 196–108.

Veblen, T. (1921). *The engineers and the price system.* New York: Viking Press.

Walton, R. E. (1989). *Up and running: integrating information technology and the organization.* Boston: Harvard Business School Press.

Weizenbaum, J. (1976). *Computer power and human reason: From judgment to calculation.* San Francisco: Freeman.

Winner, L. (1977). *Autonomous technology: Technics-out-of-control as a theme in political thought.* Cambridge: MIT Press.

Winner, L. (1986). *The whale and the reactor: A search for limits in an age of high technology.* Chicago: University of Chicago Press.

2

Reading "All About" Computerization: How Genre Conventions Shape Nonfiction Social Analysis

Rob Kling

Indiana University

DISCOURSES ABOUT COMPUTERIZATION

This chapter examines how unstated, but critical, assumptions that underlie social analyses of computerization frame our understanding. I will focus on the popular, professional, and scholarly literatures in which authors claim to describe the actual nature of computerization, the character of computer use, and the social choices and changes that result from computerization. I am not including certain kinds of writing that are also very important, but that do not claim literally to characterize the empirical world, now or in the future: ethical studies, normative policy analyses, analyses of discourse (such as this chapter), and works that are self-consciously fictional (including science fiction).

Every year thousands of articles and dozens of books comment on the meaning of new computer technologies for people, organizations, and the larger society. Because computer technologies are likely to improve significantly over the next few decades, we should expect periodic accounts of the social meanings of new technologies. Moreover, as we approach the year 2000, there will be a predictable flood of books and articles that examine the virtues and problems of computer technologies in the twenty-first century.

A large fraction of the literature about computing describes emerging technologies and the ways they can expand the limits of the possible. Faster, tinier computers can make it easier for people to access information in a wider variety of places. Larger memories can make more data accessible. Richer display devices can help people communicate more readily with computerized systems through pictures and text. High-speed networks, such as Usenet and Internet, link thousands of computer systems together in ways only dreamed of in 1970. The remarkable improvement in the capabilities of equipment from one decade to the next generate breathless excitement by researchers, developers, and entrepreneurs, as well as by the battalions of journalists who document these events in the daily newspapers and weekly magazines.

Accounts of the powerful information-processing capabilities of computer systems are usually central to many stories of computerization and social change. *Authors write about these changes in technology and social life with different analytical and rhetorical strategies* (Kling & Iacono, 1988, 1991). Some authors enchant us with images of new technologies that offer exciting possibilities of manipulating large amounts of information rapidly with little effort—to enhance control, to create insights, to search for information, and to facilitate cooperative work between people. Much less frequently, some authors examine a darker social vision in that any likely form of computerization will amplify human misery—people sacrificing their freedom to businesses and government agencies, people becoming very dependent on complex technologies that they don't comprehend, and sometimes the image of inadvertent global thermonuclear war. Both kinds of stories often reflect the conventions of utopian and anti-utopian writing. Authors craft utopian and anti-utopian writings within a set of conventions that limit what they can or will say. Even though these writings talk about social forms that the authors suggest are likely, their tacit conventions preclude their discussing important social relationships that are also likely. A genre refers to any body of work that is characterized by a set of conventions. The works that we readily identify as romantic comedies, impressionist paintings, horror films, newspaper editorials, and popular movie reviews often are constructed with a set of conventions that make them readily intelligible and accessible. Authors and artists who work wholly within the conventions of a genre also limit the kinds of themes that they can effectively examine. Authors of romantic comedies usually have trouble exploring boredom in life and the ways that people work out sustained negotiations to get by day to day. Scholars have examined the ways that literary formulas shape fiction (Cawelti, 1976), journalistic conventions shape newsmaking (Tuchman, 1978; Campbell, 1991), and academic conventions shape scholarship (McCloskey, 1990; Van Maanen, 1988).

This chapter carries these conceptions of genre formulas as epistemological envelopes further into the realm of writing that is putatively nonfictional, writing that authors position as telling us truths about the world of computerization "out there" and beyond the author's imagination. A major theme of this chapter is that many social analyses of computing are written with genre conventions that limit the kinds of ideas that can be readily examined. Conventions make works more easily intelligible. I have found, however, that scholars and professionals who read these social analyses often are unaware of the ways that works are crafted within the conventions of specific genres, and the ways in that these conventions limit as well as facilitate analysis and debate.

The utopian and anti-utopian genres of social analysis are about 500 years old, and predate the social sciences by about 350 years. Authors who work within these genres examine certain kind of social possibilities, and usually move quite freely beyond the technologies one finds in use today and beyond social relationships that commonplace today. Utopian tales are devised to stimulate hope in future possibilities, while anti-utopian tales are devised to stimulate anger at horrible possibilities. Technological utopianism is particularly influential in North America. Appreciating its epistemology helps us to understand an important aspect of North American thought.

A different kind of investigative strategy and genres of reporting one's insights are based on examining existing computerized systems as they are actually used in real social settings. These investigations and genres of writing that communicate them rest on the empiricist's faith that by examining the world as it is, we can learn something important of the worlds that might be. I will examine three major genres that rest on empirical observation: social realism, social theory, and analytical reduction. These are not the only genres of social analysis of computing. One can find works written with other conventions, such as expert surveys and personal reminiscences. But some of these five genres are commonplace, and others are important for developing systematic analyses. I am concerned with the strengths and limits of inquiries conceived and reported within these five genres: the two utopian genres and the three empirical genres. I hope that the analysis of these genres sensitizes readers to the way that any genre of social analysis has important strengths and limitations. First I will examine utopian and anti-utopian analyses of computerization.

TECHNOLOGICAL UTOPIANISM AND ANTI-UTOPIANISM

Technological Utopianism

Utopian thinkers portray societies in which people live ideal lives. The first such description appeared in Plato's *Republic*, written some 2500 years ago. But the name *Utopia* derives from Thomas More, who published a story of an ideal society named

Utopia in 1516. In Utopia people lived harmoniously and free of privation. His fanciful name, which meant "nowhere," has been picked up and applied to a whole tradition of writing and thinking about the forms of society that would make many people happiest. There have been hundreds of utopian blueprints. They differ substantially in their details: Some have focused on material abundance as the key to human happiness, whereas others have advanced visions of happiness based on austere and simple ways of life. Some utopians advocate private property as a central social institution, while many place a primacy on shared property.

The most obvious utopian sources are discourses that the authors identify as fictional accounts with traditional devices, such as made up characters and fanciful dialogue. We are concerned with discourses about computerization that authors present as primarily realistic or factual accounts (and that are catalogued as nonfiction in book stores and libraries). We will show how some of these discourses are shaped by the conventions of utopianism and anti-utopianism.

Edward Feigenbaum and Pamela McCorduck explicitly identify with utopian ideals when they close their book about the social virtues of expert systems with this observation.

> ..."Utopian" also means something we have said many times and in many ways that we desire as a human good.... all this... corresponds to Adam Smith's vision in *The Wealth of Nations* of a universal opulent society, a condition of plenty that frees the people from dependence and subordination to exercise true independence of spirit in autonomous actions. (Feigenbaum & McCorduck, 1984)

The British author Tom Stonier (1983) also illustrates the utopian tradition in writing about information technology. He ends his book about the way that information technologies can transform societies with this observation.

> To sum up, everyone an aristocrat, everyone a philosopher. A massively expanded education system to provide not only training and information about how to make a living, but also on how to live. In late industrial society, we stopped worrying about food. In late communicative society, we will stop worrying about material resources. And just as the industrial economy eliminated slavery, famine, and pestilence, so will the post-industrial economy eliminate authoritarianism, war, and strife. For the first time in history, the rate at which we will solve problems will exceed the rate at which they will appear. This will leave us to get on with the real business of the next century. To take care of each other. To fathom what is means to be human. To explore intelligence. To move out into space. (Stonier, 1983)

Utopian images are common in many books and articles about computerization in society written by technologists and journalists. I am particularly interested in what can be learned, and how we can be misled, by a particular brand of utopian thought—*technological utopianism*. This line of analysis places the use of some specific technology, such as computers, nuclear energy, or low-energy low-impact technologies, as key *enabling elements* of a utopian vision.[1] Sometimes people will casually refer to exotic technologies—like pocket computers that understand spoken language—as "utopian gadgets." Technological utopianism does not refer to these technologies with amazing capabilities. It refers to *analyses* in which the use of specific technologies plays a key role in shaping a benign social vision. In contrast, *technological anti-utopianism* examines how certain broad families of technology facilitate a social order that is relentlessly harsh, destructive, and miserable. George Orwell's novel *1984* is a representative of the genre.

Utopian Elements in Technological Blueprints

Technologists who characterize new or future technologies often rest on utopian imagery when they examine their social meaning or implications. In 1948, before there were any working electronic computers, Vannevar Bush set forth a vision of a fast, flexible, remotely accessible desk-sized computer, called "Memex," which would allow a researcher to electronically search through vast archives of articles, books, and notes electronically (Bush, 1988). He wrote:

Wholly new forms of encyclopedia will appear, ready-made with a mesh of associative trails running through them, ready to be dropped into the memex, and there amplified. The lawyer has at his touch the associated opinions and decisions of his whole experience. The patent attorney has on call millions of issued patents, with familiar trails to every point of his client's interest. The physician, puzzled by a patient's reaction, strikes the trail established in studying an earlier similar case, and runs rapidly through analogous case histories, with side references to the classics for the pertinent anatomy and histology. The chemist, struggling with the synthesis of an organic compound, has all the chemical literature before him in his laboratory, with trails following the analogies of compounds, the side trails to their physical and chemical behavior.

The historian, with a vast chronological account of people, parallels it with a skip trail which stops only at the salient items, and can follow at any time, contemporary trails which lead him all over civilization at a particular epoch. There is a new profession of trail blazers, those who find delight in the task of establishing useful trails through the enormous mass of the common record. The inheritance from the master becomes not only his additions to the world's record, but for his disciples, the entire scaffolding by which they were erected.

Thus science may implement the ways in which man produces, stores, and consults the records of the race. (Bush, 1988)

---

[1] See Howard Segal's article on technological utopianism for a description of technological utopianism in the period 1880–1930. The technologies of technological utopians can change from one era to another. But the assumption that a society that adopts the proper technologies will be harmonious and prosperous remains constant.

Bush continued by describing the ways in which the users may associate items, gather together the useful clusters of information that showed up during the search, and "instantly" project any or all of them onto displays for selective review, fast or slow.

> Presumably, man's spirit should be elevated if he can better review his shady past and analyze more completely and objectively his present problems. (Bush, 1988)

Bush envisioned a flexible, compliant research assistant able to artfully fish through vast archives of textual information and gather the useful stuff embodied in an uncomplaining ever-ready machine.[2] A seductive image indeed! This vision was ever more remarkable because the image of digital computers that dominated scientific writing at the time—and even dominates scientific thinking in today's talk about supercomputers—was high-speed calculation of numerical data.

I could have examined any number of other technological visions—of computer-based instruction to transform education (Papert, 1980), or of information systems that would enable managers to more tightly control their business enterprises, and so on. In part, these visions, like Bush's, rest on descriptions of computer-based devices and their information processing capabilities. In *The Fifth Generation*, Edward Feigenbaum and Pamela McCorduck speculate about several possible applications of artificial intelligence to medicine, library searches, life at home, and help for the elderly. Feigenbaum and McCorduck speculate in terms similar to Bush—by describing how these technologies might work under ideal conditions to help a person carry out socially useful actions. Yet they ignore key social conditions under which these technologies would be likely to be used.

A remarkably talented engineer, Douglas Engelbart, was inspired by Bush's vision. About 15 years later, he assembled a brilliant research team at the Stanford Research Institute to build computer systems that resembled Bush's Memex. At the time, computer technology had advanced to the point where room-sized computers could be "time-shared" by dozens of people and accessed through video displays in their offices. Engelbart described his project "to augment human intellect" in these terms.

> By 'augmenting human intellect' we mean increasing the capability of a man to approach a complex problem situation, gain comprehension to suit his particular needs, and to derive solutions to his problems.... We include the professional problems of diplomats, executives, social scientists, life scientists, physical scientists, attorneys, designers.... We refer to a way of life in an integrated domain where hunches, cut-and-try, intangibles, and the human 'feel for the situation' usefully coexist with powerful concepts, streamlined terminology and notation, sophisticated methods, and high powered electronic aids. (Engelbart, 1963)

Engelbart's team designed a novel system that included technologies that began to appear in the marketplace in the mid-1980s, such as the mouse, hypertext, and con-

---

[2] In another section of his article, he presaged the invention of charge cards for department stores.

text-sensitive help available with function keys.[3] Engelbart's team focused on computer systems that would enhance the performance of groups of people working together. They developed text systems that allowed different group members to have their own views of the same body of text. They built an electronic mail system that enabled people to track messages sent about various topics within their group. Today, there are some commercial "groupware" systems to facilitate the functioning of groups by allowing many people to work with common bodies of text, schedules, and so on. Visions like Bush's and Engelbart's, from which I have drawn tiny excerpts, serve as an inspiration for many technologists and aficionados of new technologies.

Visions like Bush's and Engelbart's are also flawed in the way they characterize technologies, people, and social life. They emphasize the ways that a technology should work ideally, under conditions where all the participants are highly cooperative to make things work their best. Some people call the field that researches and develops computer systems to support group activities "computer supported cooperative work (CSCW)." In this label, the work of groups is implied to be cooperative by definition. Other kinds of social relationships in work groups—such as those marked by conflict, competition, coercion, and even combat, are denied to exist by definition (Kling, 1991).

In an illustrative review of software, Derfler (1989) argued that group scheduling or calendaring software was a critical module of "workgroup productivity software," although other modules, such as text processing and electronic mail, are important to make a more usable system. Derfler goes on to say:

> Scheduling three or more busy people for a meeting, along with arranging for a conference room and a slide projector, can be a frustrating and time-consuming task, requiring at least three phone calls. If one person or facility isn't available at the time the other people or facilities are, a whole series of negotiations begins. Mathematicians refer to it as progressive approximation; you (or your secretary making the arrangements) call it frustration. Before the scheduling problem is resolved, the number of people involved and phone calls made may have increased dramatically.

> Scheduling programs… vary in how they confirm proposed events. The simpler packages assume that if the event fits on the calendar, that the people scheduled to attend will be there. Other programs ask for confirmation, while some go as far as to tie into electronic mail modules for notification.

> …The best scheduling software is utterly useless if people aren't willing to play the game by keeping their personal calendars current. Obviously, these personal calendars are at the heart of the group scheduling process—calendars that aren't readily available or easy to use will never be maintained by group participants. With this in mind, it seems imper-

---

[3] These technological innovations are most frequently used in single user systems on microcomputers such as Apple Macintoshs and IBM PCs for prosaic tasks like editing memos and papers. Engelbart's team seems to have done little to actually enhance the ability of the kinds of professionals he describes to actually solve practical problems.

ative that these programs allow you to run the personal calendar module (interactively while running other programs) and make it easy to use. (Derfler, 1989)

Derfler describes and critically evaluates key features of some major programs, and describes the best of these packages as dreams come true for busy professionals and managers. Like Vannevar Bush, Feigenbaum, and McCorduck, he describes how these programs can facilitate various kinds of group activities, such as scheduling, under the best of conditions: Machines are up and running properly; people have immediate access to the shared system to keep their calendars up-to-date; people actually keep their calendars up-to-date. Unfortunately, like many journalists, he does not explain what social conditions make these packages most effective—or even usable at all. Derfler's article is entitled "Imposing Efficiency," but he never describes why or how efficiency would be *imposed* by anyone involved with the systems he reviews. In discussing meeting scheduling, he observes, "The best scheduling software is utterly useless if people aren't willing to play the game by keeping their personal calendars current." However, he immediately moves from this central observation to a technical point: That the scheduling software should be designed so that it can "pop up" whenever a person is running some other application. That way, if a person schedules a meeting by telephone when she is doing something else, like writing a memo, she can promptly update her electronic calendars with a minimum of interruption. That's a valid point. Yet Derfler never goes beyond the technical observation to examine the social practices of "imposed efficiencies," specifically the requirement that users accept and cooperate with the demands of managers who are trying to improve productivity through computerized systems.

Utopian Visions of Computerized Societies

So far, our examples focus on computer-based systems used by relatively small groups. But powerful images that link computerization and larger-scale social change have entered ordinary language through newspapers, popular books, and advertisements. The terms include "computer revolution," "information society," "knowledge worker," "computer-mediated work," and "intelligent machine." These catch phrases have strong metaphorical associations. They are often introduced by authors to advance positive exciting images of computerization.

These new terms are often worked into common usage by journalists and authors who write for popular audiences. We live in a period of tremendous social changes. And sometimes new terms can help better capture emerging social patterns or new kinds of technologies, than can our conventional language. However, the way that many authors casually use these terms often reflects important unexamined and even questionable social assumptions.

Alvin Toffler helped stimulate enthusiasm for computerization in these popular terms in his bestseller *The Third Wave*. He characterized major social transformations in terms of large shifts in the organization of society—driven by technological change. The "Second Wave" was the shift from agricultural societies to industrial societies. He contrasts industrial ways of organizing societies with new social trends that he links to computer and microelectronic technologies. Toffler is masterful in succinctly suggesting major social changes in breathless prose. He also invented some of his own terminology to help characterize key social changes—terms like second wave, third wave, electronic cottage, infosphere, technosphere, prosumer, intelligent environment, and so on. Many of his new terms did not become commonly accepted. Even so, they help frame a seductive description of social change, and this excerpt from his chapter, "The Intelligent Environment," illustrates his approach.

> Today, as we construct a new info-sphere for a Third Wave civilization, we are imparting to the "dead" environment around us, not life, but intelligence. A key to this revolutionary advances, of course, the computer. (Toffler, 1980)

> As miniaturization advanced with lightning rapidity, as computer capacity soared and prices per function plunged, small cheap powerful minicomputers began to sprout everywhere. Every branch factory, laboratory, sales office, or engineering department claimed its own.... The brainpower of the computer... was "distributed." This dispersion of computer intelligence is now moving ahead at high speed. (Toffler, 1980)

> The dispersal of computers in the home, not to mention their interconnection in ramified networks, represents another advance in the construction of an intelligent environment. Yet even this is not all. The spread of machine intelligence reaches another level altogether with the arrival of microprocessors and microcomputers, those tiny chips of congealed intelligence that are about to become a part, it seems, of nearly all the things we make and use...

> What is inescapably clear, however, whatever we choose to believe, is that we are altering out info-sphere fundamentally.... We are adding a whole new strata of communication to the social system. The emerging Third Wave info-sphere makes that of the Second Wave era—dominated by its mass media, the post office, and the telephone—seem hopelessly primitive by contrast...

> In all previous societies, the infosphere[4] provided the means for communication between human beings. The Third Wave multiplies these means. But it also provides powerful facilities, for the first time in history, for machine-to-machine communication, and, even more astonishing, for conversation between humans and the intelligent environment around them. When we stand back and look at the larger picture, it becomes clear that the revolution in the info-sphere is at least as dramatic as that of the technosphere—in the energy system and the technological base of society. The work of constructing a new civilization is racing forward on many levels at once. (Toffler, 1980)

---

[4] Toffler defines an info-sphere as "communication channels through which individuals and mass messages could be distributed as goods or raw materials" (Toffler, 1980).

Toffler's breathless enthusiasm can be contagious—but also stymies critical thought. Like Derfler, he assumes that key people—administrators and purchasing agents—will share his enthusiasm for the new technologies. Toffler also ignores cost constraints. Today, for example, many small colleges and universities are unable to provide adequate computer support for their faculty and students; community groups and poorer organizations also have trouble affording adequate computer systems.

Toffler illustrated changes in the infosphere with The Source, a large commercial US-based computer-communication and messaging system that has thousands of individual and corporate subscribers (Toffler, 1980). Today, he could multiply that example manifold with the emergence of competing commercial systems in the US, such as Compuserve, Prodigy, and Genie, as well as tens of thousands of individually owned computerized bulletin boards that people have set up in hundreds of cities and towns. Similarly, one could ask about the social roles of other messaging systems, such as Minitel, which supports numerous sexy messageries.

However, there have been myriad other changes in the information environment in the United States that are not quite as exciting to people who would like to see a more thoughtful culture. For example, television has become a major source of information about world events for many children and adults. The popular television shows include soap operas, sitcoms, and rock video television networks like MTV. Television news, the most popular "factual" kind of television programming, slices stories into salami-thin 30–90-second segments and fits them to simple storylines. Moreover, there is some evidence that functional illiteracy is rising in the United States. The problems of literacy in the United States are probably not only a byproduct of television's popularity. But it is hard to take Toffler's optimistic account seriously when a large fraction of the population has trouble understanding key parts of the instruction manuals for automobiles and for commonplace home appliances, like refrigerators and televisions.

Toffler opens up important questions about the way that information technologies alter the ways that people perceive information, the kinds of information they can get easily, and how they handle the information they get. But his account—like many popular accounts—caricatures the answers by using only illustrations that support his generally buoyant theses. And he skillfully sidesteps tough questions while creating excitement. (For example, "The work of constructing a new civilization is racing forward on many levels at once.")

Toffler's vision is not dated, however. Ten years later two respected information systems scholars examined offices of the late 1990s.

> The office of the late 1990s can now be envisioned. Its staff of professionals and mangers are surrounded by intelligent devices that speak, listen, or interact with them to determine what is to be accomplished and how it is to be done. Contacts with other departments, other divisions, customers, vendors, and other organizations are made with little effort and without human intervention. Behind the scenes, systems are being developed by system developers equipped with versatile and highly integrated software. (Straub & Wetherbe, 1989)

This vision is similar to Toffler's, but less poetic. It portrays computerized information systems and offices similar to a spaceship in which the crew is highly automated and staffed with robots.

In a similarly upbeat manner, John Sculley, former Chairman of the Board of the Apple Computer Corporation, advocated the development of simulation, hypermedia and artificial intelligence to strengthen the United States economy and educational systems (Sculley, 1991). He argued by analogy with the role of print in the Renaissance. Sculley claims that print technology catalyzed the Renaissance, which broke the stranglehold of the church and feudal interests on the population of Europe. He argues that computer systems based on hypermedia, simulation, and artificial intelligence applied to education are the appropriate means for a similar transformation today. Sculley's article is typical of some that try to excite a positive sense of purpose for developers and users of new computer technologies by referring to big historical changes such as the Renaissance or the Industrial Revolution. They excite hope for computerization by linking it to positive social ideals that they anchor in oversimplified and sometimes distorted historical accounts.[5]

I have spent substantial space examining technological utopianism because it is a common genre for exploring the social meaning of new and future technologies in North America. And it is the genre that is most influential in the North American technological communities.

TECHNOLOGICAL ANTI-UTOPIANISM

There is a relatively small North American literature that critically examines key claims made about the social virtues of different computerization strategies. The technological anti-utopian critiques portray computerization—in almost any form the analyst can conceive—as likely to degrade social life (e.g., Weizenbaum, 1976; Reinecke, 1984; Buesmans & Wieckert, 1989). I will illustrate this genre with two examples. Weizenbaum's *Computer Power and Human Reason* is a complex critique of computerized decision systems that their users and managers do not or cannot understand. He amplifies the underside of every computerized system which he discusses. For example, he criticizes visions of computerized databases that record historical data (like Vannevar Bush's Memex, which I described earlier), because they usually eliminate important information which is too complex or costly to include:

The computer has thus begun to be an instrument for the destruction of history. For when

---

[5] For example, Sculley (1991) distorted the bases of economic expansion during the Renaissance to emphasize the value of the printing press. In a recent issue of *Daedalus*, Hillis (1992) exaggerated the role of technologies in creating an industrial revolution, and the effectiveness of certain early industrialists, such as Eli Whitney. In each case, the selective distortions serve to help these authors emphasize the value of computer technologies sold by their companies today. See Dunlop and Kling (1991) for detailed critique of Sculley's argument. See Kling, Scherson, and Allen (1992) for a corrective to Hillis' distorted historical account.

society legitimates only those "data" that are in one standard format, then history, memory itself, is annihilated. *The New York Times* has already begun to build a "data bank" of current events. Of course, only those data that are easily derivable as by-products of typesetting machines are admissible to the system. As the number of subscribers to this system grows, as they learn to rely more and more upon "all the news that [was once] fit to print,"[6] as *The Times* proudly identifies its editorial policy, how long will it be before what counts as fact is determined by the system, before all other knowledge, all memory, is simply declared illegitimate? Soon a supersystem will be built, based on *The New York Times'* data bank (or one very much like it), from which "historians" will make inferences about what "really" happened, about who is connected to whom, and about the "real" logic of events. (Weizenbaum, 1976)

Weizenbaum's observations gain more force when one realizes that journalists don't simply report "the facts." Often they rely on standard kinds of sources, voices of publicly legitimate authority, in framing stories. For example, when a university alters a curriculum, deans and professors are more likely to have a voice in the resulting news story than are students. Tuchman (1978) characterized reporters in search of a story as casting a selective "newsnet" around their favorite kinds of sources. Journalists rarely cast their nets to give equal voice to all kinds of informed parties. Although reporters are much more likely to go to "the grass roots" today than they were in the days of Vannevar Bush, each newspaper prints a mix of stories in a style that reflects a relatively stable character. Usually, even if the mastheads were interchanged, one would not confuse *The New York Times* with a small town weekly newspaper.[7] Without special design, nothing in the database technology would be likely to give a user a clue about its real limitations in representing a narrow range of perspectives. And, yet, its convenience might make it very tempting for a busy professional to rely on it as a primary source, without appreciating its limitations. That is the cautionary note that one might draw from Weizenbaum's bitter observations. However, Weizenbaum's argument is primarily polemical. He doesn't discuss any virtues of news databases or conditions under which they might not have the deleterious problems he identifies. News databases can also substantially assist in useful research as long as they do not become a sole source of information. Professional historians who have developed strong criteria for verifying events with original sources may be less likely to become their prisoners than many professionals (and students) who find them efficacious and seductive, despite their limitations. Moreover, Weizenbaum speaks with authority about future events ("soon a supersystem will be built…").

Discussions of computerization and work have been a major topic for both utopian and anti-utopian analysts (see Iacono & Kling, 1987). Some authors argue that computerization has systematically degraded clerical work through a pattern of industrialization

---

[6] The *New York Times'* masthead slogan is "All the News That's Fit to Print."

[7] For a very readable and revealing account about the way that newspapers shape the reports that appear as "news," see Manhoff and Schudson (1986).

(Braverman, 1974). Some go farther and argue that the computerization of clerical work sets the stage for the industrialization of professional work as well (Mowshowitz, 1986; Perrolle, 1991). Mowshowitz (1986) summarizes his sharp vision in these concise terms.

> Our principal point is that the lessons of the factory are the guiding principles of office automation. In large offices, clerical work has already been transformed into factory-like production systems. The latest technology—office automation—is simply being used to consolidate and further a well-established trend. For most clerical workers, this spells an intensification of factory discipline. For many professionals and managers, it signals a gradual loss of autonomy, task fragmentation and closer supervision—courtesy of computerized monitoring. Communication and interaction will increasingly be mediated by computer. Work will become more abstract... And opportunities for direct social interaction will diminish.

Like Weizenbaum, Mowshowitz writes authoritatively about distressing future events. He doesn't examine the possibility that many professionals will use their occupational power to resist the loss of autonomy and fragmented jobs that he describes. Nor does he examine how some professionals have exploited computerization to their advantage—in making their jobs more interesting and complex. Elsewhere in his article, he criticizes studies that examine such variations as concerned with "minutiae." Mowshowitz follows Braverman's line of argument that (under capitalism), managers will computerize so as to enhance their control by degrading working conditions. Braverman's thesis has been subject to significant discussion and found wanting, because it doesn't account for other processes that shape computerization (such as enhancing control over expensive resources other than labor or improving product quality in the face of competition).[8] Braverman's thesis is anti-utopian insofar as only one tragic outcome is likely. It is an important line of argument insofar as it locates computerization efforts within a logic of managerial interests, and highlights the importance of controlling labor as a key managerial interest.

Utopian and anti-utopian analysts share important common conventions. Their narratives are usually future oriented, universalize experiences with technologies, homogenize experiences into one or two groups, and portray technologies as totalizing elements that dominate important social interactions. They take extreme, but different, value positions. They portray computerization with monochromatic brushes: white or black. The technological anti-utopians' characterization of the tragic possibilities of computerization provide an essential counterbalance to the giddy-headed optimism of the technological utopian accounts. The romances and tragedies are not all identical. For example, some anti-utopian writings examine the possibilities of computerized systems for coercion, while others emphasize alienation. But the technological utopian and anti-utopian genres have some important inherent limitations that we now examine.

---

[8] See Kuhn (1989) for a careful empirical examination of Braverman's thesis. See also Wood (1989) for a discussion of the literature about Braverman's thesis.

STRENGTHS AND LIMITS OF UTOPIAN ANALYSES

I have illustrated some utopian and anti-utopian analyses of computerization, and commented on some of their strengths and weaknesses in passing. To what extent are utopian or anti-utopian visions helpful in understanding the social possibilities of computerization? Despite key limitations that I shall characterize below, I see utopian and anti-utopian analyses as important and legitimate forms of speculative inquiry. Questions about the social consequences of new technologies are central to choices about paths for development, levels of social investment, and regulatory policies. These all merit analysis to help us better understand future possibilities. All such analyses rest on theories of the interplay between technological developments and social life. Utopian and anti-utopian themes are the most common in this culture. I will examine important alternatives to utopian and anti-utopian analyses in the next section—social realism, social theory, and analytical reduction.

Utopian visions are sometimes characterized as "reality transcending" (Kumar, 1987, 1991). They play important roles in stimulating hope and giving people a positive sense of direction. But they can mislead when their architects exaggerate the likelihood of easy and desirable social changes. Writing about technological utopianism in the 1930s, Wilson, Pilgrim, and Tasjian (1986) comment:

> Belief in the limitless future potential of the machine had both its positive and negative aspects. During the 1930s this almost blind faith in the power of the machine to make the world a better place helped hold a badly shattered nation together.... These science fiction fantasies contributed to an almost naive approach to serious problems and a denial of problems that could already be foreseen.

Anti-utopian writings are far less numerous. They serve as an important counterbalance to technological utopianism. But they could encourage a comparable ineffective sense of despair and inaction. Utopian and anti-utopian visions embody extreme assumptions about technology and human behavior. But their causal simplicity gives them great clarity and makes them easy to grasp—to enjoy or to abhor. They can resonate with our dreams or nightmares. Consequently, they have immense influence in shaping the discussions (and real directions) of computerization. Their causal simplicity is their greatest strength, and also a point of entry to some crippling limitations that I examine now.

Conflict

Technological utopian analysts portray a world which is free of substantial conflict. Technological anti-utopians usually portray certain fundamental conflicts such as between social classes (Mowshowitz, 1976, 1986) or between government agencies and the public (Burnham, 1983) as almost unalterably unbalanced. One side virtually dominates while the other side mounts negligible resistance. Neither extreme characterizes the world in which social conflicts are important but in which coalitions draw complex lines and the intensity of conflict varies in place and time.

Practical attempts to establish utopian social schemes have been fraught with significant and complex conflicts. For example, the United States was founded on premises that were utopian in the 1700s. The Declaration of Independence asserts that "all men were created equal" and that they would be should be guaranteed the right to "life, liberty, and the pursuit of happiness." This was in significant contrast to the political cultures of the European monarchies of the time, where the rule of the king or queen, and her nobles, most of whom were selected by heredity, determined peoples' fates. Of course, asserting this right as universal didn't immediately make it so.[9]

Utopian ideals are hard to realize. Their advocates often have to fight hard to change social practices to better fit their ideals. Bloody revolutions were fought in the United States and France to overthrow the ruling monarchies in the late eighteenth century. Almost 200 years later, Martin Luther King and others advanced the cause of improved civil rights in the United States through aggressive confrontations: marches, rallies, court injunctions, and sit-ins, as well as through more quiet persuasion. These social changes, which altered the balance of privilege and exploitation, did not come quietly and peacefully. I have examined how Sculley underplays the level of conflict between the Catholic church and other groups during the Renaissance and thereby transforms a bloody period into one in which a key technology (the printing press) became an agent of bloodless social change.

Distribution of Knowledge

In utopian analyses of computerization, people have whatever skills they need to adequately use systems and to resolve problems as they arise. Anti-utopian analyses vary in their accounts of technological skills. Sometimes everyone is adequately skilled, but are using technologies in ways that undermine important social values. In other anti-utopian accounts, many people are confused about key social relationships and the use of technologies. In these latter analyses, either elites control key skills or sometimes no one has key knowledge (as in Weizenbaum account of "incomprehensible systems"). These accounts rarely portray people's technological skills as being distributed in complex ways: many people as having adequate technical skills for some of their activities, and muddling through on others with help from coworkers or consultants, and being confused about a few technological activities.

---

[9] In the US, for example, slaves were legally property that could be bought and sold, told where to live, and broken apart from their families until 1865. Women were not allowed to vote until 1919. But even in 1963, Martin Luther King's major speech about a country free of racial discrimination was called "I Have a Dream," not "An Old Dream Has Now Come True."

Problems Caused by Technological Development

Technological utopians sometimes recognize that new technologies cause new problems—but these are to be solved with additional technologies. Buckminster Fuller argued that it was difficult and almost pointless to teach people to drive very cautiously and to harass them with rigid laws. He argued for safer cars rather than for changing human behavior. Today's discussions that focus on computerized "smart cars" rather than smart drivers runs along a parallel line. Technological utopians would usually advocate government funds invested in stimulating the development of new technologies rather than increasing the scale and scope of regulatory bureaucracies. As another kind of example, technological utopian discussions of computerization in schools emphasize the potentials of new technologies and ignore the ways that they may be unrealized when classes are overcrowded, teachers are not very sharp, and schools spend substantial efforts in trying to regiment students (Kling & Iacono, 1988). By focusing on new technologies as agents of social change and assuming that social systems will use them effectively, technological utopians ignore the social conditions for technologies to be effective.[10] Consequently, they often overstate their social value. In contrast, technological anti-utopians often understate the social value of technological innovations and the way in which all technologies pose problems.

Necessity of Technological Effects

Technological utopian and anti-utopian analysts suggest that the changes they foresee are virtually certain to happen if a technology is developed and disseminated. Their arguments gain rhetorical force through linear logics and the absence of important contingencies. This causal simplification is, in our view, a fatal flaw of utopian and anti-utopian speculations. They explore the character of *possible social changes* as if they were the only likely social changes.

BEYOND THE UTOPIAN IMPULSE:
SOCIAL REALISM, SOCIAL THEORY, AND
ANALYTICAL REDUCTION

In the previous section, I identified four major characteristic limitations of technological utopian and anti-utopian analyses. Not all technological utopian (or anti-utopian

---

[10] For example, when motor cars first became popular in the early twentieth century, they were viewed as a clean technology. Some of the larger cities had annoying pollution problems from another primary transportation technology—horses. On rainy days, large pools of horse manure would form on busy street corners, and walking was somewhat hazardous for pedestrians. By the 1950s, we began to view cars as a major polluting technology, since smog visibly dirtied the air of major cities.

analyses) are equally coherent,[11] clear, or credible. However, other forms of social analysis can also be incoherent or baseless. So clarity does not differentiate between utopian analyses and other modes of social analysis.

Attractive alternatives to utopian analysis should be more credible in characterizing conflict in a social order, the distribution of knowledge, the ways of solving problems that arise from new technologies, and resting on less deterministic logics of social change. Most important, they would also identify the social contingencies that make technologies (un)workable and social changes benign or harmful for various social groups. I briefly identify three alternatives that are anchored in empiricism: social realism, social theory, and analytical reduction. Analyses in these three genres often acknowledge complex patterns of social conflict, yet are more open-ended and contingent than both genres of utopian analysis.

Social Realism

I use the label "social realism" to characterize a genre that uses empirical data to examine computerization as it is actually practiced and experienced. Social realists write their articles and books with a tacit label: *"I have carefully observed and examined computerization in some key social setting and I will tell you how it really is."* The most common methods are those of journalism (e.g., Frantz, 1996; Salerno, 1991) and the social sciences, such as critical inquiries (e.g., Forester, 1989), and ethnography (e.g., Dutton & Kraemer, 1985; Kling, 1978; Kling & Iacono, 1984; Laudon, 1986). But the genre is best characterized by the efforts of authors to communicate their understanding of computerization as it "really works" based on reporting fine grained empirical detail (e.g., Stoll, 1991; Office of Technology Assessment, 1986). Social realism gains its force through gritty observations about the social worlds in which computer systems will be used.

An interesting example of social realism is found in a study of instructional computing in classrooms by Sheingold, Hawkins, and Char (1984). They report on a number of ethnographic studies of instructional computing in specific classrooms, including the use of databases, a mathematical game, and LOGO programming. They carefully report different ways that teachers conceptualize the relationship between these programs and instruction (with resulting differences in ways that they integrate them into their classes). They also report a variety of ways that students use the programs, from those that fit conventional rationalist conceptions of media in learning to those that simply get the work done. In some instances the students wrote and ran their

---

[11] Sometimes utopian and anti-utopian analyses have internal contradictions. For example, one can ask of Feigenbaum and McCorduck how they expect people to engage in socially important activities that reap no profit (such as helping people in roadside accidents) when the *dominant virtue* in their Smithian world is to be individual greed. Other times, it is simply unclear how a disadvantaged social group can move from where it is to the more munificent utopian social order. In anti-utopian scenarios, it is sometimes unclear why a moderately advantaged group would tolerate relentless exploitation (see, for example, Mowshowitz).

programs as they were instructed to. They worked together so that they all participated in solving problems and also in entering programs into their computers. But the cute title of the paper, "I'm the thinkist, you're the typist" comes from their observations of the educationally inappropriate way that two girls divided their efforts in programming with LOGO. This division of labor between a girl who took control of the problem solving and her partner who handled the mechanics of transcribing the LOGO program illustrates the ways that people will organize so as to rapidly complete their work done, but not necessarily satisfy broader (utopian) educational goals.

Another example of social realism is Grudin's (1989) analysis of the *social assumptions* that designers and advocates of groupware make about the use of these packages. He argues that the meeting scheduling systems championed by Derfler (1989) work best when their users all have secretaries to help keep their calendars up-to-date. These packages are especially attractive to managers, who often have secretaries, and who often want to schedule meetings with subordinates. They can be a burden to professionals who do not have secretarial support. They can also burden people who are away from their desks in meeting out of their offices part of the day, where they are making new commitments that are not reflected in their shared calendars. More deeply, Grudin examines computer applications with a model of organizations in which resources and authority are not equally distributed. Grudin places computer systems in work worlds in which there is a political economy of effort—some people can generate work for others. And the people who generate work may not have to work as hard as do the people who have to meet their requirements. Grudin's article examines the social contingencies that make these systems (un)workable. And Grudin takes some care in identifying which kinds of groupware are more troublesome.

Social realists vary in the extent to which they weave their evidence into tight narratives. Tighter stories can leave us more satisfied. But there is a risk that important elements that don't fit the narrative are ignored (cf. Campbell, 1991). More frequently social realism offers us compelling frank portraits that suffer from particularism. Authors in this genre rarely are explicit in drawing concepts or themes that generalize across technologies and social settings from the rich literature about the social character of computerization, or in contrasting their study with many other studies or accounts in the computerization literature. Moreover, it is always debatable what the present can tell us about what the future can be like if social arrangements or technologies are substantially transformed.

Social Theory

In contrast with social realism, theoretical analysts explicitly develop or test concepts and theories that transcend specific situations. Unlike utopian and anti-utopian accounts, social theoretical works are not "reality transcending." But they are situation transcending. Some examples are *reinforcement politics* (Danziger, Dutton, Kling, &

Kraemer, 1982),[12] *web models* (Kling, 1992; Kling & Scacchi, 1982), *structuration theory* (Poole & DeSanctis, 1990; Orlikowski, 1991), *post-structuralist theories* (Poster, 1991), Judith Perolle's explication of *social control theories* (Perolle, 1988), and Terry Winograd's (1988) explication of *language-action theory.*

Web models illustrate this kind of theoretical work. Walsham, Symons, and Waema (1988) characterize web models in these terms:

> The basic tenet of web models is that a computer system is best conceptualized as an ensemble of equipment, applications and techniques with identifiable information processing capabilities. Each computing resource has costs and skill requirements which are only partially identifiable; in addition to its functional capabilities as an information processing tool it is a social object which may be highly charged with meaning. There is no specially separable 'human factor' for information systems: the development and routine operations of computer-based technologies hinge on many human judgement and actions, often influenced by political interests, structural constraints, and participants' definition of their situations.

> The network of producers and consumers around the focal computing resource is termed the 'production lattice'; the interdependencies in this network form the 'web' from which the model derives its name. The production lattice is a social organization which is itself embedded in a larger matrix of social and economic relations ('macrostructure') and is dependent upon a local infrastructure. According to web models, these macrostructures and local infrastructures direct the kind of computer-based service available at each node of the production lattice, and since they evolve over time computing developments are shaped by a set of historical commitments. In short, web models view information systems as 'complex social objects constrained by their context, infrastructure and history.' (Kling & Scacchi, 1982)

Web analyses are action-oriented and examine the political interplay of coalitions in structured—but somewhat fluid—settings (Kling, 1987). The main organizing concepts were a "focal computing technology," which was the center of analyses, the infrastructure that supported its development and operation (including production lattices), its context of development and use, and a history of organizational commitments that structured these arrangements. Researchers have applied web models to better understand a variety of cases, including dilemmas of developing the Worldwide Military Command and Control System, dilemmas of converting complex inventory control systems in manufacturing firms, the development of software in insurance firms, and the ways in which desktop computerization changes worklife in offices (Kling, in press).

Social theoretical studies of computerization offer the traditional virtues of theory: relatively concise general explanations and concepts that help guide inquiry in new situations. However, they are much less accessible to a broad audience than technological

---

[12] Reinforcement politics holds that organizations computerize so that actors with most resources gain more influence, whereas those with fewer resources lose subsequent influence.

utopian, anti-utopian and social realist accounts because of their intellectual demands: their (necessary) use of specialized terms and their frequent abstraction from the kinds of concrete situations that readers can readily visualize and perhaps identify with.

The contrast between social realism and social theory, as ideal types, is rather clear. And it is easy to find books and articles that illustrate these types. All social analyses are imbued with theoretical assumptions, however implicit (Kling, 1980). Journalists and others who are not trained in the social sciences are much more likely to write as social realists rather than as social theorists. Social scientists are more capable of developing theoretical inquiries, but they are more likely to publish social realist discourses about computerization or documents that apply existing theory to sharpen realist accounts. I believe that there is a shortage of good empirically anchored theoretical explorations of the social aspects of computerization.

Analytical Reduction

Some scholars organize their social investigations into computerization by working within a tightly defined conceptual framework. They identify a few key concepts, sometimes derived from theory or abstracted from a group of studies, and examine them in new settings. If they adopt a strictly quantitative social science approach, they operationalize all of their key concepts into variables, measure them, examine how behaviors are distributed along the variables and via mathematical relationships between variables (e.g., correlations). Although completely quantitative studies represent ideal examples of this genre, studies that focus on a few qualitatively described dimensions share enough key characteristics to be appropriate to group with them also.

Hiltz's (1988) chapter on the ways that computer conferencing systems alter productivity of groups illustrates the quantitative version of the genre. Hiltz administered questionnaires to people who used four different computer conferencing systems before and after a period of use. She grouped four survey questions items into a summary measure of productivity (e.g., quality of work with system, quantity of work with system, overall usefulness of system, and utility of system in reaching other people). She measured many aspects of the groups, their work, their usage of the conferencing systems, and the features of the systems. She bases her conclusions on the magnitude of quantitative relationships between the variables that she measured. For example, she notes

> The strongest correlates of productivity improvements for all four systems are pre-use expectations about whether the system would increase productivity. Other determinants relate to the group context: leadership skill is important and strong competitive feelings may hamper productivity (Hiltz, 1988).

In a similarly analytical approach, Suzanne Iacono and I (1988) examined the extent to which the development of a complex computerized inventory control system could best be explained by one of three different kinds of organizational choices processes: rational decision making, organizational drift, and partisan politics.[13] In this study we presented a qualitative case study, and then systematically examined it for evidence in the form of episodes and social relationships which would support or undermine each of these three models of organizational choice.

I label this genre as *analytical reduction* because the authors reduce their accounts of the social world and computer technologies to a few key concepts. Depending on one's view, this approach represents the best or worst of social science inquiry. Those who see it as a valuable genre appreciate the way that the authors[14] critically examine key concepts and examine the extent to which they shed insight into the social world of computing. They believe that our best hope for *systematically understanding* the social character of computerization will come from studies in this genre. Those who criticize, or sometimes even despise analytical reduction, see it as arcane and inaccessible except to academic specialists. They usually prefer social realist studies because they are more easily accessible and identifiably concrete. Further, the quantitative reductions are less likely to characterize the shifts of understandings that participants have over time, the nature of unusual but important events, or even the occasions when computerization becomes comical or tragic.

HYBRID DISCOURSES

I have identified five genres of investigations and writing as ideal types. While many articles and books clearly fit one of these genres, some works are hybrid. For example, some works combine key facets of social realism and anti-utopianism. David Burnham's *The Rise of the Computer State* is a passionate examination of the way that many computerized data systems operated by credit reporting agencies, medical information bureaus, police agencies, and so on reduce personal privacy in the United States. His book reports his investigation of several large data systems based on dozens of interviews. Burnham is insightful in identifying the ways that large scale personal information systems have eroded personal privacy. He views each system as a medium for personal abuse—as examples of organizations intruding unfairly on people's private lives. For example, he discusses the Parent Locator System that uses matching on a complex array of Federal and State systems to track parents (usually fathers) who avoid paying legally mandated child support by hiding, often in another state. In this discussion he criticizes the system, sometimes obliquely. But he doesn't suggest that it has any socially redeeming value, even if, on balance, he would disagree with the tradeoffs made by using it. I see his book as reflecting a strong anti-utopian orientation mixed with a social realist format. Burnham's anti-utopianism is particularly clear when his book is read in contrast with Ken Laudon's *Dossier Society*—a social realist

---

[13] We found the greatest support for partisan political models of organizational choice governing the developmental trajectory of computerization in this case.

[14] The authors of this genre are almost always academics or people with substantial academic training.

study that criticizes many key aspects of computerized police systems.

Another hybrid work is Shoshana Zuboff's *In the Age of the Smart Machine,* which is the most daunting and serious recent study that examines the labor processes and phenomenology of work with computer-based systems. She provides vivid and often brilliant descriptions of the phenomenology of work with special computer systems in specific work settings. She examines several cases of computerization in white collar offices and in the control room of a paper factory, thus giving the book the appearance of social realism. She draws on labor process theories of work, and develops an interesting theoretical argument. However, her book is also driven by a significant anti-utopian subtext since all of her white collar empirical cases (and drawings that illustrate them) conclude that computerization has uniformly degraded work. The body of empirical research literature shows that computerization has not altered white collar work in such a unidirectional manner and that there are many technological and social contingencies which Zuboff ignores (Kling & Iacono, 1989).

The books by Burnham and Zuboff illustrate only two of a myriad of hybrid patterns. Hybrid works are quite common. They can avoid some of the problems of their component genres if they are carefully developed (e.g., *Datawars* by Kraemer, Dickhoven, Tierney, & Kling [1987], which mixes social realism and analytical reduction); or they can suffer from some of the fatal problems of their underlying genres if their authors do not take special pains to resolve these limits (e.g., Zuboff, 1988; Forester & Morrison, 1990).

CONCLUSIONS

I have identified five important genres in the literature that claim to describe the actual nature of computerization, the character of computer use, and the social choices and changes that result from computerization: utopian, anti-utopian, social realism, analytical reduction, and social theory. There are other important genres that I have ignored in order to maintain some focus. This chapter indicates the way that the conventions of genres like these amplify some kinds of ideas and mute others. They also make the resulting narratives accessible and attractive to different audiences. This attention to genre conventions blurs the crisp boundaries between fiction and nonfiction.

Writings in each genre have formulaic limits, much in the way that romantic fiction (or any other literary genre) has important limits (Cawelti, 1976). Cawelti notes that "the moral fantasy of the romance is that of love triumphant and permanent, overcoming all obstacles and difficulties (Cawelti, 1976, pp. 41–42). This does not mean that we can't be entertained or our appreciation of life enriched by romantic fictions; it is simply a genre with important formulaic limits. The moral fantasies of technological utopianism and anti-utopianism similarly limit the way that they can teach us about the likely social realities of new forms of computerization: One is romantic and the other is tragic. I am not arguing for some simple "balance" in each account—and especially not for balance between the utopian and anti-utopian genres. Life is more than a balance between romance and tragedy. (For example, neither romances nor tragedies frequently illustrate effective negotiations over vexing problems.)

I am much more sympathetic to the empirically oriented genres—social realism, social theory, and analytical reduction, than to the utopian and anti-utopian lines of analysis that I find less credible. But I see the two utopian genres as legitimate, for they help explore the limits of the possible. Social realist accounts are usually so anchored in the present that they don't examine long term possibilities very well. The social theories of computerization are a relatively new mode of analysis that transcends the particularism of social realism. However social theorists tend to "totalize" their narratives by emphasizing their key concepts and underplaying events and data that don't fit the conceptual scheme. Analytical reduction can be arcane for nonspecialists and is most accessible to social scientists.

It is easy to identify the two utopian genres with Ideology and the three sociological genres with Science. This polarity captures important contrasts. But it is also too facile because all discourses, even scientific discourses, make ideological assumptions.[15] Conversely, even the most blatantly ideological analysis can make some valid empirical claims.

In the 1990s, there will be a large market for social analyses of computerization stimulated by

- the steady stream of computing innovations;
- the drive by academic computer science departments and funding agencies such as the US National Science Foundation and Defense Advanced Research Projects Agency to justify large expenditures on computing research;
- justifications for major national computerization programs, such as the High Performance Computing Initiative; and
- articles examining life and technology in the twenty-first century.

A large fraction of this literature will be written by technologists and journalists for diverse professional and lay audiences. However, utopian analyses are most likely to dominate the discourse because most authors will champion special computer technologists or align with their champions.

The causal simplicity of technological utopianism and anti-utopianism is deceptive. But utopian and anti-utopian lines of analysis are legitimate and useful genres for helping us to understand how new technologies expand the limits of the possible (Kumar, 1991). But they are insufficient for creating an adequate literature about the social character of computerization. Moreover, organizations that have tried to computerize with utopian blueprints have often found that actual technologies are much more costly,

---

[15] In Kling (1980) I show how empirical studies of computerization are shaped by various theoretical perspectives, such as the human relations tradition, symbolic interaction, organizational politics, and class politics.

complex, and problematic while providing much less value than the utopian analysts suggest when they are taken literally.

The actual uses and consequences of developing computer systems depend upon the "way the world works." Conversely, computerized systems may slowly, but inexorably, change "the way the world works"—often with unforseen consequences. A key issue is how to understand the social opportunities and dilemmas of computerization without becoming seduced by the social simplifications of utopian romance or to be discouraged by dystopian nightmares. I see both kinds of images as far too simplified. However, to help identify an interesting and important set of social possibilities.[16]

The main alternatives, social realism, social theory, and analytical reduction, are less likely to be produced in a comparable quantity. They are relatively subtle, portray a more ambiguous world, and have less rhetorical power to capture the imagination of readers. However, social realists have not developed systematic strategies for analyzing the social character of powerful technologies that are not yet available, in use, for the kind of highly nuanced empirical observation that is the hallmark of the genre.[17] Journalists probably produce the largest number of social realist accounts, although they also write stories that fit within the utopian genres. Social theory and analytical reduction are the specialty of social scientists and relatively inaccessible to non-specialists. Few scholars have examined computerization with a social theoretical perspective. The scholarly literature about computerization is relatively unknown to journalists, computer scientists, and computer professionals.

Even though they are much more scientific than the utopian genres, the sociological genres don't seem to appeal to many scientists and engineers. Some technologists dismiss social realist accounts as "primarily anecdotal," and they have little patience for social theory. For example, articles from these genres are rarely published in highly visible North American journals such as *Scientific American*, *Science*, and IEEE publications. Fortunately, they appear periodically in some ACM journals, such as *Communications* and *Transactions on Information Systems*. I see the development of systematic social analy-

---

[16] New technologies do serve to expand the range of the possible. Jet planes make it possible for an intact nuclear family to have dinner in a different time zone each night next week. But the envelope of typical activities is much smaller than the world of the possible. Most intact nuclear families will have dinner in the same time zone every night this week. This does not mean that jet planes are useless. Nor do the periodic crashes of jet planes and failures of complex systems—which on rare but important cases, fail badly—mean that we should take their failures as a way to predict their everyday behavior. But even when infrequent failures are also routine, they cannot be wholly ignored, such as when systems are designed and staffed to insure safer operations.

[17] There are high-quality social realist accounts which examine the social dilemmas of emerging computerized systems. See, for example, Bellin and Chapman (1987) and Laudon (1986). However, these studies are highly particularistic. The articles in Bellin and Chapman's book examine computerized weapons systems without giving a clue how one might undertake social realist examinations of other kinds of computerized systems. Similarly, Laudon examines the social dimensions of large police data systems without giving many clues about how one might study future computerized systems in very different kinds of settings, such as automated battlefields.

ses of computerization—that are both credible and compelling—as a major challenge for the 1990s.

It is ironic that computing—which is often portrayed as an instrument of knowledge—is primarily the subject of a popular and professional literatures that are heavily weighted toward the less reliable utopian genres. Conversely, the more trustworthy empirically anchored genres often have much less appeal in the scientific and engineering communities.

A major purpose of the chapter is to advance our understanding of the social aspects of computerization by examining the kinds of stories that we tell ourselves and our audiences. The recent advances in applying and developing social theories pertinent to computerization have given us one important basis for some more credible and compelling stories. But social theory also has important limits based on the conventions of theoretically writing. I don't believe that we can develop "conventionless genres," even though we can benefit from new genres that situate computerization in credible social worlds. At this time, it's tempting to explore new genres that combine the richness of social realism with the future orientation of the utopian genres.

But we gain much by understanding the way that the conventions of any genre of social analysis amplify the possibility of some kinds of insights while moving other kinds of insights from view. I believe that we have the most to learn from rich literatures about computerization in social life that give us diverse credible narratives. This is different from hoping that some new genre will help answer all critical questions in a compelling manner. We are much better off with a diverse collection of credible materials that can tell us different kinds of insightful stories about the social aspects of computerization.

ACKNOWLEDGMENTS

I have sharpened the ideas discussed here through lively discussions and correspondence with Jonathan Allen, Pat Bentley, Werner Beuschel, Charles Dunlop, Jonathan Grudin, Bonnie Nardi, Mark Poster, Thomas Standish, Leigh Star, John Sonquist, Karen Weickert, Luc Wilkin, and Joseph Weizenbaum.

REFERENCES

Bellin, D. & Chapman, G. (Eds.). (1987). *Computers in battle: Will they work?* Boston: Harcourt Brace.

Braverman, H. (1975). *Labor and monopoly capital: The degradation of work in the twentieth century.* New York: Monthly Review Press.

Buesmans, J. & Wieckert, K. (1989, August). "Computing, research and war: If knowledge is power, where is responsibility?" *CACM 32*(1): 939–951.

Burnham, D. (1983). *The rise of the computer state.* New York: Pantheon Books.

Bush, V. (1988). As we may think, in *The Atlantic Monthly,* 1948. Reprinted in Greif, I. (Ed.), *Computer-supported cooperative work: A book of readings,* San Mateo, CA: Morgan-Kaufmann.

Campbell, R. (1991). *60 minutes and the news: A mythology for middle America.* Chicago: University of Illinois Press.

Cawelti, J. (1976). *Adventure, mystery and romance: Formula stories as art and popular culture.* Chicago: University of Chicago Press.

Danziger, J., Dutton, W., Kling, R., & Kraemer, K. (1982). *Computers and politics: High technology in American local governments.* New York: Columbia University Press.

Deng, Y., Glimm, J., & Sharp, D. H. (1992). Perspectives on Parallel Computing. *Daedalus 121*(1)(Winter): 31–52.

Derfler, F., Jr. (1989, Sept. 26). Imposing efficiency: Workgroup productivity software. *PC Magazine 8*(16). 247–269.

Dunlop, C., & Kling, R. (Ed.). (1991). *Computerization and controversy: Value conflicts and social choices.* Boston: Academic Press.

Dutton, W. H., & Kraemer, K. L. (1985). *Modelling as negotiating: The political dynamics of computer models in the policy process.* Norwood, NJ: Ablex.

Engelbart, D. (1963). A conceptual framework for the augmentation of man's intellect, in *Vistas in information handling*, vol. I (Howerman, P., ed.) (pp. 1–29). Washington DC: Spartan Books. Reprinted in *Computer supported cooperative work: A book of readings* (Grief, I. Ed.), San Mateo CA: Morgan Kaufman Publishers (1988).

Feigenbaum, E., & McCorduck, P. (1983). *The fifth generation: Artificial intelligence and Japan's computer challenge to the world.* Reading, MA: Addison-Wesley.

Forester, T. (Ed.). (1989). The myth of the electronic cottage, in *Computers in the human contest: Information technology, productivity, and people.* Cambridge, MA: MIT Press.

Forester, T., & Morrison, P. (1990, June). Computer unreliability & social vulnerability, *Futures*: 462–474.

Frantz, D. (1996). B of A's plans for computer don't add up, in R. Kling (Ed.), *Computerization and conroversity: Value conflicts and social choices* (2nd ed.; pp. 161–169). San Diego: Academic Press.

Fulk, J., & Steinfeld, C. (Ed.). (1990). *Organization and communication technology.* Newbury Park, CA: Sage.

Grudin, J. (1989). Why groupware applications fail: problems in design and evaluation. *Office: Technology and People, 4*:245–264.

Hillis, W. D. (1992). What is massively parallel computing and why is it important? *Daedalus 121*(1)(Winter): 1–16.

Hiltz, S. R. (1988, December). Productivity enhancement from computer mediated communication: A systems contingency approach. *Communications of the ACM 31*(12): 1438–1454.

Iacono, S., & Kling, R. (1987). Changing office technologies and the transformation of clerical jobs, in *Technology and the transformation of white collar work* (Robert Kraut, Ed.). Hillsdale, NJ: Erlbaum.

Kling, R. (1978, June). Automated welfare client-tracking and service integration: The political economy of computing. *Communications of the ACM 21*(6): 484–493.

Kling, R. (1980, March). Social analyses of computing: Theoretical orientations in recent empirical research. *Computing Surveys 12*(1): 61–110.

Kling, R. (1987). Defining the boundaries of computing across complex organizations, in Boland, R. & Hirschheim, R. (Eds.), *Critical Issues in Information Systems Research.* London: Wiley.

Kling, R. (1991, December). Cooperation, coordination and control in computer-supported work. *Communications of the ACM 34*(12): 83–88.

Kling, R. (1992). Behind the terminal: The critical role of computing infrastructure in effective information systems' development and use, chapter 10 (pp. 153–201) in *Challenges and Strategies for Research in Systems Development.* Cotterman, W. & Senn, J. (Eds.). New York: Wiley.

Kling, R., & Iacono, S. (1984, December). The control of information systems developments after implementation. *Communications of the ACM 27*(12): 1218–1226.

Kling, R., & Iacono, S. (1988, June). The mobilization of support for computerization: The role of computerization movements. *Social Problems 35*(3): 226–243.

Kling, R., & Iacono, S. (1989). Desktop computerization and the organization of work, in *Computers in the human context: Information technology, productivity, and people.* Forester, T., (Ed.), Cambridge, MA: MIT Press.

Kling, R., & Iacono, S. (1991). Making the computer revolution, in *Computerization and controversy: Value conflicts and social choices.* Dunlop, C., & Kling, R., (Eds.). (pp. 63–75). Boston: Academic Press.

Kling, R., & Scacchi, W. (1982). The web of computing: Computer technology as social organization. *Advances in Computers, 21*: 1–90.

Kling, R., Scherson, I., & Allen, J. P. (1992). Massively parallel computing and information capitalism, in *A new era of computing.* Hillis, W. D., & Bailey, J., (Eds.). Cambridge, MA: MIT Press.

Kraemer, K. L., Dickhoven, S., Tierney, S. F., & Kling, J. L. (1987). *Datawars: The politics of modeling in federal policymaking.* New York: Columbia University Press.

Kuhn, S. (1989). The limits to industrialization: Computer software development in a large commercial bank, in *The transformation of work: Skill, flexibility and the labour process.* (Wood, S., Ed.). London: Unwin Hyman.

Kumar, K. (1987). *Utopia and anti-utopia in modern times.* New York: Blackwell.

Kumar, K. (1991). *Utopianism.* Minneapolis: University of Minnesota Press.

Laudon, K. (1986). *Dossier society: Value choices in the design of national information systems.* New York: Columbia University Press.

Manhoff, R. K., & Schudson, M. (Eds.). (1986). *Reading the news.* New York: Pantheon Books.

McCloskey, D. N. (1990). *If you're so smart: The narrative of economic expertise.* Chicago: The University of Chicago Press.

Mowshowitz, A. (1976). *Conquest of will: Information processing in human affairs.* Reading, MA: Addison Wesley.

Mowshowitz, A. (1986). The social dimensions of office automation. *Advances in Computers, 25.* New York: Academic Press.

Office of Technology Assessment (1986). *The social administration and information technology.* Washington, DC: U.S. Government Printing Office.

Orlikowski, W. (1991) Integrated information environment or matrix of control? The contradictory implications of information technology. *Accounting, management and Information Technology, 1*(1).

Papert, S. (1980). *Mindstorms: Children, computers and powerful ideas.* New York: Basic Books.

Perrolle, J. (1991). Intellectual assembly lines: The rationalization of managerial, professional and technical work, in *Computerization and controversy: Value conflicts and social choices.* Dunlop, C., & Kling, R., (Eds.). Boston: Academic Press.

Perrolle, J. (1988). The social impact of computing: Ideological themes and research issues. *Social Science Computer Review 6*(4)(Winter): 469–480.

Pfaffenberger, B. (1989, January). The social meaning of the personal computer: Or, why the personal computer revolution was no revolution. *Anthropological Quarterly 61*(1): 39–47.

Poole, M. S., & DeSanctis, G. (1990). Understanding the use of group decision support systems: The theory of adaptive structuration in *Organization and communication technology* Fulk, F., & Steinfeld, C., (Eds.). (pp. 173–193). Newbury Park, CA: Sage.

Poster, M. (1991). *The mode of information.* Chicago: University of Chicago Press.

Reinecke, I. (1984). *Electronic illusions: A skeptic's view of our high tech future.* New York: Penguin.

Salerno, L. (1991). What happened to the computer revolution? In *Computerization and controversy: Value conflicts and social choices.* Dunlop, C., & Kling, R., (Eds.). Boston: Academic Press.

Sculley, J. (1991). The relationship between business and higher education: A perspective on the twenty-first century, in *Computerization and controversy: Value conflicts and social choices.* Dunlop, C., & Kling, R., (Eds.). Boston: Academic Press.

Segal, H. P. (1986). The technological utopians, in *Imagining tomorrow: History, technology and the American future* Corn, J. J., (Ed.). Cambridge, MA: MIT Press.

Sheingold, K., Hawkins, J., & Char, C. (1984). 'I'm the thinkist, you're the typist:' The interaction of technology and the social life of classrooms. *Journal of Social Issues* 40(3): 49–61.

Stoll, C. (1991). Stalking the Wiley hacker, in *Computerization and controversy: Value conflicts and social choices* (Dunlop, C., & Kling, R., Eds.). Boston: Academic Press.

Stonier, T. (1983). *The wealth of information: A profile of the post-industrial economy.* London: Methuen London Ltd.

Straub, D., & Wetherbe, J. (1989, November). Information technologies for the 1990s: An organizational impact perspective. *Communications of the ACM, 32*(11): 1329–1339.

Toffler, A. (1980). *The third wave.* New York: Bantam Books.

Tuchman, G. (1978). *Making news: A study in the construction of reality.* New York: Free Press.

Van Maanen, J. (1988). *Tales from the field: On writing ethnography.* Chicago: University of Chicago Press.

Walsham, G., Symons, V., & Waema, T. (1988). Information systems as social systems: Implications for developing countries. *Information Technology for Development 3*(3).

Weizenbaum, J. (1976). *Computer power and human reason.* San Francisco. Freeman.

Wilson, R. G., Pilgrim, D. G., & Tasjian, D. (1986). *The machine age in America: 1918–1941.* New York: Harry Abrams.

Winner, L. (1992). Silicon Mystery House, in *Variations on a theme park: The new American city and the end of public space.* New York: Noonday Press.

Winograd, T. (1988). A language/action perspective on the design of cooperative work, *Human-Computer Interaction 3*(1): 3–30. Reprinted in Greif, I., (Ed.), *Computer-supported cooperative work: A book of readings.* (pp. 623–653). San Mateo, CA: Morgan-Kaufmann.

Wood, S. (1989). The transformation of work, in *The transformation of work: Skill, flexibility and the labour process* Wood, S., (Ed.). London: Unwin Hyman.

Zuboff, S. (1988). *In the age of the smart machine: The future of work and power.* New York: Basic Books.

3

*Questions to Ask and Techno-Fallacies to Avoid in the Consideration of New Information Technologies**

Gary T. Marx

University of Colorado

At the DIAC conference in 1990 in Cambridge, MA, cheerleaders for still another new technology—virtual reality—praised it with all the enthusiasm of a millenarian who has just talked to God. Not expressed were doubt, self-deprecating humor, attention to

*This chapter draws from commentary offered at the DIAC conference in Cambridge, MA, 1991 and extends on G. T. Marx, 1994, *Undercover: Police Surveillance in America* (Berkeley: Univ. of Calif. Press), ch. 10; "Technology and Privacy" *The World and I*, September 1990; and "No Soul in the New Machine: Techno-Fallacies in the Electronic Monitoring Movement" (with Ron Corbett) *Justice Quarterly*, Sept. 1991.

risks, opportunity costs, trade-offs, unintended consequences, empirical proof, and the mechanisms by which wondrous social changes were to arrive.

At this conference I had the familiar sense of *deja vu* that is almost always present when information technologists and marketeers publicly discuss their activities. They all too often offer solutions in search of problems and substitute answers for questions.

In considering new computer-based tools a cartoon captures a fundamental distinction between many technologists and humanists. It shows a Woody Allen-type character with a friend at the circus. They are watching endless clowns pour out of a small Volkswagen Bug. The friend says, "I always wonder how they get all those clowns into one little car." To which Allen replies, "That's the difference between us. I always wonder why." The "why," of course, refers not only to a scientific explanation involving the compression of matter, but to an explanation in human terms. Why was a technology developed? What are the rationales and motives for its use? What assumptions are made about how it will be used and the consequences it will have?

Before technical innovations are blindly and blithely adopted, it is important to examine the broader cultural climate, the rationales for action, and the empirical and value assumptions on which they are based. Although it is true of neither redwoods nor new technologies, that if you have seen one you have seen them all, the same basic questions should be asked about any new technology. In moderating the session on virtual reality, I asked the panelists to consider at least some of the following questions.

- What human needs or goals is the technology intended to serve?

- What other means are (or might be) available for obtaining the same goals? How do these compare to the proposed technology? If no other means are available, how does the cost of using the new technology compare to doing nothing?

- Who needs or wants the technology?

- Where does the pressure to develop and apply it come from?

- What groups are most involved in making decisions about the form of the technology and how it will be used?

- What groups are likely to profit most, or be hurt most, by the technology?

- What are the likely social impacts of the technology on things such as the economy, the environment, the physical and mental health of those who manufacture, work with and use it, the uses of power, equality, democracy, access to information and participation, autonomy, civil liberties, privacy, crime, victimization, and justice?

- How valid, reliable, and effective is the technology?

- What can go wrong as well as right? What are the major short- and long-run risks associated with it and the likelihood of their occurring?

- What unintended consequences might occur?

- What safeguards should be in place to minimize problems?

- How available and easy to use will the technology be? (For example, will it be available primarily only for large organizations, the wealthy, or the technically sophisticated?)

- Will it be designed to maximize choice and growth on the part of the user?

- Are there ways that it can be used without the subject's knowledge or consent?

- Where it will be used in a conflictual or coercive context, are principles of due process followed?

- What forms of recourse are available if the technology is misused and individuals and groups are harmed by it?

- What precedents does use of the technology create?

- What are the best and worst scenarios involving the technology that can be imagined for the next 10 years and the next 50 years?

- What factors are operating to push us toward or away from these outcomes?

- What lessons can we learn from earlier technologies already in place and from the experience of other countries?

These questions are not asked in an antitechnology tradition, but in a skeptical social science tradition. This tradition stresses the importance of asking about social stratification, power, ideology, unintended consequences, and the social and cultural correlates of what is produced and used in a society, in order to understand and evaluate the social impact of new technologies.

As is common, at the conference where these questions were asked by the moderator, the virtual reality panelists chose to ignore them in favor of celebratory oration. The presenters saw themselves as inventors, explorers, and entrepreneurs with a technical job to do. They were interested in the "how" not the "why." As in singer Tom Lehr's parody of Werner von Braun, sending the rockets up was their job, being concerned about where they came down was someone else's.

The presentations on virtual reality suffered from *premature enthusiasm*. Grandiose claims were made for which no documentation was offered. Conclusions seemed to be more based on magic or faith than on empirical evidence. We need dreams and visions, and marketplace rhetoric may have a role in creating a place for new ideas in the face of resistance from a conservative status quo, yet this may bring obvious dangers. To ask for caution and moderation is not to ask for inaction. A flashing yellow light is different from one that is red or green.

With the emphasis on the *means*, the goals were unclear. One presenter said that his job is "to build tools that do the best job." However, he did not define what the job was. Here ends become subservient to means.

When goals were specified, in particular for military and commercial uses, some audience commentators offered another more value-based and personal criticism—they were the *wrong goals*. If funds are not available for big projects from consumer, peace, or environmental groups should they be taken from whatever source offers them? Scientists and engineers unreflectively may become hired guns. The question of whether the technology will be developed and applied in such a way as to broadly serve the public interest (assuming we can define it), rather than the more narrow interests of sponsors is not considered.

Virtual reality, along with other machine-mediated forms of interaction and communication, raises important social and psychological issues. The issues this raises for children are particularly important. What are the dangers of *creating socially incompetent and escapist persons* who are more comfortable interacting with, and through, machines than in conventional ways? The late Timothy Leary was an advocate of the technology. It requires no great insight to ask about parallels between drugs and virtual reality and whether virtual reality is a functional equivalent. If it is, is it harmless? Is there a danger of addiction and of difficulty of negotiating one's way back and forth between worlds?

In permitting the rearranging of conventional reality and the seeming alteration of customary natural laws, will the technology be mentally disorienting for some? Can humans safely maintain the multiple, inconsistent realities that the technology may bring? Will the technology offer a platform for experimenting in a "safe" way with antisocial fantasies and serve as an escape valve, or will it encourage antisocial and psychotic behavior? Or will it have an opposite effect, extending experience, making for more well-rounded persons who can more confidently and competently face new situations, since they have already had a simulated experience with them?

Our confidence in the world may decline in the face of the rich *possibilities for creating alternative realities* offered by such technologies. Given the technology's power to alter images of conventional reality, will trust decline and skepticism increase about whether things are what they appear to be?

Through statements such as "We have to face it," "We have to get used to it," and "I'm only one person," presenters implied that the *technology was autonomous and unstoppable*, driven by an unseen all-powerful hand. However, there is nothing necessarily inevitable about technical developments. They involve human choices. Individuals have important responsibilities and can make a difference. There is no hidden hand or predetermined reality. Individuals create history within the broad constraints of their environment.

Other concerns expressed about the technology involved asking if "virtual reality" was the best name for it, since this may carry unwanted connotations. Less grandiose, epistemologically charged and emotion-laden terms, such as "virtual environment" or "high fidelity simulation," were suggested. The question also was raised as to whether there is anything new here. The assertion by one speaker that virtual reality offers "a world where there has been nothing before" and "all has to be created" seemed doubtful. Computer-based video simulation is not new. A common social science finding is that there are multiple social realities in which people may experience the same incident very differently. Even if there are new elements, the way the technology is developed and used and what people bring to it reflect the past.

AVOID TARNISHED SILVER-BULLET TECHNO-FALLACIES

The presentations on virtual reality nicely illustrated a number of the beliefs that can be labeled techno-fallacies. The failure to ask the questions posed at the beginning of this can lead to assumptions and statements that are highly questionable empirically, ethically, and practically. An academic analyst should offer theories, concepts, methods, and data. But he or she also hopefully should offer wisdom. A part of the wisdom arises in being able to identify and question the web of tacit and taken-for-granted assumptions that undergird action.

As an ethnographer I watch and listen. Sometimes I hear statements that seem wrong, whether empirically, logically, or normatively—much as a musician knows that certain notes are off key. Some examples include: "turn the technology loose and let the benefits flow"; "you can't stop progress"; "do away with the human interface"; "when you choose to make a phone call you are consenting to have your telephone number released"; "the public interest is whatever the public is interested in watching"; "the social security number will only be used for reporting income and wages"; "there is no law against this"; "the technology is neutral"; "that has never happened"; "if the data is available we'd be foolish not to use it"; "if we have the technology we ought to use it."

As a participant in many working groups, conferences, and hearings over the last decade dealing with new information technologies, I have encountered a number of "tarnished silver bullet information age techno-fallacies." Moving from general fallacies regardless of the technology, to those that apply primarily to information and communication technologies, we can note:

1. The fallacy of imminent development and use, which holds that if a technology can be developed it should be, and that if it is developed, its use cannot be stopped.

2. The fallacy that greater expenditures and more powerful technology will continually yield benefits in a linear fashion.

3. The fallacy that pragmatism and/or efficiency should automatically overrule other values such as fairness, equity, and external costs imposed on third parties.

4. The fallacy of thinking that the meaning of a technology lies only in its practicality or material aspects and not in its social symbolism and historical referents.

5. The fallacy that the means will never determine the end (or if you can't fix the real problem fix whatever the technology permits you to fix).

6. The fallacy of the free lunch or painless dentistry.

7. The fallacy of perfect containment or nonescalation (or the Frankensteinian fallacy that technology will always remain the solution rather than become the problem).

8. The fallacy of thinking that a given, carefully circumscribed change will not create a precedent.

9. The fallacy of technical neutrality.

10. The fallacy of societal consensus and homogeneity in which it is assumed that conflicts and divisions are nonexistent and what's good for those with economic and political power is necessarily good for everyone else.

11. The fallacy of implied consent and free choice.

12. The fallacy of quantification.

13. The fallacy of the short run.

14. The legalistic fallacy that just because you have a legal right to do something it's the right thing to do.

15. The technocratic fallacy that the experts always know what is best.

16. The populist fallacy that the people always know what is best.

17. The fallacy of lowest common denominator morality in which if the competition or others push moral limits, you are justified in doing the same.

18. The fallacy of permanent victory.

19. The fallacy of the 100% fail-safe system.

20. The fallacy of delegating decision-making authority to the machine.

21. The fallacy of a passive, nonreactive environment.

22. The fallacy of believing that because it is possible to successfully skate on thin ice, it is acceptable to do so.

23. The fallacy of assuming that if a critic questions the means, he or she must also be against the ends.

The following apply particularly to information technologies:

24. The fallacy of assuming that only the guilty have to fear the development of intrusive technology (or if you've done nothing wrong you have nothing to hide).

25. The fallacy of assuming that personal information on customers, clients, and cases in the possession of a company is just another kind of property to be bought and sold the same as office furniture or raw materials.

26. The fallacy of assuming that data are simply there waiting to be delivered or plucked from the data tree (the social and political factors involved in collection–construction are not seen).

27. The fallacy that the facts speak for/produce themselves.

28. The fallacy of assuming that because our privacy expectations are historically determined and relative, they must necessarily become weaker as technology becomes more powerful.

29. The fallacy that if a value such as privacy is relatively new or new in form, or applies to only a fraction of the world's population, it can't be very important.

Finally, there follows a more general fallacy:

30. The fallacy of rearranging the deck chairs on the Titanic instead of looking for icebergs (or responding to an overflowing bath tub by mopping the floor instead of turning off the faucet).

These fallacies differ in kind—some can be shown to be empirically false or logically suspect, and hence, if the argument is correct, persons of diverse political perspectives could agree that they are fallacious. Others will be seen as fallacies only when there is agreement about the values or value priorities on which they are based. Someone holding different values might come up with a different list including items such as "the fallacy of listening to academics who make broad generalizations." The fallacies also differ in seriousness and some are in conflict. My basic point is not to argue strenuously for this particular list, but to argue for the importance of undertaking a critical examination of the assumptions that we make about new technologies.

Let me end with a joke that I hope is not apocryphal. Three people are about to be guillotined in the not-too-distant future. The first, a very religious person, has his head put on the block, the rope is cut, but the blade fails to fall. He looks up and says, "It's the will of God" and is let go. The second, a political activist, has her head placed on the block, the rope is cut, and again it fails to fall. She looks up and says, "It's the will of the people" and is let go. The third person, a computer scientist with an MBA looks up and says, "Hey, wait a minute, I think I can fix that." I hope in our noble efforts to use computer technology to fix our society that none of us end up committing self, corporate, or social suicide!

4

*Knowledge in Production**

Jim Davis
Michael Stack

At a certain stage of their development, the material productive forces of society come into conflict with ... the property relations within which they have been at work hitherto. From forms of development of the forces of production these relations turn into their fetters. Then begins an epoch of social revolution. With the change of the economic foundation the entire immense superstructure is more or less rapidly transformed.

—Karl Marx, 1968

But if robots indeed are able to take the place of human labor, critical questions arise.

—Lewis, 1990

INTRODUCTION

The designations "Information Age," "Second Industrial Revolution," and "Electronics Revolution" are all attempts at uniting under one banner the totality of recent develop-

* A version of this chapter originally appeared in *Directions and Implications of Advanced Computing 1992 (DIAC-92 Symposium Proceedings*, Computer Professionals for Social Responsibility, Palo Alto, CA.

ments in computers, digital telecommunications, robotics, bioengineering, and materials science. Use of the word "revolution" recognizes the nature of these new technologies as qualitatively different from that which has gone before.

Technology can be defined as the sum "of the means employed to provide objects necessary for human sustenance and comfort" (*Webster's New Collegiate Dictionary, 1975*). As such, "technology" comprises not only the machinery and tools required for production, but also workers' skills and the organization of production. In this chapter, we hold that the technologies of this new era are distinguished from technologies of the industrial age by their high *knowledge* content—they can be characterized as knowledge-intensive. This distinction, which will be explored in more detail later, is warranted for two converging reasons. First, our widening understanding of Nature, especially in the life and material sciences, is yielding dramatic benefits in productivity, thereby reducing labor, machinery, and raw material requirements in production. Second, the ability to *record* workers' skills (another form of knowledge), and encode it using digital electronics into the instruments of production, and to "play back" the knowledge in the absence of humans, reduces labor requirements in production. With the diminishing contributions of machinery and raw materials and labor, knowledge emerges as the dominating component in production.

We consider in this chapter the implications for the organization of production based on knowledge-intensive technologies. As knowledge's role in production becomes dominant, it threatens the stability and viability of a system organized around the exchange of goods based on ability to pay. Briefly put, the new technologies undermine current social relations. This chapter pays particular attention to the effect on labor.

For the purposes of this chapter, we define "data" as raw perceptions captured by some data collection device. The Landsat satellite, for example, is capable of photographing the entire Earth's surface every two weeks, and has been operating for 20 years. Ninety-five percent of the images have never been seen by human eyes (Gore, 1991).

"Information" is data with human labor applied to it. In its broadest sense, information includes experiences, perceptions, symbols, imagery, signals, and data that have been collected, organized, perhaps analyzed, and then expressed in some form. The key point here is that information is the product of human intellectual activity—effort has been expended to put the data into a form capable of satisfying some need or want. Using the Landsat example, the satellite photographs that have been examined and catalogued would qualify as "information." Information also includes transactions, customer lists, mail, news, research reports, and so forth.

"Knowledge" is a further refinement of information. It too is a product of human labor. It is information that has been systematized and integrated, organized so that it is relevant to natural and social processes. Pursuing the Landsat example, an understanding of weather patterns, climate trends, mineral deposits, or land usage might be examples of knowledge derived from the catalogued and studied photographs. In this chapter we focus on knowledge as a component of production.[1]

THE NATURE OF KNOWLEDGE IN PRODUCTION

Production cannot take place without knowledge. Some understanding of the production process is required so that production can take place. Just as knowledge enables production, more knowledge enhances it, that is, it increases productivity. In one of its most obvious forms, additional knowledge, in the form of a worker's superior skill, enables him or her to accomplish a task more quickly, more easily, and with less waste.

Knowledge in production takes many forms. In addition to being brought to the production process by the worker as *skills*, it might be contained in the *organization* of production like the "assembly line" or the "work team," or in the *design* of tools or machinery, or in the production *process*, or in the chemical *formulae* or in the molecular *structure* of a composite material or the DNA *sequence* of a bioengineered protein, or in the software *algorithm*. Knowledge might be represented by the conservation *techniques*, or *methods* of utilizing waste and byproducts, or inventory management *theories*. Knowledge mobilizes the benefits of nature. Scientific and technological knowledge—the universe as understood by society—is Nature's bounty discovered. It deepens or enhances or enlarges the environment in which production (and all other human activity) takes place. Knowledge has a *material* basis. Knowledge cannot exist separate from some material "container"—memory, books, computer disks, and so on. Knowledge, in and of itself, cannot create a house or a loaf of bread or a computer. Its usefulness only manifests itself through the production process. Knowledge can only generate useful things by having labor apply it during production. Knowledge can be disseminated, but is useless without the labor to apply it.

Knowledge has a *social* origin—it is the result of people interacting. Technology and invention are not the products of solitary inventors or scientists; rather, inventors and scientists build on the past accomplishments, experiences, and discoveries of generations of scientists, engineers, authors, production workers, and so on.

Finally, we should note that knowledge has peculiar qualities that distinguish it from labor, machinery, raw materials, and other components of production. Two people can simultaneously use some bit of knowledge, it can be duplicated ad infinitum at almost no cost, it can circulate around the globe in seconds, it is not "consumed" or exhausted as it is used, and the more it is shared, the more it grows.

---

[1] There are certainly other important aspects of information in today's economy. Large quantities of information are required to circulate goods in a global market; and information itself has become a commodity (Schiller, 1988). The reproduction of labor power requires transmitting the knowledge required to continue production, through the educational system and publishing. Entertaining and propagandizing to preserve the social order is handled by and large through "information industries," including the news media and entertainment industry. Methods of coercive social control (via the police and military) keep pace with technology as well.

(Cleveland, 1985; see also Toffler, 1983). These qualities give knowledge a unique and subversive role in commodity production.

Throughout history, humans labor, and as a result of that labor, society learns more about the universe. The amount of knowledge increases. This knowledge shows up in technology. The development of the means of production is the accumulation of the experience of workers, refined by them into knowledge, and congealed in technology.

One of the general processes throughout the evolution of technology has been the transference of human skills and attributes to the machinery and techniques used in production. The need for humans as a source of physical power began to disappear with the domestication of animals and the harnessing of wind and water power. Later, the need for humans as a dexterous manipulator of materials began to disappear with the development of machinery that used gears, ratchets, springs, cams, and so on to replicate human motion. Most recently, the human functions of "operator" and "decision-maker" have been usurped as the workers' knowledge is abstracted and programmed into numerical control ROMs, and the decision-making is replaced by "artificial intelligence" programs. This last stage has only been possible with the development of cybernetics, information theory, transistors, and a host of other technologies in the period around World War II. These technologies laid the basis for replicating functions of the human brain in inanimate electronic equivalents harnessed to machinery. With the invention in the late 1960s of low-cost programmable microprocessors and memory chips, knowledge could be converted into sequences of computer code and processed by semiconductors at a speed of millions of simple instructions per second to direct machinery. In the past, the machine operator served as guide and overseer, steering and monitoring—qualities difficult to reproduce using only mechanical means. But the advent of new technologies allowed the machine operator's function to be abstracted and encoded, eliminating the need for an operator at all. Thus began the assault on the last outpost occupied by humans in the production process. One key factor of knowledge-intensive production, then, is that the human aspect of production is "recorded," as it were, digitized, and is *now capable of being "replayed" ad infinitum.* Knowledge becomes a "direct force of production."[2] What remains of the laboring process is the ever-shrinking pool of tasks, like servicing or designing, that are still beyond the dexterity or "programmability" of evolving technology; or tasks for which the cost of the automated machinery exceeds the labor required to carry it out.

The knowledge brought to mass manufacturing by workers (in the form of skills) or embodied in the machinery do not comprise the total required: Knowledge also is embedded in the organization of production itself. The traditional assembly line was

---

[2] "Nature builds no machines, no locomotives, railways, electric telegraphs, self acting mules etc. These are products of human industry; natural material transformed into organs of … human participation in nature. They are *organs of the human brain, created by the human hand;* the power of knowledge objectified. The development of fixed capital indicates to what degree general social knowledge has become a *direct force of production* (Marx, 1973, p. 706).

set up once, after which it ran without variation for month after month. Workers were consigned to one task. Change necessitated extensive revision and reaadjustment. Current trends such as "lean production" are not hard-coded in this way but are intentionally malleable so that they can take advantage of new knowledge as it becomes available. This "new knowledge" appears as the outcome of ever-evolving experience with a particular manufacturing process; or as changes ordered by management; and (a recent "innovation") the taking and rewarding of input from those who actually carry out the work. In the latter case, a "neotaylorism" emerges, where instead of the dictates coming down from above as they did in the past, workers in teams on the shop floor study ways to tailor themselves more tightly to the task.

A production system with more knowledge applied to it will be more productive. Differentials in labor, energy, and material costs of course are important, but it is not these factors that are credited for the marketplace success, say, of Japanese manufacturers, the originators of "lean" (i.e., knowledge-intensive) production methods. "A critical point was reached [in the development of production technologies] when the American automobile industry finally acknowledged that Japanese firms had established a real production advantage based on the more effective use of capital—that is, in the effective organization of labor and equipment—not on low-cost labor" (Cohen & Sysman, 1987, p. 118; see also footnote 3).

In knowledge-intensive production, significant amounts of scientific research (mental labor) are carried out outside of and prior to actual production. The product of research is then brought to production in the forms of designs, new materials, techniques, algorithms, biotechnologies, and so on. The products of this scientific effort employ a deeper understanding of natural processes, down to the molecular and atomic level. Some new materials "remember" qualities when exposed to light or temperature changes; others are superconductive; still others facilitate data transmission at the speed of light. Toffler describes this leap in productive forces.

> Second Wave industries used brute force technologies—they punched, hammered, rolled, beat, chipped and chopped, drilled and battered raw materials into the shapes we needed or wanted.... The Third Wave industries operate at an altogether deeper level. Instead of banging something into shape, we reach back into the material itself and reprogram it to assume the shape we desire. (Toffler, 1983, p.20)[3]

As a result,

> new materials and biotechnologies, along with information technologies, undercut the value of many existing sources of natural resources, since they allow the replacement of

---

[3] Toffler used "waves" to describe in broad strokes these stages: the First Wave corresponds to the era of primarily agricultural-based manual labor; the Second Wave corresponds to mechanized industrial production; the Third Wave corresponds to the knowledge-intensive production based in electronics, biotechnology, and new materials (see also Toffler, 1980).

one material with another, or permit the more efficient use of already available objects. (Goldhaber, 1985, p. 61)

Intellectual work beforehand substitutes for material (and labor, as described above) in production. This has always been the case, but the rate of substitution has accelerated, and its application is facilitated by new technologies (e.g., telecommunications technologies disperse them, and flexible manufacturing methods enable their ready implementation).

Developments in science and technology reinforce the fact that we have made a radical break with our industrial past. Electronic technology and cybernetics enable instructions and information to be coded in digital electrical pulses, instead of gears, ratchets, and springs. The result is components (e.g., digital communication switches) that do not suffer from friction or fatigue, and operate at speeds and load levels orders of magnitude greater than their mechanical counterparts. A constantly repeating sequence of instructions does not wear out a processor chip the way repeated actions eventually wear out a piston or camshaft (League For Programming Freedom, 1990). Beyond solid-state electronics, the developing field of "molecular electronics" utilizes the properties of proteins and bacteria in production.[4] The possibility of bacteria tirelessly creating polymers in a laboratory vat (now a possibility), without the cost of locating, drilling, pumping, transporting, and processing oil to achieve the same result suggests a level of productivity that is qualitatively different from previous forms of productive forces.

Or consider the particular case of the computer software industry. Software, the instructions that direct machinery, is knowledge encoded. It is distilled experience and learning listed out in instructions for hardware. Forty years ago, there was no software industry. In 1990, the global market for packaged software was estimated at $43 billion, and is expected to reach $100 billion by 1995.[5]

But where does software stop and hardware begin? The distinction becomes fuzzy when machinery incorporates chips with instructions "burned into" them. Chip masks for semiconductor production have been legally defined as a form of writing, and once a mask of acceptable quality is developed, it becomes something like a printing plate for reproducing chips (and money). Even the metals and composite ceramics used in production are now spoken of as being "smart," as in, "The smarter the material, the less it weighs" (Altehpohl, cited in Cleveland, 1985).

---

[4] "A protein isolated from bacteria found in salt marshes is proving to be a promising device for data storage in a molecule...." A group of researchers from Syracuse University reported they optically stored and retrieved data in three dimensions in a tiny block made of molecules of bacteriorhodapsin...." The article goes on to say that six 1-cm cubes of the molecules can store the entire Library of Congress (Amal Kumar Naj, "Bacteria protein may help to miniaturize computers." *Wall Street Journal.* September 4, 1991. p.B-4).

[5] These figures are for the "packaged software market", and do not include computer programming services or in-house computer programming.

In examining the nature of knowledge in production, we might look for quantitative measurements to justify calling the new technologies "knowledge-intensive." Knowledge (admittedly a soft term) can take the form of "already known" knowledge, in the form of existing technology, training, education, copies of software, and so on, or of "newly known" knowledge, the results of research and development.

The extensive training required to master new technologies, and the need for ongoing education to keep current with a given field indicates the volume of "already known" knowledge required for contemporary production. Or one might use the number of instructions built into a machine in a state-of-the-art factory, or years of education per worker to measure "knowledge-intensity."

One measurement of "newly known" knowledge might be the relative portion of *design* effort that goes into a product, versus the actual *production* effort. "[I]nformation, design, research and development and software represent a growing proportion of the value of most products," note the authors of *Beyond the Casino Economy*, an analysis of Great Britain's economy. "As the importance of research and development rises relative to that of direct production, the purpose of labour is increasingly the production of knowledge, in the form of designs or production processes" (Costello, Michie, & Milne, 1989).[6] The recording of knowledge in the form of software makes up ever greater proportions of pivotal tools and industries. Software becomes a larger and larger cost of increasingly complex production systems: "Software now accounts for about 80 percent of the development expense for new systems," according to *Computer Design* magazine in 1987 (Hayes, 1989, p.87). Even in manufacturing, software plays a central role. "Retooling," with the new "flexible manufacturing systems," simply means changing the software that guides the machines. The assembly line (hardware) remains unchanged. The robots, hardly pausing, begin exercising different actions in obeyance of the newly loaded programs.

Lash (1991) has suggested that the number of models per design serves as a crude indicator of the relative amount of knowledge that goes into a good, That is, a model of a car of which only 10,000 "copies" are made has a higher design or knowledge content than a model of which 20,000 are made. The trend in manufacturing has been toward smaller production runs, with more frequent model changes, suggesting therefore a higher design/knowledge content. Finally, we might look at employment statistics as an indicator of the changing character of the productive forces. By 2000, one study estimates that two-thirds of the employed workforce in the United States will be working in education/knowledge/information-related jobs, whereas manufacturing, commerce and industry will account for only 22%, and agriculture for 2%. In 1920, 9% worked in information/knowledge/education jobs; 53% in manufacturing; and 28% in agriculture (Cleveland, 1985). But the lines between these categories are blurring as the knowledge component in each sector increases. In a report on high-tech

---

[6] A recent *Business Week* pointed out "automation has whittled hands-on labor to 15% of manufacturing costs, and in high-tech industries, it's closer to 5%" (Kelly, 1991).

tractors, a modern farmer was quoted, "Farming you used to do with your back; now you use your mind" (Rosenfeld, 1991).

KNOWLEDGE IN THE PRODUCTION OF COMMODITIES

A common problem in discussing "knowledge" as a factor in production is determining its "value," and what value it adds to goods during production. Toffler (1989), for example, says that "knowledge adds value" (p.82). But what *is* "value"? An economics textbook defines "value added" as simply "the revenue from selling a product minus the amounts paid for goods and services purchased from other firms" (Baumol & Blinder, 1979, p. 322). This definition is unsatisfactory. Is "value" only realized through the "selling" and the "purchasing"—in the realm of circulation? What about the production process? Is value really only tied to the vagaries of fluctuating supply and demand? What if the "goods and services" can't be sold, say, because potential users do not have the money to purchase the product? Does the product therefore have less (or no) value?

Recognizing the central role of commodities in capitalism, Marx began *Das Kapital* with an extended analysis of the question of the "value" of commodities. He identified two different kinds of "value" in commodities. In order to be exchanged, a commodity must fulfill some need or want for another human being. Marx called this subjective and qualitative aspect of a commodity its *use value.* At the same time, in order to exchange goods of different use values, Marx argued that there needs to be some common basis of assessing a value of the commodities, some quantitative, measurable aspect. Marx identified "socially necessary labor" as that "thing" common to all commodities. It represents the amount of abstract human labor added during production, and the "dead" labor embodied in the raw materials and machinery used up during production. Marx called this aspect of commodities *exchange value.* The purpose of production, the reason that humans come together and engage in economic activity, Marx argued, is to create use values, to satisfy needs and wants. The process of production, however, is the expenditure of past and present human labor, measured as exchange value. The exchange value of *knowledge,* then, is the "socially necessary labor" that goes into the research, the analysis, and the expression required to develop it.[7]

Marx (1967) defined "socially necessary labor" as "that required to produce an article under the normal conditions of production, and with the average degree of skill and intensity prevalent at the time" (p.47). The concept of "socially necessary labor" that defines the exchange value of a commodity recognizes an "average" technology stage or platform upon which production takes place. The "socially nec-

---

[7] Workers who process information can create surplus value (i.e., are productive workers in the Marxist sense)—researchers and data collectors are the miners of information production; programmers, the tool and die makers; computer operators, the forge hands; desktop publishers, the trim workers.

essary labor," then, implies also a certain common level of knowledge about production processes. The use of computerized typesetting in newspaper production, robotics in automobile manufacture, and crop rotation in agriculture are examples of a technology platform. Some producers may be ahead of the average, because of some special knowledge or technique, and some may be behind the average, because they are unaware of a technique, or have not invested in state-of-the-art technology. A commodity made by a worker employed by the "behind the average" company with outdated technology or using outdated techniques does not have more value because the worker took longer to make it. *Nor does the commodity have less value if an especially productive worker, using state-of-the-art equipment with the latest techniques, takes less time to make it.*

In the latter example, a capitalist enterprise can realize extra profit from use of some particular knowledge as long as the knowledge enables him to produce commodities whose value is less than the "average" value of that commodity from all producers, both slow and fast, both backward and advanced. The advanced producer's commodities contain less than the socially necessary labor—the enterprise ahead of the innovation wave is producing commodities more cheaply than its competitors, but selling them at the same price on the market. Thus, certain kinds of knowledge become sought-after resources; and competition drives forward technological development, although in a haphazard and socially hazardous way, because maximum profitability is the overriding goal.

Once knowledge becomes the new social average (that is, it becomes widely disseminated so now everyone is using the new technique), its ability to enable the innovator to accumulate extra profit is lost. To *maximize* profit from knowledge, then, the capitalist must enjoy the *exclusive* use of it.

In order to preserve the value of knowledge for the originator, knowledge used in production must be contained, and prevented from becoming the social average. The innovator tries to keep new techniques that give the firm an advantage hidden from competitors. At the same time, however, competing capitalists want to get hold of the newest technology to effectively compete. The patent and copyright system was developed, and continues to develop through laws and the courts, to attempt to resolve these two contradictory demands by competing capitalists—*protection of profit* (protecting the producer of the knowledge or technology) versus *access to profits* (access by competitors who want the knowledge or technology).[8] Copyrights and patents are the legal mechanisms for maintaining exclusive rights to a particular technique. They are treated as assets on company balance sheets and represent sources of revenue, like mineral deposits or trade routes or rights-of-way.

The economics of "knowledge production" are such that the initial version requires a substantial investment (a high fixed cost), but subsequent copies have a relatively low

---

[8] (See, e.g., Hindle & Lubar, 1986; Stallman, 1985; Wincor & Mandell, 1980.) We are assuming here that the business is not the production of knowledge, like software companies. Their task is to sell the technology as widely as possible, while retaining ownership over the technology.

reproduction cost.[9] Thus, the exclusive, original copy of the knowledge has high exchange value. But just as machinery loses value as cheaper versions come into use, copies of knowledge, because of the relatively low cost of duplicating knowledge (hence, cheaper versions of the original), quickly depreciate the exchange value of the original knowledge.[10] For subsequent users, the knowledge, once it has become the social average (i.e., widely known or distributed), continues to add to the mass of use values, but transfers little or no exchange value to commodities in the course of production. Each copy (book, computer disk, tape, etc.) of "knowledge" consumes almost no material relative to its development cost, so has little exchange value to transfer to the final product. Compare this with, say, a machine cutting tool. Each "copy" of the cutting tool consumes additional steel, energy, labor, and so forth, so it may have a substantial exchange value to transfer to the final product.

A century and a half ago, Marx (1967) noted that "[a]ll means of production supplied by Nature without human assistance such as land, water, metals in situ, and timber in virgin forests" fall into a category of things which transfer use value, without transferring exchange value (p.197). Elsewhere, Marx (1967) referred to the "gratuitous" work of machines, the result of the machinery mobilizing natural forces.[11] He also recognized that "the productive forces resulting from cooperation and division of labor cost capital nothing. They are natural forces of social production. So also physical forces, like steam, water, etc. when appropriated to productive processes cost nothing" (p. 365). "Cooperation" and "division of labor"—learned ideas of how to organize production—are examples of knowledge. Once discovered, knowledge costs nothing (i.e., transfers little or no exchange value) but enhances productivity, and thus adds to the mass of use values. This is the character of contemporary productive forces.

---

[9] Knowledge-intensive companies like Microsoft (software) or Merck (pharmaceuticals) can be extremely profitable if they have a successful product. Microsoft has two-and-a-half times the profit of Apple on a third of the sales. (*Business Week*, November 18, 1991) Software companies are peculiar in that they carry virtually no fixed assets, and have few direct manufacturing costs. A computer program that takes person-years to develop can be duplicated in a matter of seconds using a personal computer. *Soft*letter*, a software-publishing industry newsletter recently surveyed its readership regarding manufacturing costs. "The typical personal-computer-software company now spends 18 percent of its revenues on what accountants call 'cost-of-goods sold,' a category that includes product components, manufacturing operations, fulfillment, and shipping." The median unit cost of software products (disks and manuals) was $10.20; for products in the $300-999 price range, it was $20.98 (Tarter, 1990).

[10] "But in addition to the material wear and tear, a machine also undergoes what we may call a moral depreciation. It loses exchange-value, either by machines of the same sort being produced cheaper than it, or by better machines entering into competition with it. In both cases, be the machine ever so young and full of life, its value is no longer determined by the labour actually materialised in it, but by the labour-time requisite to reproduce either it or the better machine. It has, therefore, lost value more or less (Marx, 1967, p. 381).

[11] "After making allowance [for wear and tear and auxiliary consumption like oil and coal, machines] each do their work gratuitously, just like the forces furnished by Nature without the help of man (Marx, 1967, p. 365).

So when Toffler says that "knowledge adds value," he is correct in the sense that it adds to the mass of *use* values. But in another sense he is wrong, because knowledge reduces the *exchange* value of commodities.

Adding machinery to production increases the constant portion of capital. It is development based on expansion of requirements—more raw materials, more fixed capital. Knowledge, on the other hand, *reduces* the constant portion of capital and production requirements, while *expanding* output. The cost of computing power, for example, has plummeted because of new materials and new designs (see, e.g., Forester, 1987). Miniaturization, computerized controls, conservation techniques, and new composite "smart" materials reduce raw material and energy requirements in manufacturing and agriculture. Computerized inventory control and digital telecommunications reduce inventory requirements and speed the turnover of capital. Some economists assign a majority, and in some countries, over 75%, of the postwar economic growth in the West to improved productivity via technology, as opposed to growth resulting from increased inputs like more labor, raw materials, and machinery (Berliner, 1976). Knowledge, as a special form of information, now dominates production itself, and overwhelms the contributions from traditional inputs to the final product.[12]

THE IMPACT ON LABOR

The twofold process we have been describing—knowledge-intensive production is able to "record" and "play back" human effort many times in the absence, for all practical purposes, of human beings; and at the same time, knowledge mobilizes the *in situ* benefits of Nature, extracting use values possessing little or no exchange values—points to the elimination of labor from production. Exchange value is the measure of human labor power consumed in production. A drop in exchange value represents a drop in human labor requirements.

Concretely, new technologies affect the labor market in different ways. Forester identifies four "causes of concern" regarding the impact of high technology on jobs: (a) traditional manufacturing jobs (e.g., in automobile and steel production) are disappearing, and will never come back; (b) new manufacturing industries will not create many new jobs, because of automation; (c) there are doubts about the capacity of the service sector to create any more new jobs; and (d) the high tech sector itself, even though it might grow, will create only a modest number of jobs (Forester, 1987).

Under capitalism, one of the primary reasons for introducing new technology is to reduce costs (toward maximizing profit), including labor costs. The greater the savings, the greater the incentive to innovate. Robotics and numerical control technology enable firms to eliminate high-paid production jobs. In a recent interview, Heidi and

---

[12] From this, it follows that, in a knowledge-based economy, the production and distribution of knowledge becomes the leading sector of the economy, much like the railroad sector of the late nineteenth century.

Alvin Toffler describe a new factory in Israel. It "is a cutting tool factory that doesn't have a single worker in it. Even machines get their parts from a robot that goes from machine to machine and resupplies them." What work is done is moving information around either as "technical specialists" or helping the products circulate, "working in bookkeeping or in sales (NeXTWORLD Interview, 1991). The NeXT computer factory in Fremont, CA "requires only five manual assembly workers and fewer than a hundred other workers, mostly engineers, for a line capable of producing $1 billion of computers a year" ("All NeXT's Factory Lacks is Orders," 1990).

Better data access and analysis as a result of computers, improved telecommunications, and networking enable firms to also eliminate middle management positions. Digital telecommunications, improved transportation technology, and modern manufacturing methods enable the globalization of production and the labor market. This makes it economically feasible to transfer work that can be moved, like manufacturing, as opposed to work that cannot be moved, like personal services to cheaper labor markets; and at the same time squeezes domestic wages. Recent figures from the US Bureau of Labor Statistics indicate that the same number of people will be employed in manufacturing in 2000 as in 1970. This means that the number of people employed in manufacturing, as a percent of total employment, will shrink from 24% in 1970 to 14% at the turn of the century. From 1970 to 1988, however, manufacturing output has remained a steady 20% or so of the GNP, whereas the output, in constant dollars, has grown by more than 50%. Other figures indicate that, over the last ten years alone, 1 million manufacturing jobs have disappeared in the United States In 1982 dollars, the average weekly earnings (including overtime) for private industry production and nonsupervisory workers was $298 in 1970; in 1989 it was $264, an 11% drop (U.S. Bureau of the Census, 1991).[13] Fewer manufacturing workers are producing more, and in general, making less.

At the same time a relatively small, well-paid, knowledge-rich (highly skilled) section are still eagerly sought after by firms. "Not all parts of the labor market are shrinking. Engineers and technicians are still in demand, depending on their specialty, even at companies that otherwise are paring workers" ("Help Not Wanted," 1991). The working class is splitting into a well-paid, knowledge-rich (highly skilled) section that works in capital-intensive design and production work, and a larger, relatively low-skilled (or no-skilled) section consigned to work that is too expensive to automate, with an ever-widening gulf growing in between (Fusfield, 1988).[14] The polarization of income has been dramatic. A recent *Business Week* article points out that "it's only those in the top 20% who show a respectable gain in real incomes over the 15-year span." The bottom 60% have seen their incomes drop, whereas the richest 5% have seen their income

---

[13] According to the labor theory of value, as the value (exchange value, that is) of other commodities drop, so does the value of labor power, itself acommodity. Since price gravitates around exchange value, the price of labor power, that is, wages, would drop as well.

[14] See also Gandy, 1987, for a discussion of "information-rich" versus "information-poor."

grow 60% and the richest 1% have seen rates of growth twice that ("The Rich Get Richer," 1991).

Whole sections of the U.S. population are being cast out of the sphere of production. The cast-outs are neither consumers nor producers; they aren't even needed as a "reserve army of the unemployed." Drugs, disease, illiteracy, homelessness, or prison are their lot. "High-wage slavery is being replaced by low-wage slavery. Low-wage slavery is being replaced with no-wage slavery—people who work without wages, but who are 'paid' in survival coupons" (Miller, 1991). The members of this latter group are marginally maintained by society through shrinking welfare payments and food stamps, and forced to earn their meager keep through modern versions of slavery like workfare or prison labor.[15] The "cost of production" of marginalized workers exceeds their usefulness as laborers—in the logic of capitalism, they are people with no value (Peery, 1992).

The "well-paid, knowledge-rich" section of the working class is by no means immune from the pressures on wages and "redundancy" originating in the information economy. Behind the drive for object-oriented programming (OOP), for example, is the need to cut costs and raise productivity by bringing software production techniques at least to the level of the interchangeable part—something achieved in industrial production 150 years ago. A *Business Week* editorial argued,

> There's already evidence that object-oriented programming can help corporate computing departments reduce the outlandish amounts of money and time spent on creating their own programs. This could spell substantial savings, since corporations now spend most of their information-technology budgets on software—about 60% more than they spend on hardware, according to market researchers. ("A Great Leap," 1991)

The next technological step beyond OOP is computer-aided software engineering (CASE), which could bring software production up to the electronic age, by having computers themselves write the software.[16]

The current recession has pummeled the electronics industry, as much as any other. IBM has announced that an additional 20,000 jobs will be cut in 1992, on top of the 20,000 cut in 1991. IBM will have eliminated 75,000 jobs—almost 20% of its workforce—since 1986. Some 90,000 jobs were lost nationally in the electronics industry during the year ending in September 1991 ("Thousands of Electronic Jobs Vanishing," 1991). The mini- and mainframe computer companies like Digital, Bull, Wang, Burroughs, Tandem, Amdahl, and IBM have been victims of the rapid "downsizing" (replacing large, old computer systems with small, cheap,

---

[15] "New York State's prison system has quietly imposed mandatory work policies, locking inmates who refuse work in their cells for 23 hours a day and then blackballing them when they come up for parole.... For [their labor] they are paid 60 cents a day at the start for a normal 40-hour workweek" ("New York Prisoners Work or Else," 1992).

[16] This process is no different than earlier efforts to break the power of skilled production workers. The automatic spinning mule, the cylinder textile printing machine, and the wool-combing machine all undermined the power of specific skilled textile trades. (Barsalla, 1988).

more powerful systems) in hardware and software driven by new technology and the recession.[17] Under the euphemism of "restructuring," workers in these technology firms are being cut loose, ironically due, in part, to even more powerful computer technology.

There is also no reason why data entry, computer programming or data analysis cannot be done in low-wage areas like India, Ireland, or Eastern Europe, with the product of the labor, computer code or data, transmitted instantaneously electronically to customers on the other side of the world.[18] A recent *Wall Street Journal* article described how data processing and other "back-office work" is being moved offshore to cheaper labor markets. It's not only low-skilled data entry work that's moving.

> Wright Investor Services has 85 employees in its Shannon [Ireland] office. Most of them are young financial analysts earning less than the equivalent of $20,000 a year organizing financial information from companies around the world for Wright's databases. That is far preferable to hiring American business school graduates at $45,000.... It is precisely these kinds of higher-level jobs—financial analysts and technicians—that the Irish government is trying to attract. And much the same can be said for Jamaica, Singapore and, for that matter, many U.S. communities. So the future may bring intensified worldwide competition for these high-skill computer-based tasks. ("American Firms," 1991)

The article goes on to describe how software developer Quarterdeck employs 20 workers in Ireland to field nearly a thousand technical support calls a week. During the day, calls are handled by the U.S. staff, "but after hours, the head office [in California] throws a switch and the calls are routed automatically to Ireland." Intercontinental Software in Palo Alto, CA, founded by a Bulgarian emigre, brokers well-trained but relatively inexpensive East European programmers for American firms seeking to lower software development costs.[19]

---

[17] "Both Tandem and Amdahl make large computers. That segment of the industry has suffered as customers move computing tasks to networks of inexpensive desktop machines" ("Two Computer Makers Report First-Ever Losses," 1992).

[18] Or Colorado or Texas, for that matter. Apple built its latest factory in Colorado, and located its technical support staff in Texas, because costs were cheaper there than Silicon Valley ("American Firms" 1991).

[19] Describing a recent arrangement between a Russian computer design team and US computer manufacturer Sun Microsystems, *The New York Times* reported: "The [Russian] team's full-time effort will come at an astoundingly low price for Sun. Its members will be paid a little more than their current salaries of a few hundred dollars a year in American dollars.... Top American computer designers sell their services for $100,000 a year or more, but both Sun officials and Mr. Babayan said the Russians on the new team could not be paid that handsomely without engendering bitter feelings among their colleagues or causing inflation in the Russian economy.... Other high-technology companies are searching for similar windfalls" ("Russian Computer Scientists," 1992).

CONCLUSION

Knowledge costs almost nothing to duplicate, especially if it appears in digital form. As a greater percentage of goods become knowledge, the nature of production as resource-exhaustive, labor-consuming, and scarcity-bound becomes obsolete. The new productive forces are resource-conservative yet generate an abundance. "Ownership" becomes an irrelevant concept if many people can possess the same thing simultaneously. Property rights as we have known them simply get in the way, and hold back development. The holding back takes many forms: incompatible standards that needlessly complicate learning new skills and sharing information; unnecessary and wasteful duplication of research and development; expensive lawsuits, ultimately paid for by the consumer, over ownership of interfaces; increased surveillance to catch "information pirates"; decreased access to public information as databases are privatized and information is commodified; skewed priorities as profitability and not social need are the determining factor in research, development, and distribution of knowledge; and even the criminalization of knowledge itself as it is classified as weaponry, lest it get into the wrong minds.[20] Society is harmed, and social development is held back.

With fewer jobs and lower wages as a result of the new knowledge-intensive forces of production, the circulation of commodities in exchange for wages becomes impossible. Wages are simply not high enough nor extensive enough to absorb the productivity of the economy. Private property laws separate the destitute worker from the means of survival. So apartments sit empty, while homeless people sleep in doorways or in prison-like shelters.[21] Food sits in warehouses or is destroyed, while children suffer from malnutrition. Illiteracy rates climb, while teachers are laid off. Meanwhile, the capitalist scrambles to protect his position by locking up knowledge, by looking for new areas to commodify and convert into sources of profit, and by further revolutionizing production. More workers are laid off, or jobs eliminated through "early retirement"; this only exacerbates the crisis.

Sivanandan (1990) described the revolution in technology as "emancipating" capital from labor:

> [T]he more Labour tries to hold Capital in thrall by withholding its labour, the more Capital moves towards its emancipation through yet more information technology, yet more labour-less productive regimes, yet more recourse to the captive labour force in the periphery. The relations of production, that is, have changed with the changes in the level of the productive forces: information (in the sense of data fed to computers, robots, etc.)

---

[20] The Boston 3 case is a recent example. The technical skills of three engineers, who were active in Irish support, was used against them by the prosecution. Knowledge, when combined with political conviction, now seems to be sufficient grounds for prosecution and conviction.

[21] According to US census figures some 7% of US housing is vacant US Bureau of the Census). San Francisco, with an estimated homeless population of 6,000 to 12,000, has 22,000 vacant housing units (*San Francisco Examiner*, April 24, 1991).

increasingly replaces labour as a factor of production; Capital no longer needs living labour as before, not in the same numbers, in the same place, at the same time; Labour can no longer organize on that basis, it has lost its economic clout and, with it, whatever political clout it had, whatever determinancy it could exercise in the political realm.... And this is what moves the battle from the economic to the political. (p.8)

The problem becomes not how to produce wealth, but how to distribute it. As such, the struggle is not around wages, or job security per se—economic struggles—but around property relations and social relations, around the social contract and social convention of ownership, around social control and survival—political issues.

A syndicated article by Robert Lewis appeared in November 1990, in the *San Francisco Examiner* (ironically, in the employment want ad section) with the headline "Will the age of the robots produce a workless society?"

Imagine a society where material needs are provided by "smart" machines, where people manage to break the link that equates self-worth with a job and are able to live comfortably from the fruits of robot labor....

Computer scientists Hans Moravec of Carnegie Mellon University and Kalman A. Toth, founder of the Silico-Magnetic Intelligence Corp., predict robots will be commonplace in 10 years. In 50 years they say, robots will have replaced most if not all human labor....

Experts say the widespread entry of robots into the workplace could raise the living standards unlike any invention during the industrial revolution. But if robots indeed are able to take the place of human labor, critical questions arise.

First, how should the wealth produced by enterprises operated with robot labor be distributed to those who don't work or who work part time? Toth says he envisions that nonworkers would receive "citizen pay" on a basis that would have to be worked out.

Between people's needs, and the immense productivity of the knowledge economy, stands a system of property relations. These relations are historical—"private property," as a social convention, developed, not without much struggle, during the beginning of the capitalist period in the sixteenth and seventeenth centuries (see, e.g., Hill, 1975). Such a system of property relations was required for private ownership of means of production, and the protection of newly acquired wealth from both the feudal powers and the emerging "property-less" classes. There is nothing "natural" about property rights, nor are they universally recognized (Branscomb, 1986). Rather, they are conventions struggled over, formally and informally, by various social forces. Different sections of society respond to these developments in different ways. Among the most destitute section of society, it takes the form of struggling to open empty HUD houses to the homeless, to distribute food in government warehouses to the hungry, or to provide livable welfare grants by raising taxes of the wealthy.

Marx and many other writers have pointed out that social relations eventually must correspond to the level of productive forces. We now live in a time when productive forces have raced far ahead of social relations. The knowledge-intensive productive forces are straining against the chains of private property relations. The qualities of knowledge, to be fully maximized, require a system based on cooperation and sharing, because cooperation and sharing generates more information and social wealth. Such a system would emphasize education, because education builds the infrastructure for expanding social wealth. Such a system would require the distribution of goods on the basis of need, because the cost of production eliminates scarcity and wages. This, of course, is a radically different system. Then again, the technology we use to produce goods now is radically different.

REFERENCES

"A great leap for software—and business," *Business Week* editorial, September 30, 1991.

"All NeXT's factory lacks is orders," *New York Times.* December 24, 1990.

"American firms send office work abroad to use cheaper labor," *Wall Street Journal.* August 14, 1991.

"Bacteria protein may help to miniaturize computers," *Wall Street Journal.* September 4, 1991.

Barsalla, G. (1988). *The evolution of technology.* Cambridge: Cambridge University Press.

Baumol, W. & Blinder, A., (1979). *Economics: principles and policy.* New York: Harcourt Brace Jovanovich.

Berliner, J. (1976). Prospects for technological progress, In *Soviet industry from Stalin to Gorbachev.* Berliner, J. (ed.), Ithaca, NY: Cornell University Press.

Branscomb, A. W. (1985). Property rights in information, in *Information technologies and social change.* Guile, B. (ed.). Washington, DC: National Academy Press.

Cleveland, H. (1985). The twilight of hierarchy, in *Information technologies and social change.* Guile, G. (ed.) Washington, DC: National Academy Press.

Cohen, S., & Sysman, J. (1987). *Manufacturing matters: The myth of the post-industrial society.* New York: Basic Books.

Costello, Michie, & Milne (1989). *Beyond the casino economy.* London: Verso.

Forester, T. (1987). *High tech society.* Cambridge, MA: MIT Press.

Fusfeld, D. (1988). *Economics, principles of political economy.* Boston: Scott Foresman and Company.

Gandy, O. (1987). *The political economy of communications competence, in The Political Economy of Information*, Mosco, V. & Wasko, J. (eds.), Madison, WI: University of Wisconsin Press.

Goldhaber, M. (1985). *Reinventing technologies.* Washington, DC: Institute for Policy Studies.

Hayes, D. (1989). *Behind the silicon curtain.* Boston: South End Press.

"Help not wanted," *Business Week.* December 23, 1991.

Hill, C. (1975). *The world turned upside down.* New York: Penguin.

Hindle, B., & Lubar, S. (1986). *Engines of change: The American industrial revolution 1790–1860.* Washington: Smithsonian Institution Press.

Kelly, K., (1991). "A bean-counter's best friend" *The Quality Imperative, Business Week* Special Issue, 1991.

Lash, S. (1991). Disintegrating firms, *Socialist Review.*

League for Programming Freedom (1990). *Against software patents.* Cambridge, MA:LPF.

Marx, K. (1967). *Capital, Vol. I.* New York: International Publishers.

Marx, K. (1973). *Grundrisse*. New York: Vintage Books.

Marx, K. (1968). *Selected Works*. New York: International Publishers.

Miller, S. (1991). *The electronic chain gang*. Unpublished draft.

"New York State prisoners work or else," *New York Times*. January 27, 1992.

"NeXTWORLD Interview: Alvin and Heidi Toffler," *NeXTWORLD*, vol. 1, No. 2, March/April 1991.

Peery, N. (1992). Talk presented in San Francisco, February 21, 1992.

"Russian computer scientists hired by American company," *New York Times*. March 3, 1992.

Sivanandan, A. (1990). All that melts into air is solid: the hokum of New Times. *Race and Class*. London: Institute of Race Relations.

Tarter, J. (1990). Soft*letter's manufacturing survey, *Apple Direct*, April, 1990. Cupertino: Apple Computer, Inc.

"The rich are richer—and America may be poorer," *Business Week*. November 18, 1991.

"Thousands of electronic jobs vanishing," *San Francisco Chronicle*. December 4, 1991.

Toffler, A. (1980). *The third wave*. New York: Bantam.

Toffler, A. (1983). *Previews and premises*. New York: Bantam

Toffler, A. (1989). *Powershift*. New York: Bantam.

"Two computer makers report first-ever losses," *San Francisco Chronicle*. January 24, 1992.

US Bureau of the Census (1991). *Statistical abstract of the United Staates: 1991*. Washington, DC.

Wincor, R., & Mandell, I. (1980). *Copyright, patents and trademarks: The protection of intellectual property*. Dobbs Ferry, NY: Oceana Publications, Inc.

5

Moral Issues Involved in Protecting Software as Intellectual Property

Natalie Dandekar
Churchville, MD

Most of us have undoubtedly done something considered piracy by sellers of intellectual property. Copying computer programs or using them on more than one machine at the same time are examples of alleged infringing activities. Hettinger (1989) claims that, "These phenomena indicate widespread public disagreement over the nature and legitimacy of our intellectual property institutions." However, few companies bother to prosecute individuals for such minor infractions. Rather, when companies seek the protection of computer copyright they seem to be primarily concerned with creating a market monopoly for some owner of a software program vis a vis the marketers of other software programs. Generally speaking, ownership can be understood as involving several component rights.

1. the right to use an item (to employ it to advance one's aims);

2. the right to possess it (the right to exclude others from using it);

3. the right to manage it;

4. the right to the income from it (the right to the proceeds derived from putting it to productive use); and

5. the right to the capital in it (the right to sell, consume, waste, modify, or destroy it) (Becker, 1977; Honore, 1961; McMahon, 1989).

Copyright is sought as one possible way of protecting both the third-mentioned right, that is, the right to manage property, involving the right to determine who may use it and how they may use it, and that which is mentioned fifth, the right to sell it.

I want to explore the question of whether and to what extent computer software deserves copyright protection in a world where computer literacy is becoming an important element of employability and computer software is a necessary part of technology transfers between countries with highly developed economies and countries with less developed economies.

First, it must be recognized that copyright is only one possible form of protection. Within the United States, for example, those interested in marketing computer software can protect market share in a number of ways. Traditional legal forms of protection include trade secrets, trademarks, patents, and the law of unfair competition as well as copyrights. In addition, Congress has passed computer crime legislation that specifically makes it a federal crime to use computers as tools in the conduct of criminal activity. Bills on personal privacy also protect information against access, and so on. Businesses sometimes use technological controls, such as encrypting programs against piracy. It is alleged that some computer software developers even resort to implanting computer worms or viruses or otherwise infecting a program so that a copyright infringer suffers disastrous consequences. Each of these methods has advantages and disadvantages worth discussing. I have put some of these considerations into Appendix A.

The most favored procedure for protecting software in the United States during the 1980s has been the use of copyright; because only in this way can the owner avail herself of protection against reverse engineering. In fact, if she reaches copyright first, her market share is even secured against independent invention. Most important, however, given the costliness of developing computer software and the relatively modest cost of reinventing alternative approaches, copyright can be interpreted to give some protection against a whole range of knockoffs, duplicative programs that achieve the desired external effects of look and feel, that is, the look of the screen design and the feel of the user controls, without duplication of precisely the same code. The legal history of this approach, with citation of important legal decisions, is provided in Appendix B.

These background considerations, however, do not address the more basic question of when, if ever, it is just that one inventor or designer should be able to make exclusive claims to intellectual products as property. Why should anyone have an exclusive right to possess something that all people could possess and use concurrently? Intuitively, this is less than obvious. As Hettinger puts it:

> One reason for the widespread piracy of intellectual property is that many people think it is unjustified to exclude others.... Also, the unauthorized taking of an intellectual object does not feel like theft... taking an intellectual object deprives the owner of neither possession nor personal use—though the owner is deprived of potential profit. (Hettinger, 1989, p. 35)

Historically, the justification for providing the designer or inventor with a monopoly on potential profit falls under five headings.

1. Natural rights arguments. These extend the Lockean argument for property rights to include intellectual properties. One had mixed one's labor and created new value while still leaving "enough and as good"[1] for others. Although this may not be true of all technological advances that receive protection, software seems to fit the Lockean proviso more than most, since although it presents one (presumably convenient) solution to a problem, problems can be solved in different ways. So, alternative solutions are still available for those willing and able to develop them.

2. Reward by monopoly. The argument claims that since society in the aggregate enjoys the benefit of this invention, the inventors therefore are owed a just recompense for the benefits conferred on the various members of society by their inventiveness.

3. Monopoly profits incentives. Monopoly privileges, whether just or not, are seen as necessary economic incentives to encourage inventive activity and its financial support, which in turn, positively affects the economic well-being of the society. The threat is that if inventors don't receive marketing monopolies they will lack incentives and therefore, inventors will turn their attention to more profitable activities. The stream of inventions will slow to a trickle and the national economy will slow as other countries take the lead in technological development.

4. Monopoly for the diffusion of technology. If inventors rely on alternative ways of using their invention for a profit, they will probably turn to the alternative provided by trade secrets. If they rely on secrecy, however, the progress of technology will slow. Everyone else will have to reinvent every wheel. As in discussed earlier, the feared consequence will be that the stream of inventions will slow to a trickle and the national economy will slow as other countries take the lead in technological development.

---

[1] John Locke *Two Treatises...2d Treatise on Government.*

5. The transformation of unowned potential into actual utilities. Rather than basing property on labor, as with the Lockean natural rights claim, the basis is described here as creativity. As Hegel put it, "When I impose a form on something, the thing's determinate character as mine acquires an independent externality (not) restricted to my presence here and now" (Hegel, 1962, p. 54). On this basis, aspects of one's created property may be sold, while other aspects are retained. For example, Hegel specifically notes that in the case of a reproduction, use of one may be sold without relinquishing ownership to the sale of further reproductions.

Taking these in order, the Lockean Natural Rights argument, although it may provide a basis for recognizing intellectual property, is, in itself, insufficient ground for claiming *monopoly* on that intellectual property. Inasmuch as one's natural rights cease at the point where others are harmed, if it can be shown that a marketing monopoly of software does harm others, as I try to show later, then it may be that property in software does not justify fully the privilege of a marketing monopoly. Rather, even were one to accept software as property, justice might preclude the legitimacy of granting that it is the sort of property that is held monopolistically so as to bring profit in the marketplace. "The right to receive what the market will bear is (only) a socially created privilege," not itself a product of natural rights (Hettinger, 1989, p. 40).

As for the second historical argument in favor of granting a monopoly on intellectual property, few today would argue that the profits thus maximized guarantee a *just* reward. Often it seems that the basic work, and the mathematical genius, which merit the greatest reward are the very aspects that are in no way subject to monopoly control. Rather:

> financial gains obtained through a patent (or copyright) bear little relation to the effort and costs expended in the invention's creation or to its usefulness to society. Moreover, inventions grow out of a social stream of intellectual developments. Patents ascribe degrees of merit to individual participants in an arbitrary and, some would argue, clearly unjust manner. (Benko, 1987, p. 17)

The third-mentioned ground, economy incentives, disregards claims about justice to pursue social welfare. This may be a tenable moral basis, but then it seems one must determine whose social welfare is to count, and how heavily. I discuss some typical difficulties of determining such a balance in the second part of this chapter.

As for the fourth ground, the idea seems to be based on an apparent contradiction, that is, by slowing down the diffusion of technical progress it ensures that there will be more progress to diffuse. This presumption has never been tested, and alternative approaches, less significantly contradictory, do seem possible. For example, Robert Benko suggested that a grant funding system, something like that used by scholars to obtain support for research, might create an alternative but equally productive climate for technical invention.

Finally, the fifth-mentioned ground, that of creative transformation as engendering a special set of ownership rights in intellectual property, logically includes a rarely noticed limitation, that is, by the logic which legitimates market monopoly on ideas, one may limit sales of the thing copyrighted, but not new transformations based on those ideas. Thus, Hegel writes that just as intellectual property originates from transformative rethinking, so others, too, may rethink those thoughts, and by learning, make these thoughts newly owned. In that case:

> Others may regard as their own property the capital asset accruing from their learning and may claim for themselves the right to reproduce their learning in... new form. (Hegel, 1962, p. 55)

On the basis of this very brief review of the five grounds on which monopoly rights to intellectual property are supposed to be justified, only the monopoly incentives, the diffusion of technology and the Hegelian creativity position, which in different ways argue that market monopoly serves to promote social welfare, seem capable of sustaining even the most cursory logical analysis. This suggests that copyright protection, if it is justified, and for whatever length of time it is justified, rests on claims to enhance/serve social welfare. It is also very probable that the moral basis of monopoly in intellectual ideas is necessarily limited in the way Hegel describes, by the condition that the monopoly not extend to rethinking and learning, and thus not constrain *new* transformations that might also promote social welfare. Putting aside the question of whether alternatives to a market monopoly might also serve to forward social welfare, one important question remains—whose social welfare is to count?

Let us grant that a marketing monopoly can serve to promote social welfare. Then a number of further difficulties can be distinguished. First, one can ask whose social welfare is at stake. We live in a world economy. Therefore is it appropriate to consider the social welfare of all the inhabitants of all the countries involved in this economy? Since we do not have a world government that can legislatively protect intellectual property, such legislation is the prerogative of sovereign states. It is tempting, therefore, for legislators to consider the problem of social welfare as if it is merely a national issue, and the questions of social welfare discussed by legislators tend to focus on only three aspects: the probable future of their national economy; what is fair to the inventors and those who have invested capital in these inventions; and what measures promote the basic rights of the citizens.

Even with such an unrealistically narrowed perspective, the problems posed are very difficult. For example, legislators in the United States have traditionally sought to provide free public access to information.

> Public libraries ... and similarly public schools ... were created in the belief that only an educated literate society can govern itself. (Weingarten, 1983, p. 5)

This means that as society turns more and more around an informational and technological axis, individuals will need greater access to knowledge and information if they are to participate effectively in citizenship. If they are to share equitably the benefits of an information society, they need the ability to gain and use information. However, if the market price is inflated as a monopoly would tend to do, and if intellectual property is narrowly owned for maximal profit, then the outcome may be a new underclass based on lack of access to education and information. Lobbyists expect legislators to show sensitivity to these concerns. Thus, when the draft version of the Computer Software Rental Amendments Act of 1989 exempted only libraries from a bill that would make it illegal to rent or lend software without the permission of its publisher, EDUCOM, an organization representing 580 colleges, submitted written testimony arguing that the legislation could restrict or terminate software lending programs at many universities where the college libraries are not prepared to handle software loans and their computer resource centers, which currently handle such loans, would not be able to afford negotiations with the scores of software developers over permission to lend software. Steven Gilbert, a vice president of EDUCOM, argued specifically that restrictions on lending procedures would have the greatest impact on "economically disadvantaged students" who rely on the laboratories because they cannot afford their own computers (DeLoughery, 1989).

Other concerns, however, may provide a basis for a counter argument in favor of granting great protections to those developing intellectual property. For example, development costs tend to be very high, whereas what are called knockoff costs are comparatively low. If those who underwrite product development cannot be guaranteed returns, it may be that the market forces will lead inventors to turn to products that are less useful socially but more likely to turn a quick profit. Venture capitalists will cease to underwrite the more expensive, slow to pay off educational software and instead concentrate on supporting inventions likely to make a quick profit in, for example, the mass market in video games.

Even if the preceding issues of fairness were resolved, and even if fairness is to be assessed only at the narrowly nationalist level, the moral appropriateness of legislatively granting monopoly may be questioned further in terms of considerations about a quite different, but important, public policy issue. What is the appropriate role of Congressional legislation? Should Congress consciously change copyright law to favor one product or service that seems more in the public interest. Should the law promote one type of technology over another? Or should the law merely attempt to provide a level playing field for the economic competitors?

When one takes the broader focus of asking what effect intellectual property protections have in the world market, the disparity in resources between less developed countries (LDCs) and highly developed countries (HDCs) becomes focal. LDCs take the position that Western technology is unjustly expensive. What might be a reasonable price where the average monthly wage is $500 becomes outrageous when $500 is the average yearly wage. Moreover, restrictions on use serve to perpetuate and strengthen the split between LDCs and HDCs.

With the existing resource mixture in most LDCs, the most easily realized tactic for development is the adoption of less-advanced, more labor intensive technologies (Small Is Beautiful). But, this development strategy would also serve to solidify the technological gap and with it the economic developmental gap. LDCs would become permanently disadvantaged even as they developed. The citizens in a country that successfully adopted labor intensive development strategies over a period of years might consider their situation to be somewhat improved compared with the impoverishment suffered by the less well off in LDCs today. However, most people simply do not consider their current situation compared to that from which they have come. They also compare themselves with other contemporaries. Consider the case of two LDCs, where one chooses the Small Is Beautiful route to self-improvement and the other invests in technological advances and basic education suited to scientific development. Both "improved" countries compare their relative advancement with the advancement potential in HDCs using technologically advanced development strategies. The poorer classes in a post-development, Small Is Beautiful LDC will be relatively even worse off compared with the citizens of the advanced HDCs. With worldwide communications already in place, such comparisons are probable.

Recognized relative impoverishment in itself can be seen as a specific kind of harm (Honore, 1984b). So a less advanced, labor intensive development strategy may be seen to produce long-run harm by widening the economic development gap.

For LDCs to close the economic development gap, they must practice infant industry strategies that can rectify current trade disparities. For this, they must have access to advanced technologies. Benko suggests that intellectual property monopoly rights are not compatible with such policy priorities. Thus, LDCs act rationally when they choose to promote weak domestic laws for protecting intellectual property. Often they practice inefficient enforcement of these laws the better to further their own technological advancement.

The consequence follows that no matter how protective the patent and copyright protections accorded to developers of software in the United States, knockoffs still will be sufficiently easy for those who manufacture them in LDCs. For example, the Brazilian government has rejected the notion that traditionally understood copyrights are the appropriate means of protecting computer software. Like Japan, the former Soviet Union, Greece, and Brazil are considering a special software "copyright" law, but for shorter periods. The Brazilian measure would extend protection for only 10 years, and even then, protection would be subject to compulsory licensing. This latter technique would force a manufacturer covered by Brazilian protection to begin production in Brazil within a specified length of time. If the manufacturer failed to do so, Brazil would license an indigenous firm to begin manufacture internally, thereby cutting development costs to nothing.

As it is, a recent study by Future Computing, in cooperation with the Association of Data Processing Service Organizations and 11 publishers of software, estimated that piracy cost the US software industry $1.3 billion in lost revenue between 1981 and 1984. When market analysts for MicroPro International Corporation examined the Brazilian market, they found copies of their software already for sale (Benko, 1987). Nor is Brazil unusual. Thailand has a copyright law that makes no mention of software. US officials estimate that software piracy in Thailand alone cost American software firms between

$3 and $4 million in losses in 1987. In Thailand, dealers provide free software for life to people who buy a computer. The Reagan administration tried to pressure the Thai government into amending the country's copyright law. The attempt backfired, however.

> When a government backed bill was introduced that would have amended Thailand's copyright law, one of the major parties in the ruling coalition balked, resulting in a vote of no confidence, resulting in new elections, that put in office a new Prime Minister who is standing firm against American pressure. (*Boston Sunday Globe*, March 26, 1989, pp. A6–7)

Countries that face severe technological lag can and do argue that they are rationally promoting their own nation's interests in playing catch-up by rules that do not include respect for intellectual property monopolies, whatever the term set by copyright.

This last argument, that it is rational to serve to forward one's national interest by promoting weak domestic laws for protecting intellectual property or by practicing inefficient enforcement of stronger laws for protecting intellectual property, should be subject to criticism in that it might serve to promote short-term gain but it will not help the LDC over the long run, inasmuch as it will not even encourage the citizens of the "pirate" country to become software authors. Rather, the question these countries should seek to address is what set of ground rules will encourage innovation, facilitate international trade, and respect the interests of all the countries involved (Benko, 1987).

If knowledge is the common heritage of humanity, then it should be made available at the lowest possible cost. However, even if one accepts the possibility that knowledge can become, in some ways, or for some time, the property of an inventor, one may still argue that development is in the interests of all nations, and on that ground, the HDCs should provide technological information at low cost and with a minimum of restrictions on its use. As things are now:

> In the real world, costs and benefits are spread disproportionately among nations. Short term private benefits as well as longer term social benefits (of technological knowledge diffusion) accrue almost exclusively to the developed nations. LDCs simply endure the costs and enjoy precious few of the gains.[2]

Alternatives to copyright exist. If they did not, fairness would demand that they be invented and used. Otherwise, the protection of intellectual property by granting copyright in computer software so as to give firms a marketing monopoly is liable to telling criticism in a world of variable technological development. Justification of copyright measures was found to rest on social welfare arguments, augmented by the perception that knockoffs are unfair. Opposition arguments focus on whose welfare is to count and

---

[2] I am indebted to the careful and generous analysis provided by an anonymous reader for the DIAC conference whose comments pointed out these aspects of irrationality of an LDC seeking to maximize development at the expense of international respectability.

bring potential future disadvantages and harmful consequences to our attention. Overall, a utilitarian calculus seems to make equitable international technology transfer a more important ethical goal than the effort and cost of imposing and enforcing copyright. Fortunately, software developers are ingenious and have developed alternatives. The simplest method is just lowering the price. If it does not pay to sell a program for less, knockoff artists lose interest. This system could be combined with a process of grant-support awards especially for developing expensive and socially useful "educational" software. Such a system would undercut the claim that without a monopoly grant to market shares protected by copyright no one will have a motive for doing necessary development work. A third technique is currently being used by some developers who provide "90-day trial samples" that are protected against copying and programmed to degrade after three months. Alternatively, software copyright law could be deliberately used to promote alternative approaches to marketing. Thus, shareware, in the United States, plays off the profitability margin afforded by copyright in that it allows satisfied users to benefit monetarily by sharing software, thus turning the user into part of the shareware sales force.[3] However it is done, I believe that we must recognize the responsibility to promote policies that will open educational opportunities to the much less well-to-do, and, in this way, promote a more just world.

APPENDIX A

Advantages–Disadvantages of the Different Types of Protection Available to Owners of Intellectual Property

Typically, businesses choose either to patent an invention or to hold it as a trade secret. Trade secrets provide advantages in that they do not require disclosure, but require the business make strong efforts to protect secrecy. Patents and copyrights require public disclosure. Also patents have a limited term, 17 years, initially set as equal to the training life of two apprentices, of little economic relevance now. Copyrights have a longer term, generally the life of the author plus 50 years. If the author is anonymous or pseudonymous, or the work is made for hire, then the copyright extends 75 years from the date of first publication or 100 years from creation, whichever expires first. Trade secrets resemble standard cases of ownership in that they have no term.

It is sometimes claimed that trade secrets involve less cost than acquiring and defending a patent, but given the cost of establishing and maintaining an atmosphere of secrecy for software products, this purported advantage may not apply.

Trademarks are mere registries of name, and encourage spending on image rather than development. They fail entirely to protect against knockoffs.

---

[3] I am indebted to Dawn Motyka and Charlie Manske for pointing out the fact that shareware logically depends on the enforcement of software copyright laws for a least part of its effectiveness.

APPENDIX B

Important American Case Law Decision on Computer Software

1. *AppleComputer, Inc. v. Franklin Computer Corp.*, 714 F 2d 1240, 1247 3rd Cir. 1983, cert dismissed, 464 U.S. 1033 (1984). This court decision protected the operating system program as copyrightable, held that computer programs either in object or in source code were copyrightable and a computer program was still copyrightable even if embedded in the function ROM of a computer.

2. *M. Kramer Mfg Co., v. Andrews*, 783 F 2d 421 (4th Cir. 1986) A video poker game was copied, the ROM board configuration was changed, and words in the video display of the program also were varied, but ultimately the game was similar to the original game. The court found copyright infringement of the screen display. The Court of Appeals held that under the authorities copyrightability of video games as audiovisual works cannot be disputed and a copyright in the audiovisual display protects also the underlying computer program to the extent the program embodies the game's expression.

3. *Digital Communications v. Softklone Distributing Inc.*, 639, F. Supp 449 (N.D. Ga 1987). The defendant clearly intended to exploit the innovative Crosstalk XVI screen but also intended to avoid copyright infringement by writing Mirror in a different program code. Despite the different program codes, to the consumer they appeared identical.

    The court rejected the argument that the display was an audiovisual work, but held the screen to be copyrightable as a compilation. The court thus found a textual display copyrightable.

4. A new copyright ruling, effective as of June 1988, limits the number of copyrights that may be held on a software program to just one. This will have a major effect on future litigation, but it is too soon to predict what that will be.

5. *Manufacturer's Technologies v. CAMS, Inc. and Chempro Data Sciences Corp.* (Conn. 1989). US District Judge T. F. Gilroy Daly held "look and feel" to constitute a "unique expression of an idea" the sequencing and flow of the screens in the sequence constitute a copyrightable expression.

6. Patent 4, 823,108 awarded to Gary Pope (June 1989) for "An Improved Display System and Memory Architecture and Method." Quarterdeck patents the multitasking DESQview environment specific process—a method of dealing with ill-behaved software that circumvents the operating system for its displays—allowing it to work properly in a multitasking environment.

7. *Lotus v. Paperback Software and Mosaic Software*, U.S. Dist. Ct. Feb. 1990, Judge Robert E. Keeton decided a "look and feel" case (See #5). The Lotus case established a clearer precedent, so that software companies will know when they can claim exclusive rights to aspects of a software program's "look and feel."

REFERENCES

Becker, L. (1977). *Property rights*, London: Routledge & Kegan Paul.

Benko, R. P. (1987). *Protecting intellectual property rights: Issues and controversies.* Washington, DC: American Enterprise Institute for Public Policy Research.

DeLoughery, T. J. (1989) Copyright amendment could restrict borrowing of software, colleges fear in *The Chronicle of Higher Education*, May 17, A13.

Hegel, G. W. F. (1962). *Philosophy of right* (Knox, T. M., Trans.), Oxford: Clarendon Press.

Hettinger, E. C. (1989). *Justifying intellectual property*, Philosophy and Public Affairs, *18* 1 (Winter). pp. 31–52.

Honore, A. M. (1984a). Ownership, in (Becker, L., & Kipnis, K., Eds.). *Property: cases, concepts, critiques* (pp. 78–87). Englewood Cliffs, NJ: Prentice Hall.

Honore, A. M. (1984b). Property, title and redistribution, in *Property: cases, concepts, critiques* (pp. 162–170) (Becker, L., & Kipnis, K., Eds.). Englewood Cliffs, NJ: Prentice Hall.

Honore, A. M. (1961). Ownership, in *Oxford essays in jurisprudence*, (pp. 107–147) Guest, A. M., (Eds.). Oxford: Clarendon.

Locke, J. *Two Treatises… 2d Treatise on Government*.

McMahon, (1989, October). Managerial authority, *Ethics 100* 33–53.

Sholkoff, J. (1988), Breaking the mold: Forging a new and comprehensive standard of protection for computer software, *Computer/Law Journal VIII 4* (Fall).

Weingarten, F. (1983). "New Information Technology and Copyrights," Testimony before Congress, July 21, 1983, reprinted in *Computers and Society, 13*(3), pp. 4–8.

6

"Virtual Reality" —Really?*

Thomas B. Sheridan
David Zeltzer

Massachusetts Institute of Technology, Cambridge, MA

A mechanical engineer has completed work on the design of a multilegged walking machine for traversing rough terrain. Donning a head-mounted display, and putting on a special glove, she feels as if she is looking around in a rugged landscape. She makes a gesture with her gloved hand, and a computer simulation of her robot walking

*A highly edited version of this unpublished essay appeared in Technology Review, MIT Press, October, 1993.

Authors' addresses: Thomas B. Sheridan, Department of Mechanical Engineering, MIT, Room 3-346, Cambridge MA 02139; e-mail: sheridan@mit.edu. David Zeltzer, Research Laboratory of Electronics, MIT, Room 36-763, Cambridge MA 02139; e-mail:dz@irts.mit.edu.

Thanks to Barbara Shinn-Cunningham and Mandayam Srinivasan for helpful comments about auditory and haptic displays.

machine appears beside her. Even though she's been working on the design for days on end, she's startled to see how big the machine really is when the life-sized model appears in this simulated landscape. With another gesture of her gloved hand, the machine begins to walk, and she watches intently as it slowly moves its legs. For the next few hours, she'll put the walking robot vehicle literally through its paces, to see if it will perform as it was designed to do.

Our engineer has been working in a *virtual environment* (VE)—a computer simulated world consisting of mathematical and software representations of real (or imagined) agents, objects, and processes; and a human-computer interface for displaying and interacting with these models. The interface has two parts: a *logical* interface that specifies what parameters of the VE and its models can be changed and when; and a *physical* interface consisting of visual, haptic, and auditory displays for presenting the virtual world to the human participants, and a set of sensing devices to monitor the actions of the humans.

As in the example, today's VE systems often use *head-mounted displays* (HMDs)—a pair of miniature liquid crystal TV screens mounted one in front of each eye for stereo viewing, with optical elements to generate a wide field-of-view, and a sensing device that measures the wearer's head motions. For any given change in head position the graphic images displayed on the HMD can be updated as if the human were looking around in the synthetic world. Graphics workstations are now capable of updating simple scenes relatively fast, so that when viewed through an HMD, the feeling of *presence*—of being immersed in the virtual world—is quite compelling. Not all applications, however, require visual interfaces as dramatic as an HMD, although realistic sound effects, and the ability to manipulate the models by hand, add a great deal to one's feeling of involvement in the virtual world, and help one to interact with the computer system in an easy, natural way.

Unfortunately, in the last few years, we have heard the words "virtual reality" (known to the cognoscenti as "VR") applied to a confusing variety of ideas and technologies. This includes what used to be thought of simply as interactive three-dimensional computer graphics, as well as rather conventional simulation systems such as modern flight simulators. The term refers also to notions about shared "data spaces," culminating, perhaps, with computer-based systems augmented by novel displays and input devices that seem to make the user feel as if he or she is "there" in a computer-generated environment, much like in the rather speculative example involving the engineer and the robot walker.

In part because these so-called "immersive interfaces" can be so compelling, and perhaps because of the high-tech mystique, VR is in high fashion. Public curiosity and appetites seem insatiable. In the last three years there have been numerous symposia on the subject, and technical sessions at otherwise staid and conservative technical meetings, not to mention a barrage of newspaper and magazine articles, movies, and TV stories.

This developing bundle of technologies and research ideas collectively called "VR" has, we think, many promising and powerful applications. At the same time, a number of difficult problems remain to be solved before this potential can be fulfilled. We ourselves prefer the definable and less-hyped descriptor "virtual environment" (VE) to refer to the scientific and engineering efforts we are pursuing and will discuss in this chapter.

How does VE technology work? What is new, compared to flight simulators and computer games? What is the current state of the component technologies—display hardware, for example, or simulation and modeling software? What is it good for? Is there a behavioral science of "presence"? And are there social or other pitfalls?

WHAT'S REALLY NEW?

One can muster arguments that nothing is really new in VE technology. In the early 1940s entrepreneur Edwin Link pioneered flight simulator technology, along with Admiral Luis DeFlorez (who founded the Naval Training Devices Center, funded the DeFlorez design prize at MIT, and was the only person with permission from the MDC to land his seaplane in the Charles River basin when he made his visits to MIT to award the prize). All major airlines, for a decade or two, have trained pilots in takeoffs and landings in simulators so realistic (in terms of their simulated displays and controls, the way they "handle" dynamically, and the corresponding view out the window) that in many cases the pilots' first flights in new aircraft types have been with passengers.

One can also point to other "simulation" technologies that have been around for a very long time. In 1965, primitive head-mounted displays were demonstrated by Raymond Goertz at Argonne National Laboratory and by John Chatten of Motorola. With a closed-circuit television link between this head-mounted display and a pair of remote TV cameras, one could look through the HMD and safely peer into a so-called "hot cell"—where radioactive materials were handled experimentally, or processed in small production quantities for energy or medical applications. And in 1968, MIT graduate student Ivan Sutherland, now a vice president at Sun Microsystems, demonstrated use of the head-mounted display for viewing computer-generated images.

Force feedback was also first developed in Goertz's laboratory for hot cell remote manipulators in 1954, and later adapted to hand contact with computer-generated virtual objects. Around the same time, Michael Noll at Bell Labs developed a three-dimensional "machine communication tactile device"—a motorized, three-axis joystick that allowed a human to literally "feel his way" around in a computer-generated world, seeming to bump into obstacles or move along the surface of a wall.

Going back still further, one can cite the "virtual reality" of film and video, radio, still photography, and the theater. Indeed, for millennia, artists, musicians, writers, and storytellers have sought to involve our senses and imaginations in worlds that have no physical basis. For such "technologies" all that has been required on the part of the participant is a bit of attention, some imagination, and some modest effort to suspend disbelief that one is not "really there." Rather than offering entirely new experiences, we can say that our new electronic tools in many ways merely transform media with which we are already familiar. So what's really new?

Today, computer-based simulators with human operators in the control loop are applied in many contexts. Not only are there flight trainers, but also automobile driving simulators, simulators to teach ship pilots how to navigate through treacherous harbors, simulators to train locomotive engineers, simulators for nuclear power plant crews to practice their team responses to emergencies, simulators to teach military offices how to command their diverse and distributed resources in battle, and simulators to teach surgeons and anesthesiologists.

However, these are the "older" type simulators. They create a sense of presence in the real situation because the space in which the user moves around is physically mocked up to be like the real cockpit, automobile, ship's bridge, locomotive, power plant control room, military command post, or operating room. The computer may simulate the view "out the window," but the "window" in these simulators is fixed.

The "new" VE simulators currently under development are different. In this case, the whole environment will exist only as software inside the computer, and will be conveyed only through the computer displays—visual, auditory, and haptic. Because physical mockups would no longer be required, such simulators should be cheaper to build and maintain. For the same reason, these VE systems would be portable. Navy pilots, for example, could train and practice with VE simulators on shipboard, rather than having to wait for the next visit to a large and expensive land-based simulator.

However, perhaps most interestingly, the VE system would be reconfigurable in software. On one day pilots could train in an F/A-18 flight simulator, and the next day, aircraft mechanics could use the same system to practice jet engine repair. Pilots and mechanics would all use the same interface equipment for visual, auditory, and haptic feedback, but the computer models displayed to them would be very different. In the head-mounted displays, a pilot would see ocean and sky through the cockpit canopy, as well as seeing and feeling the cockpit displays and controls. For the mechanics, the VE system software would be reset to display realistic views of a parked aircraft. They would be able to see, hear, feel, and manipulate computer models of their tools, the aircraft's equipment bays and hatch covers, and the aircraft systems that they'd need to inspect and repair.

HOW DOES IT WORK?

Visual Imagery

Computer animation—the generation of moving synthetic images—is now highly developed. Driven in large part by the entertainment media, as well as by hardware and software advances by industry and university research groups, image quality, resolution and the speed of updating pictures have steadily increased over recent years. Coupled with this have been improvements in our understanding of how to simulate the way limbs move as people or animals walk, and how natural or artificial objects appear to the eye—all enabling better computer models of what we see as we move through the world (or as the world moves relative to us).

Add to this mix the improving capability to measure the position and orientation of a person's head or other body parts. With an HMD, a person *wears* the computer display, and the measured position-orientation of the wearer's head is fed to the computer. In this way the computer can generate those pictures—a slightly different view for each eye—which the observer would see corresponding to where he or she is looking. The user of such equipment can not only "look around" in the seemingly three-dimensional computer-generated environment, but can walk through doorways, crawl through holes, or defy gravity and fly through the artificial world and feel very much "present" in it.

Difficult problems in generating visual imagery remain, however. Many common objects and phenomena—such as clouds, smoke, fire, clothing, skin, and hair—still lack efficient modeling and display techniques needed for realtime display and interaction. Even though computer processing speeds have increased dramatically, realistic display of complex and interesting scenes can still bog down our fastest computers.

Another serious shortcoming of today's VE systems is the visual displays themselves. The healthy human eye is capable of discriminating details as small as one-half to one minute of arc (roughly the size of a quarter viewed from 100 yards away). Most standard displays cannot come close to this resolution at a comfortable viewing distance. Liquid crystal displays (LCDs) have rather large *pixels* to begin with, and when mounted in front of the eye, and viewed through the optics needed to expand the field of view (FOV) to match the nearly 180 x 120 FOV of the human eye, the pixels become unacceptably large, and one sees the distracting texture of the pixels themselves, rather than a smooth, continuous picture. That is, the resolution of current LCD-based HMDs, is, frankly, poor. Miniature CRTs can provide far better resolution, but at the expense of color. Moreover, even though CRT resolution is better than LCDs, it still cannot match human visual acuity.

Because it takes a nontrivial amount of time to update the visual displays as the wearer of an HMD moves their head, because there are further lags introduced by the devices that track head position, and because the FOV and display resolution are woefully inadequate, the view through an HMD is apt to be rather disappointing. When you turn your head, there is a noticeable lag before the display is updated to match your new direction of view. And the imagery you see is low-resolution and suffers from many artifacts common to real-time, computer-generated imagery—jagged edges that should be smooth, lack of shadows and indirect lighting. Worse yet, the view can be disorienting—it's easy to get lost in a VE with its paucity of landmarks, and without the feeling of place we get from sensing the movements of our body.

This lack of body motion leads to yet another difficulty. It's quite easy to write programs that will allow the VE participant to seem to "fly" through the virtual world, say, in the direction they are looking, or pointing their gloved finger. But what happens when we do this? Our eyes receive visual cues that tell us we are moving. However, our vestibular system—the organs in our inner ear that sense our linear and angular velocity, that tell us which way is "up"—is telling us we are sitting or standing in place. It is just this *sensory disparity* between our visual and vestibular systems that is thought to be responsible for the motion sickness one might get from reading a book while riding in a car, for the space sickness that astronauts feel on reaching orbit where there is no "up," and for the simulator sickness that pilots feel after spending time in a flight simulator that cannot match the physical motions of a real airplane—which can be extreme and violent for a high-performance jet fighter.

These shortcomings of today's visual displays and computer-generated imagery mean that it will be a long time—if ever—before we can truly fool the discriminating eye sufficiently well that the participant in a VE will not be able to distinguish a visual simulation from physical reality.

Auditory Imagery

Our two organs of hearing, together with their still somewhat mysterious appendages *(pinnae)* we normally call "ears," measure subtle time and amplitude differences of sound patterns reaching the two sides of our head from a common source. This provides us a sense of auditory space, and the ability to close our eyes and identify where sounds are coming from and how they are moving.

Several companies offer systems that try to synthesize these spatial auditory cues. For example, scientists at NASA Ames Research Center, together with Crystal River Engineering, have developed a system called the Convolvotron to synthesize auditory space. The user, sitting still and wearing hi-fi earphones, hears different sounds at different locations—musical instruments or people talking. The sounds can be programmed to move in given patterns in the auditory space. Further, if head position and orientation are measured, these sounds can be made to sound fixed in location or move in prescribed patterns, just as one would hear them if one were to turn one's head or walk around in a room at a party. In other words, this is the auditory equivalent of the head-mounted display technique described earlier.

As with visual imagery, serious challenges remain for those wishing to accurately simulate the sounds of the physical world. Current auditory simulations are capable of providing directional information about sound sources relatively well. Careful listening, however, reveals that the virtual auditory environment still fails to match listening in natural environments.

Research is needed before we can generate more accurate simulations of different reflecting surfaces—for example, brick walls, carpets, and pavement. *Reverberation*—echoes, sounds bouncing around a room—is hard to reproduce accurately and efficiently. Sound sources far away can be captured adequately, but simulation of near-field sources, inclusion of nonuniformly radiating sources, the simulation of doppler shift for nonstationary sources—these are all familiar properties of our everyday auditory world that remain very hard to simulate properly. In addition, pragmatic issues such as system time delays, inadequate signal-to-noise ratio and dynamic range in the computation, and algorithmic approximations made in the simulation all contribute to the lack of realism in today's best virtual auditory worlds. Finally, although directionality can be conveyed with some accuracy, little effort has been made to synthesize sound sources in the simulations. Instead, sources are sampled from real-world sounds, and simply manipulated to provide dynamic, directional cues.

As with visual imagery, it will be a long time, if at all, before we can generate a simulated world that sounds indistinguishable from the natural world to the discriminating ear.

Haptic Imagery

Haptics refers to the senses we have in our muscles, tendons and joints, together with those in the skin. The muscle and tendon senses measure limb position and movement (respectively called *proprioception* and *kinesthesia*) as well as gross forces on the limbs. Our *tactile* sense—the feeling of "touch"—is controlled by force sensing organs within the skin. Obviously these sensory mechanisms work together, but do so in ways not fully understood.

Haptic imagery can be generated by providing artificial stimulation to the skin that is triggered by the computer when the measured hand position corresponds in the computer's model of where the hand should be to touch a particular object. Commercial devices (including the DataGlove and Exos Dexterous Handmaster) are already available to measure the position of the hand as well as the pose of all the fingers. Using tactile stimulators and hand position measuring devices, graduate student Nicholas Patrick, at MIT's Man-Machine Systems Lab, has demonstrated the ability to "reach out and touch someone—or some thing" (which isn't really there).

The technology of simulated haptic experience is currently the most difficult. Measuring limb position is not so hard; there are commercial products that do it, albeit not as accurately as one would like. What is particularly difficult is generating mechanical forces that suitably mimic those felt when one taps a hard surface, or handles an object, or runs a finger across a textured piece of cloth. The mechanical actuators (motors, really) must have extremely fast and accurate response characteristics, much better than today's commercial motors. Furthermore, to simulate tactile sensation—moving some skin surface across some external object so that a touch pattern is continually imposed on new areas of skin—requires many miniature force actuators acting in parallel. Researchers have tried many different approaches to impressing computer-driven touch patterns on the skin: piezoelectric vibrators, jets of air, direct stimulation of the skin by electric current. Many of these approaches have been explored for decades by bioengineers seeking to provide blind persons with means to read or navigate in their environments. However, none has proven satisfactory, none has come close to the tactile equivalent of the video display.

Research is required to better understand the sensorimotor abilities of the human haptic system, and the biomechanical properties of soft tissues in contact with interface devices. More accurate and efficient models of human soft tissues and nonrigid objects must be developed. In addition, people are very sensitive to the *timing* of sensory signals. If the expected smooth movement of objects in the visual field is not seen as smooth, or if the expected sights are not exactly sychronized with corresponding sounds and haptic sensations, the observer easily detects that and in some cases can be made ill by it. Simulator sickness is common in aviation and automobile driving simulators in which sensory cues are not properly timed.

It has been said that as small insects evolved to mammals, touch and haptics developed first, and hearing and vision came only much later in evolution. Technological development seems to have done the reverse: We have hi-fi for the ears and television for the eyes, both highly refined. Currently, artificial means to display electronically generated patterns of force to the skin and other haptic sensors essentially do not exist.

WHAT IS THE NEW "VIRTUAL REALITY" GOOD FOR?

The technology of simulating visual, auditory, and haptic experience still has a long way to go. In addition to the need for much better displays and modeling software, we still don't understand all the issues involved in interacting with interesting and dynamic synthetic worlds.

For example, complicated computer systems present the human operator with dozens if not hundreds of "control knobs," and a poorly designed and organized interface will result in a system that is unmanageable or even dangerous. Moreover, an immersive interface with DataGloves and an HMD will enable the human participant in a VE to manipulate virtual objects in a natural way, but how should more prosaic system functions for example, "Turn up the sound," or "Shine more light on the workpiece," be initiated or modified?

We also need to learn how to provide access to complex computer models at varying levels of abstraction. During the simulation, the engineer in our opening example will want to work with her walking machine as if it were a real physical device, but will surely want to reprogram and modify the software as bugs are discovered and diagnosed. This requires different interfaces—for both an end user and a programmer—with very different requirements. How should they be designed to take best advantage of VE interface devices? Can and should the user move freely between them?

Navigation in an unfamiliar environment is not easy. The task is hard enough in the physical world, but in computer-synthesized environments, many sensory cues and visual landmarks are often absent. We need to learn how to navigate easily and effectively in complex 3D virtual spaces without getting confused, lost, or sick (due to "simulator sickness").

In spite of all these difficulties and unanswered questions, there is great potential. It is fairly clear that VE technology will find its place in entertainment. This is already being exploited in a few commercial ventures in the United States, Japan, and the United Kingdom.

VE technology will be used to enhance existing training simulators for piloting vehicles (airplanes, cars, and so on) and in a few other skill-development applications. More than that, however, the technology will be adapted for a host of new training situations, perhaps for sports, industrial skills, and so on.

Marketing is a third potential application that has received some attention. For example, one can walk into the main kitchen showroom of Matsushita Electric Works in Tokyo, don a head-mounted display, a DataGlove, and earphones connected to a Convolvotron, and walk through any one of a number of alternative kitchens (which, of course, exist only in the computer), open the cabinet doors, drop dishes or glasses on the sink, and hear them break in just the right location. This one demonstration of marketing is sure to spawn many more.

A fourth application has been called "scientific visualization." Many new possibilities emerge from the capability to experience visual, auditory, or haptic force patterns that correspond to elements of the world but are not normally visible, hearable, or palpable. For example, Fred Brooks of the University of North Carolina has for several years been using computer models combined with visual and haptic virtual environment technology to explore how molecules can fit together. Others are discussing the possibility of superposing, on photographic or video images, computer-generated symbols or graphic data representing variables that correspond geometrically to the visible image that themselves are not visible (e.g., temperatures, pressures, radiation levels).

At the same time, many applications call for "augmented reality" in which graphics, video, and text are superimposed on real-world imagery viewed through an HMD with semitransparent displays. Surgeons, for example, might use such a system in the operating room. With a see-through HMD, a surgeon could look at a patient and see ultrasound or CT-scan imagery superimposed on the patient's body, giving the surgeon, in effect, "x-ray vision."

Another application may be in communication. One person may send a message to another which is a programmed facial expression, or handshake, or hug (of course responding to the particular gestures of the target individual when that person logs in to receive the message).

Surely there are many other potential applications that have not yet been imagined.

IS THERE A BEHAVIORAL SCIENCE OF "PRESENCE"?

We know from experiments with human subjects that when multiple senses tell us the same thing, the information is more believable. Both the authors have experienced this in their own laboratories, where a user moves his hand, sees in the computer display the (simulated) hand contact an object, and at the same time feels the corresponding forces that would be felt in actual contact. In spite of the fact that computer resolution may be poor and the force feedback may not precisely replicate the physical interaction, the combined effect is compelling. Add hearing and it is more so.

Curiously, however, our understanding of these phenomena is still very much at the anecdotal level. A true scientific understanding of what makes us feel "present" in a virtual environment is lacking. Just now we are observing new interest by psychologists to perform such controlled experiments, to establish valid measures of presence, and to correlate them with measures of performance. With others the authors are participating in a new MIT Press Journal called *Presence: Teleoperators and Virtual Environments,* which hoped to encourage better science in the field.

SOCIAL AND OTHER PITFALLS

The positive side of virtual environment technology is evident, and many small as well as large firms are currently making investments in the technology. Costs will continue to decrease, and the size, resolution, and speed of response of visual, auditory, and haptic display technology will improve. Are there negatives?

One aspect to be worried about is that many expectations about VE, driven by media hype, will simply not materialize on anything like the promised time scale. At least one pioneering firm, VPL, which developed the well-known and widely used DataGlove and EyePhone, has already gone bankrupt.

A second concern is that VE panders easily to violence. Already some entertainment applications enable the user to experience violence vicariously—fighting with animals, or diving a vehicle at high speed off the road, or doing worse violence to people, identifiable or otherwise. As much as teenage males are known to be drawn in by computer games, virtual reality has the prospect of attracting them even more. Further, the line between the simulation and reality can become so fine that they might engage in what seems like harmless violence in the simulator, only to go out in to the look alike world and do the same.

Many of our children already have access to sophisticated and very compelling virtual environments—the ubiquitous hand-held video game. Even without HMDs and other whizbang gadgetry, these systems capture far too much time and attention. But the more sophisticated interface gadgetry is coming. What will we do when our children are confronted with this powerful computer presence technology outside or inside the home? Each of us may have wondered how we can help our own children to want to read more, to ask more questions, to browse through a library, finding things out. Surely, virtual environments have the potential to spark real enthusiasm and motivation about learning. But beyond the technological research that will enable these systems, we need to better understand the learning process itself.

CONCLUSION

Like many other technologies—the telephone, the automobile, the airplane, TV, the fax machine, and the robot—VE did not spring into existence overnight. There are many antecedents. Public awareness, and concomitant fashion, have occurred within the year. Perhaps this has been because of the catchy terminology; perhaps it was because the experience itself does stir the imagination. The promise for entertainment, training, scientific visualization and other applications is truly there, as are some frightening possibilities. However, it will be years before we see full commercial realization of virtual reality. Really.

REFERENCES

Aukstakalnis, S., & Blatner, D. (1993). *Silicon mirage: The art and science of virtual reality.* Berkeley CA: Peachpit Press

Earnshaw, R. A., Gigante, M. A., & Jones, H. (Eds.) (1993). *Virtual reality systems.* London: Academic Press.

Sheridan, T. B. (1992). Defining our terms. *Presence: Teleoperators and Virtual Environments,* Spring 1(2), 272–274.

Sheridan, T. B. (1992). Musings on Telepresence and Virtual Presence. *Presence: Teleoperators and Virtual Environments,* Winter, 1(1), 120–125.

Sheridan, T. B. (1992). *Telerobotics, automation, and human supervisory control.* Cambridge MA: MIT Press.

Zeltzer, D. (1992). Autonomy, Interaction and Presence. *Presence: Teleoperators and Virtual Environments,* March, 1(1), 127–132.

7

Computerization and Women's Knowledge

Lucy Suchman
Brigitte Jordan
Xerox Palo Alto Research Center

INTRODUCTION

Evelyn Fox Keller opens her *Reflections on Gender and Science* with the following quotation from Simone de Beauvoir:

> Representation of the world, like the world itself, is the work of men; they describe it from their own point of view, which they confuse with the absolute truth. (1985, p.3)

Although de Beauvoir overstates it for us (it is only in a very particular sense that we are willing to grant the world to be the work of men) we also recognize what it is that she could be talking about. Part of what we are involved in is to see the world as a place populated by women, working in spheres of knowledge and competence rendered invisible by prevailing representations of what competence involves. There is a realm of practice—embodied, deeply rooted in experience, working from concerns of both heart and mind—that compels us in our own work and that we want to embody in our designs. Our sense is that it is in the realm of practice that involvement lies, and that it is for lack of tapping that realm that so many women have been alienated from the technological enterprise.

As a way in to this question of involvement in relation to the design and use of technology, we introduce the notion of *"authoritative knowledge."* Authoritative knowledge is that knowledge taken to be legitimate, consequential, official, worthy of discussion and useful for justifying actions by people engaged in accomplishing a given task (Jordan, 1987a, b). We begin from the view that there is an intimate relationship between the setting of human activities, as both physical environment and technology, and the distribution of authoritative knowledge. Changes in the former inevitably have consequences for the latter. Technological change can therefore be a resource for either the expansion of existing forms of authoritative knowledge, or for their transformation.

Both design and use of technology involve *appropriation.* Where technologies are designed at a distance from the situation of their use (as most are), there is an ineveitable gap between scenarios of design and circumstances of use. Inevitable, because to some extent technologies have to be designed for unknown users, in unknown circumstances. To get off the ground, designers need to project a scenario of use, the adequacy of which will depend on the adequacy of their understanding of the actual situations of use. However adequate the designers' understanding, the gap will exist and will have to be filled by the user as the technology is interpreted with respect to local concerns and circumstances. In this sense, design is only fully completed in use.

Appropriation can be either a matter of design as we conventionally think of it (that is, an engagement with the technology as such) or of use (that is, an engagement with something else, some other activity, by means of the technology as a tool). In either case, appropriation is ultimately a matter of ownership, of integration of a technology into one's activities in a way that constitutes the basis of one's competence. This is, at least in part, what we mean by involvement, by being engaged with something, and it is the thing that we observe to be noticeably absent from women's relations to computers.

If we put these two concepts—authoritative knowledge and appropriation or involvement—together, two radically different, but distinctively women's spheres of activity with which we are familiar—childbirth and office work—provide strikingly similar lessons with respect to technology and women's knowledge. In setting these superficially disparate cases side by side we find the relations between them. In both cases, ideological commitments that override the realities of what women know dictate a model of the activity that, when embodied in technologies, enforces the ideology.

THE MAYA CASE

The first case involves cross-cultural work by Brigitte Jordan on childbirth practices or ethno-obstetrics in relation to international development (Jordan, 1983). In the

Yucatan peninsula of Mexico it is the local collectivity of Maya women who hold authoritative knowledge about birth; that is to say, the knowledge that is considered consequential for making decisions about and managing the event. Childbirth takes place either in the woman's own house or that of her mother, and technologies are familiar household objects. There are unquestionnably experts involved: a midwife, with extensive experience of many births, supported by other women of the family, each of whom has her own experience on which to draw. But moment-by-moment knowledge of the event is produced collectively by the participants and draws centrally on the authority of knowledge of her own body granted to the woman herself.

Into this system, designers of development programs to promote Western biomedicine introduce new technologies developed in the context of the high technology hospital. A case in point is the sterile scissors, introduced as an alternative to the local practice of burning the umbilical stump with a candle to prevent infection. The gap between the context of its design and the local conditions of its use (in particular, an absence of stoves) led to a reinterpretation of the technology from a sterile scissors to a pair of scissors dipped briefly into a bowl of hot water. Observation by traditional birth attendants of a subsequent increase in infant tetanus resulted ultimately in their rejection of the scissors in favor of the former, clearly more effective practice of cauterization.

Transported to high technology hospitals, the familiar territory and authoritative knowledge of Maya women are lost to them. As the process of childbirth is transformed into a medical event, knowledge becomes privileged, protected and mediated by exotic technologies. In the United States, where childbirth is considered a high-risk pathological process that is best managed with the resources of medical technology, pharmacology, and surgery, the person in charge is typically a male doctor, most frequently a doctor with specialist training in obstetrics and gynaecology (which in the United Stataes is a surgical specialty). In such births the joint production of information which prevails in traditional births no longer obtains. The woman is transformed from the interactional focus of a collaborative group, an actor, an individual who provides authoritative information about the event, into a mere passive data source as her body is colonized by machines and technical procedures such as stress tests, ultrasounds, and fetal monitors. The artifacts and technologies employed, from hospital gowns to heart monitors, are unfamiliar to her. The machines on whose output the management of her labor is based are inaccessible physically, in the sense that they cannot be touched or manipulated, and experientially, in that what the output could possibly mean is beyond her technical competence. Advanced technologies and procedures depend for their interpretation on professionals with specialist training. As a consequence, authoritative knowledge and the attendant power to make decisions in such systems is redistributed.

The case of Maya obstetrics illustrates what we call *the fallacy of the empty vessel;* that is, the belief by those who design new technologies that there is nothing there in advance of their arrival. In the attmpts to "upgrade" traditional ways of handling pregnancy and birth in the direction of western biomedical practice, the fact that the new procedures interact with a pre-existing ethno-obstetric system is generally not acknowledged. Time and again, the design and imposition of new technologies that fail to recognize the realities of local conditions leads to a degrading of the local environment or rejection of the technology. In the Yucatan, and increasingly in industrialized settings as well, hospital birth is rejected, where possible, in favor of the control afforded by remaining on one's home ground.

THE OFFICE CASE

We can find other examples of the fallacy closer to home. In the case of office automation, the allocation of so-called procedural office work to women in this century, followed by the attempt to delegate it to machines, is made possible by a systematic blindness to the real practice involved in the work (Suchman, 1983). Following the tradition of scientific management initiated by Frederick Taylor in 1911, many system developers take office work to be essentially procedural in nature, involving the execution of a prescribed sequence of steps. Taking the meaning of "procedure" in the office to be the same as in the construction of computer programs, analysts have developed models of office work that represent it as a collection of ordered tasks. Office work seems, on this view, to be an activity ready-made for computerization. Interest in artificial intelligence has led to more "plan-based" approaches to office activity which emphasize the goal-directed and contingent nature of actions. More recently, those models have been extended by analogy with distributed computing, people and machines being represented as homogeneous systems of "cooperating agents." In all of these cases, the extent to which office activities remain "informal" or "unstructured"—that is, resistant to algorithmic representation—is seen as a problem for system design.

The design of so-called office information systems is based not in an understanding of the pratical, situated accomplishment of office work but in a priori, rationalized models of the office as a system of disembodied information flow. In the process, women office workers' knowledge and the technologies on which it rests are rendered invisible.

A detailed study of work in an accounting office suggested that organizational procedures, although oriented to by office workers, in no way provide instructions for what to do next (Suchman, 1983). Rather, procedures describe general guidelines for how things should go and requirements for what they should come to in the end. Those guidelines and requirements are necessarily underspecified, insofar as what it could mean to, for example, "process an account according to procedure" is contingent on the details of the particular case. The work of the office is precisely to achieve a relationship between the standardized procedures and the unique circumstances of actual cases. It is the accomplishment of this mutual accountability between procedures and real-world events, evidenced in and mediated by the record, that makes up the worker's expertise.

Careful observation of what actually goes on in offices, in other words, reveals that these "unstructured" activities involve both fine-grained structures and, more importantly, a crucial and unacknowledged form of expertise. Like the accomplishment of childbirth, the expertise of office work involves judgment, responsibility, negotiation and knowledge of how to interpret relevant events. The community of co-workers is the resource for that knowledge, bringing information to bear at the time and place that it is needed. An interaction analysis of collaborative work on a single accounting record, for example, shows how while searching files for a missing invoice co-workers continually produce comments that, as assessments of what each is finding, allow the other to monitor their joint work. This monitoring allows for the possibility that either collaborator might "know better" the sense of what the other is finding than the other does herself. And the continual monitoring provides for the possibility that their respective searches might, at any point, develop into concerted attention to any of a number of findings.

Also as in the case of childbirth, workers' knowledge and competence is based in their familiarity with their physical environment. The office worker's environment includes the spatial arrangement of the workplace, the technologies on which she relies and the others with whom she routinely interacts (Suchman & Wynn, 1984). Paper documents, the traditional office technology, are available for physical arrangement in ways that can be read for work to be done and work completed. While the organization of desks, files, and so on is partially inherited from previous owners, workspace arrangements are transformed by each individual in the course of actually doing the work. In this sense territory is appropriated to personal style and individual difference, and the most efficient or satisfactory arrangements are discovered rather than prescribed.

In the office as in other places of women's labor, the introduction of new technologies can bring about disempowerment by transforming previously familiar environments unto unfamiliar ground. New computerized systems affect all aspects of the office environment, transforming the physical workplace (including moving some part of it "into the machine"), the technology base and the social organization of office work. To the extent that technology is designed by specialist practitioners working in other settings and imported into the office, the new technology is inherently unfamiliar. And lack of familiarity, we have argued, undermines the basis of competence. This suggests a reinterpretation of the common wisdom that people (women and managers in particular) are inherently conservative or resistant to innovation. Good reasons for the rejection of new technologies might arise from an implicit recognition of the ways in which models on which the design is based ignore the basis of actual competence. Women are not alone of course in suffering the effects of such models. Our society is specialized to the extent that even managers have technologies imposed on them from a distance, and rationalistic models do no more justice to the realities of managerial work than of clerical work. The crucial difference is that managers can reject new technologies, whereas women clerical workers are forced to adapt.

What are the lessons we can draw from these cases?

1. There is a politics of technology that comes from the intimate relation of ownership and control of technology to authoritative knowledge and competence. Cross-culturally and historically, women's and men's spheres of influence have in many cases operated as "separate but equal," each holding authoritative knowledge within their culturally allocated arenas of activity. But particularly with the spread of

industrial development, the spheres in which men hold influence have systematically been elevated in value and become dominant. In settings where women are primary participants, conversely, the legitimacy of their knowledge has often been subordinated to claims on authoritative knowledge advanced by men.

2. Technological innovation has been a resource for that subordination in two ways. Indirectly, through the representations of knowledge and expertise on which the design of new technology is based. And more directly in the form of ideological commitments manifest in the development and implementation of the artifacts produced. Current models for the design of computer technologies represent activity as rationalized, cerebral, and standardized, while suppressing the work's contingent, embodied, and differentiated nature.

3. Changes imported from a distance generally are characterized by a design/use gap that must either undermine the pre-existing base of competence, result in work-arounds or adaptations of the technology, more and less satisfactorily, to local conditions or, where users have the power to do so, lead to rejection of the technology. Note that, although they may be required to be users of computer technologies designed by people who do not understand the local conditions and competencies of their lives, women have effectively rejected those technologies en masse.

A STRATEGY FOR SYSTEM DEVELOPMENT

How can we develop new technology in ways that would be sensitive to women's knowledge and concerns, engage their hearts and minds and expand their spheres of competence? In general, we argue that system design must take into account existing technologies and practices, out of which we can identify problems and possibilities for change. One could well imagine a different approach to the design of midwife training courses in the Yucatan, which would take the local ethno-obstetric system seriously, determine which problems it cannot handle, and then design collaboratively with the midwives and women in the community a program that is more sensitive to the material circumstances and cultural realities of childbirth in the region (see Jordan, 1987c). In a similar vein, the design of office technologies could be informed by the expertise and work practices of the women who do this kind of work. Only a concerted effort to demystify technology and legitimize the authority of local knowledge will realize that possibility for women.

One implication of our analysis is a radical change in the way that we view the knowledge and skills that go into system design; namely, that we view those of the prospective users of the technology as central, and that we incorporate into the design process as sophisticated an understanding of the social world as of the technology involved. Our own research strategy is to undertake studies of everyday work practice in a range of settings and bring them to bear on the design of appropriate computer systems. Two related methods of inquiry support our research: ethnographic studies of practice and interaction analysis.

Ethnography, the traditional method of social and cultural anthropology, is the intensive analysis of some activity or set of activities in a complex social setting. The goal is what Anselm Strauss has described as "a conceptually dense theory" (1987, p. 1) articulating the significance of activities and relationships between them in terms of members' beliefs, practices, conflicts, commitments, projects, and the like. Such theorizing requires extended participation in the internal life of a setting combined with a critical analytic perspective. Interaction analysis is concerned with detailed empirical investigation of the interaction of human beings with each other and with their physical environment, including technology. Video records constitute the "microscope" for these investigations, where the relevant dimension is time and the requirement that we somehow capture an inherently fleeting phenomenon for systematic review.

Recent challenges to the prevailing systems development process, particularly from Scandinavian computer scientists, suggest the possibility of taking computerization as an occasion to articulate unacknowledged forms of expertise and to take that knowledge seriously as a basis for design (see e.g., Bjerknes, Ehn, & Kyng, 1987; Bodker, 1987; Ehn, 1988; Greenbaum, 1987). In her article "Outline of a Paradigm Change in Software Engineering" (1987), Christianne Floyd draws on her own experiences as a professor of computer science at the Technical University of Berlin. Floyd characterizes the difference between what she calls "product" and "process-oriented" perspectives on software design as "an on-going controversy between rivaling ideas and attitudes underlying our scientific and technical work in software engineering" (p. 193). As Floyd describes it, the "product" perspective views software as essentially a program and associated documentation, and rests upon the following assumptions.

1. For the design of high-quality computer programs, it is sufficient to consider (formalized) information-processing aspects of the usage context. They can be considered on their own, other aspects being ignored ("abstracted from"). These other aspects include the importance of social communication and cooperation for meaningful work; the role of our body and our senses in dealing with real objects rather than with their computer-simulated counterparts; the environmental conditions under which we perform our work.

2. Human information processing and decision-making is largely equivalent to the functioning of computer programs. The division of work between people and computers is therefore arbitrary and should be determined by technical feasibility. There is no guideline as to what should and what should not be automated from a human point of view.

3. The suitability of a program in the context of work processes is determined by the information it produces. There is no consideration of how this information can be meaningfully used in communicative action. (p. 199)

In the product perspective, the interaction between the program and its environment is considered to be prescribed by the program's design. The "referent system," or "the part of the real world which we take into account when developing programs" is preselected for aspects relevant to the software, whereas the software development process itself is outside the bounds of the analysis. In the process perspective, in contrast, the referent system is composed of "human work, learning and communication" (p.194), which are assumed to be subject to continuous development in relation to the software system and vice versa. The interaction between program and environment on this view must continuously change as designers and users change their relation to the technology and as the software is modified to meet new situations and changing work processes. In place of linear "phases" of system development, the work of defining objectives, establishing requirements, specifying functionality, designing, implementing, and evaluating comprises different "universes of discourse" that meet through the collaborative interaction of participants in a complex set of activities "interwoven in time" (p. 202).

The words "oriented" and "perspective" are chosen by Floyd to convey the sense not of an opposition or mutually exclusive disjunction, but of prioritization.

> In this paper I have contrasted two perspectives and not two communities of people holding these perspectives. We all argue and act from both of these perspectives. The criticism implied in my argumentation refers to the fact that existing methods and scientific approaches in software engineering embody the product-oriented view almost exclusively. Working towards overcoming this is both highly imperative, considering the role of information technology in the living human world, and also inspiring since it will provide the opportunity for deep insights into the nature of cognitive processes, for richer relations with the people we meet in our work, and thus for personal development and growth while doing high-quality work in technology. (p. 208)

Floyd's call is for a reprioritization, a kind of affirmative action for the process perspective and its associated concerns. The process perspective focuses designers' attention on the particular settings, activities, interactions between people, and relations between people and machines that Floyd calls the "living human world" (p. 193). More importantly, it directs our attention to the problem of developing a systematic, nonreductionist, experientially based way of designing technology to fit that world.

ACKNOWLEDGMENTS

Our thanks to Paula Goossens for her comments as referee, and to Randy Trigg for helpful comments on an early draft.

REFERENCES

Bjerknes, G., Ehn, P., & Kyng, M. (1987). *Computers and democracy: A Scandinavian challenge*, Aldershot, UK: Avebury.

Bodker, S. (1987), *Through the interface: A human activity approach to user interface design*. Aarhus, Denmark: Aarhus University

Ehn, P. (1988) *Work-oriented design of computer artifacts*. Stockholm: Arbetslivscentrum.

Floyd, C. (1987). Outline of a paradigm change in software engineering, in *Computers and democracy: A Scandinavian challenge*, Aldershot, UK: Avebury.

Fox Keller, E. (1985). *Reflections on gender and science*. New Haven: Yale University Press.

Greenbaum, J. (1987). *The head and the heart: Using gender analysis to study the social construction of computer systems*. Denmark: Aarhus University.

Jordan, B. (1983). *Birth in four cultures*. Montreal: Eden Press.

Jordan, B. (1987a). The hut and the hospital: information, power and symbolism in the artifacts of birth. *Birth: Issues in Perinatal Care and Education 14*(1):36–40.

Jordan, B. (1987b). High Technology: The Case of Obstetrics. *World Health Forum 8*(3):312–319.

Jordan, B. (1987c). Modes of Teaching and Learning: Questions raised by the training of traditional birth attendants. Technical Report #004, Palo Alto, CA: Institute for Research on Learning.

Strauss, A. (1987). *Qualitative analysis for social scientists*. Cambridge, UK: Cambridge University Press.

Suchman, L. (1983). Office Procedures as Practical Action: Models of work and system design. *ACM Transactions on Office Information Systems, 1,*(4):320–328.

Suchman, L., & Wynn, B. (1984), Procedures and Problems in the Office. *Office: Technology and People, 2*:133–154.

8

*Thinking About Computers and Schools: A Skeptical View**

Hank Bromley

State University of New York at Buffalo, Buffalo, NY

INTRODUCTION

In the last 15 years, since microcomputers were first introduced into American schools, their numbers have grown explosively. Many observers have predicted this influx will produce a "revolution" of some sort in schooling. Some foresee a utopian future, prais-

*An earlier version of this chapter appeared in *The Journal of Computing and Society* 1:2 (1991). Portions of the text also appeared in my more thorough essay "Culture, Power and Educational Computing," in Chris Bigum and Bill Green (eds.), *Understanding the New Technologies in Education*, Deakin University (Australia), 1992. Many thanks are due to: Michael Apple, my advisor at the University of Wisconsin, for all his guidance and support; Michael Streibel, for providing a crucial exemplar of thinking about computers and culture—and

ing microcomputers for their democratizing potential; they imagine a society characterized by universal information access, with each person engaged in a process of self-
directed lifelong learning, freely mining the collected knowledge of humankind. In this
vision, centralized power is neutralized and instead dispersed among countless individuals by virtue of their access to large volumes of information and ease in establishing
links with like-minded counterparts. Other, less optimistic, observers fear a dystopian
future, with the homogenizing power of the computer spawning standardization, reg-
imentation, and universal surveillance. They doubt that equal access to information
would itself equalize power, and further deny the likelihood even of equal access: They
anticipate rather a two-tier society, divided into the information-rich, who possess the
resources enabling effective use of information, and the information-poor, who do not.

Much is at stake. But how are we to assess the likelihood of these (or other) scenarios, and to judge what actions might bring about (or prevent) each one? The issues
clearly involve the fundamentals of how we view ourselves as a society. What is initially phrased as a question about technology—"What is the effect of 2.5 million computers in US schools?"—is in fact a question about social processes and priorities. The
first requisite to understanding the issues is therefore an adequate approach for thinking about technology *in its social context.*

Thinking about Technology

Most writing about computers and schools has a narrow, internalistic focus. It
implicitly assumes that technology is beneficent, sure to bring us a better tomorrow if
we simply attend to a little fine-tuning now and then. Thus the myopic concern with
the technology itself and with how to do things with it. Some critics of technology
make the opposite assumption: Technology is inherently evil, and properly dealt with
only through complete avoidance. Both positions are ahistorical, in the sense that they
assume the impact, or meaning, of a given technological artifact is constant at all times
and in all places. They fail to see that the impact can vary with the context, according
to the purposes of the humans involved in the particular situation. They attribute too
much to the technology itself, and not enough to the social context of its use. We need
to shift our focus from the technology per se to the surrounding culture.

However, overemphasizing the social context can lead to another problem: The
technology may come to be seen as a "neutral tool" whose impact is wholly determined
by the intent of its users. This line of thought is extremely common; references to computers as intellectual tools, flexibly applied to whatever problem one wishes, have pro-

encouraging me to disagree; Daniel Pekarsky, for his careful reading and analysis of my work; Chris Bigum,
for his very substantial comments on the essay he solicited, his patience, and his unfailing good cheer; and
the many others who offered helpful and insightful comments, including Elizabeth Ellsworth, Bill Green,
Danny Kleinman, James Ladwig, Elaine Marks, Andy Oram, and the anonymous reviewers for the DIAC
conference. None, of course, bear any responsibility for what I've done with—or despite—their suggestions.

liferated wildly. The tool metaphor is appealing, but misleading: Tools can be flexible, but only within certain limits; their design inevitably favors some applications and prohibits others. The claim that a hammer can be used to build anything overlooks the fact that hammers don't work particularly well with screws. Calling computers neutral tools amenable to any application utilizes the same logic as the slogan "guns don't kill people, people kill people"—it is true that guns can murder only through the agency of human murderousness, but guns as a technology lend themselves to certain uses. They have a built-in propensity to be used in certain ways, toward certain ends. They may depend on human action to consummate those ends, but the predisposition exists in the design of the artifact before it ever gets used.

What I have said thus far may have suggested an opposition between a technology's predispositions and its context of use, with one located "in the technology" and the other "in society." But that apparent opposition exists only if we limit our view to the present. Where did the built-in propensities—what is now located "in the technology"—come from? They originated in the social context in effect when the technology was designed; they reflect the goals and assumptions of the people who created the technology. So there is no opposition between built-in factors and social factors, for what is now built-in is simply a petrified form of past social factors. The two considerations, then, of predisposition and context of use, are really both social. One derives from a social environment of the past (the environment of the technology's genesis), and the other from the social environment of the present.

It's important to recognize both considerations as rooted in the social so that we remember both result from human action, rather than some immutable fact of nature. Of course, what's past is past, and a given technology's propensities, being the sediment of the past, cannot be changed. Once a piece of technology has been designed, its predispositions are locked in. However, if we keep in mind that what is now fixed needn't have turned out as it did, that it might have been different, we will prepare ourselves for actively shaping the technologies of the future, instead of passively adjusting to whatever happens to come along.

What, then, would constitute an adequate analysis of the likely impact of a technological artifact (the computer, for instance)? On the one hand, we need to look at the site where that artifact is put to use, we need to consider who's using it and why, what goals those people have and how they're likely to utilize the technology in pursuit of their goals. Otherwise we risk assuming the artifact will have the same impact everywhere, under all circumstances. At the same time, we need to examine what the technology carries with it into any context, what predispositions constrain how it may be used (keeping in mind that however stuck we now are with those predispositions, they were not inevitable, and also resulted form someone's pursuit of their goals), lest we fall into thinking from the artifact as a neutral tool equally applicable to any purpose.

But one further element needs to be present: Both halves of the analysis must attend to the operation of power. In classrooms, as elsewhere, some groups and individuals have more power than others, and are consequently in a position to parlay the presence of a new technology into even greater advantage than they previously possessed.

Understanding the effect of adding a potent artifact like the computer to the classroom hence requires perceiving whatever aspects of the social structure entail power differentials. Social relationships rooted in unequal power must change if we are to control the effects of new technologies.

A Look Ahead

The remainder of this chapter reflects the twin concerns outlined earlier. One major section considers the context of use, the conflicts now ongoing in educational settings and how computers are utilized by the parties to those conflicts. The other major section focuses on the propensities built into computing technology, the baggage it carries as a result of its cultural heritage and the institutional setting of its development. In the language of the previous section, we trace the effect of the *present* social environment on educational computing, and then the effect of *past* social environments (those in which the technology was developed). Finally, we offer some concluding observations.

The cultural and political import of classroom computing is, I believe, to be found in these twin explorations, taken together. And it is critical that they be, in fact, taken together. Although I have separated the two for discursive clarity, both are always present in any actual situation. They will arrive wedded together in any real classroom, and their relative impact will depend on the specific circumstances.

THE SITE OF USE: RECRUITING COMPUTERS INTO ONGOING SOCIAL CONFLICT

Understanding the full educational impact of any computer-based curriculum necessarily involves matters well beyond the technical, and even well beyond the classroom. Many proposed computer curricula acknowledge the shortcomings of previous initiatives, yet make recommendations still addressing only technical questions. My frustration with such purported "advances" led me to the conviction that ongoing social dynamics in the classroom, long predating the introduction of computers, are of crucial importance. No matter how painstaking the design of a computer-based curriculum, what actually happens when it reaches a given classroom will depend partly on what's already going on in that classroom. The question of how the new technology gets swept up into its users' pursuit of their pre-existing goals is what I referred to in the introduction as the context of use, the effect of the social environment on educational computing. This part of the chapter will explore that social context at some length.

The issue here is how the pre-existing dynamics of the educational realm affect the utilization of computers. I'll begin by outlining some notable aspects of the overall situation in the United States, then indicate what impact the various responses to these factors have on schools, and finally, show how these circumstances bias the likely classroom uses of computers, as actors in educational settings employ the technology according to their own present needs.

The United States in the Late Twentieth Century

Volumes have been written on the gradual changes of recent years in US economics and demographics. Only a few aspects of this transformation that bear on life in schools will concern us here. First, the world standing of the United States, after several decades of clear dominance by any measure, is now more uncertain. Although obviously still very powerful, it is no longer the unquestioned center of the world's economy. The new status, along with other global conditions affecting all countries equally, has contributed to substantial shifts in the US economy. The previously vigorous manufacturing sector that had formed its core is seriously weakened, and what growth occurs is now in the provision of services. The economy increasingly hinges not on the production of goods, but on less tangible kinds of activities, particularly those related to communication and the handling of information.

One result of this transformation has been a general tightening of the job market, along with a slant toward jobs that are part-time, short-term, low-paying, without advancement opportunities, or all of the above. Given this shrinking availability of good full-time work, many working-class and middle-class white males perceive the continuing growth in the proportion of women who work outside the home and the expanding population of people of color as threats to their traditional opportunities. (The fear is misplaced, as these new workers are mainly competing for a different—and less desirable—set of jobs, but nonetheless the fear exists and is itself a significant factor in US politics.)

One strategy for coping with these dislocations would be increased social control of the economy, tempering the destructive potential of the free market. Although there are a few hopeful signs, such as the current moves toward establishing some sort of national health plan (the United States still rates with South Africa as one of the only two industrialized countries without one), for the most part the opposite strategy is being adopted: Rather than being curbed, the free market is being extended. The danger of collapse in one area is answered with the opening of new ones. Aspects of life that had been wholly noncommercial are now undergoing commodification—assessed via some efficiency measure and assigned a price. This extension of market logic has encompassed educational institutions no less than other sectors of society.

New Pressures on Schools

As various actors try to adjust to this novel situation, their reactions create new forces impinging on schools, as well as new tensions within them. Let's take a closer look at what's happening, beginning with expectations placed on schools by business interests and politicians.

With the general tightening of the economy, funding for education is more difficult to come by. School officials thus face difficulties maintaining existing levels of support. And even where spending is not actually reduced, owing to the expansion of free market thinking, they face demands for higher "productivity." The pressure, then, is to provide some sort of "output" (measured student performance), at higher and more predictable levels, with less "input" (funding). One result is an intensification of teachers' labor, as administrators respond to this pressure by passing it on to their staff members.

There are also new demands regarding what students will be taught. Because of the shifting center of economic activity, towards communication and information services, the "national interest" requires young people prepared for a high-technology workplace. This is, in fact, a two-part requirement: On the one hand, a relatively small number of elite trainees are needed for planning and design roles in the new economy. But a very different sort of training is urged for the preponderance of new workers—they need preparation for highly routinized and constricted jobs using advanced technology. It may well be that meeting this expectation has more to do with what behavioral characteristics students acquire than their intellectual abilities: One "prepares" for such a job less by learning how to think than by learning how to stand still and repeatedly perform a simple task without variation.

Another sort of service sought from schools is the provision of a market. Given the overall economic contraction, corporate officials are searching for new outlets, in non-traditional places. Schools are a popular target, for products ranging from the millions of microcomputers now in classrooms to news broadcasts with paid advertising.[1]

Schools also experience pressure from parents concerned about the economic prospects of their children. Parents, too, expect a high-tech future, and they want their children prepared. (Whether all these high-tech predictions are accurate is irrelevant—what matters here is that many parents believe they are, and act accordingly.) Common opinion has it that facility with computers will be a prerequisite for virtually all jobs before long, and no one wants to be left behind. Groups whose participation in the mainstream economy is already marginal fear being totally closed out if their schools don't keep up. And groups which historically had little difficulty securing more lucrative positions are finding it increasingly difficult. What was once virtually automatic, for instance, upon receiving a college degree, is now not so easy to obtain. Given wider distribution of educational credentials, combined with shrinking opportunities, the same credentials no longer buy what they once did. The result is an attempt by the histori-

---

[1] In Whittle Communications' controversial "Channel One" program, schools are given free video equipment in exchange for a promise to show students a regular newscast produced by Whittle, carrying paid advertising. That is, the schools guarantee to deliver an audience that Whittle can use to sell ads. Channel One now reaches over one third of all US missle school and high school students.

cally privileged to redifferentiate themselves. I will suggest in the following how computer-based education fits into this effort.

Computers and Conflict

Having prepared the way with these first two sections, on overall conditions in the United States and consequent pressures on schools, I will now explore how this social setting affects the way computers are used in schools, as classroom actors recruit the technology to assist them in ongoing conflicts.

Beginning at the top again, schools are under enormous pressure to boost their "efficiency" and the predictability of their "output." Of the various kinds of instructional software available, one is notably more responsive to such concerns: drill-and-practice programs. Such software allows precise control over, and tracking of, student activities. The activities themselves are arguably much impoverished, but the programs do train students to perform at known levels on multiple choice exams. Voilà, efficient and predictable output. From a technical point of view, the computer is just as amenable to running an open-ended simulation as a drill-and-practice program. But in the current social context you tend to see one a lot more than the other, because it's much easier to measure a student's performance on a standardized test than to verify that he or she has learned, for instance, to ask good questions.

One may also see a lot of computers sitting in schools without any well-thought-out plan for what to do with them. This phenomenon is also a result of pressure on school officials, in this case pressure to do something—*anything*—about America's faltering economy, about Japanese and European competition, about students' job prospects, about the impending information age. The problem of how to appear to be doing something about these assorted crises is easily solved: Buy some computers. The problem of how then to render the machines educationally useful is a good deal more challenging. Outcome: swarms of classroom computers without a clear mission. Expensive public relations insurance, paid for out of instructional funds.

One frequent function for such aimless computers is most definitely not educationally useful. Administrators are under pressure to cut costs; one means for cutting costs is to contain the number of teachers (or, equivalently, increase the work load for each teacher). Computers are supposed to save teachers time by handling routine instructional and administrative tasks that would otherwise have to be done manually. Therefore, if we have a lot of computers around the school, we must need fewer teachers. This line of reasoning is one way to justify the intensification of teachers' labor mentioned in the previous section.

But since the teachers are indeed experiencing work intensification, they will in fact do whatever they can to save time—including use the computers, regardless of why they were installed in the first place. And what kind of educational software most reliably saves the teacher time? Drill-and-practice programs, once again. Whichever students are using them will be wholly occupied, in a known activity with few surprises to require the teacher's attention, for a predictable amount of time. That can be very use-ful to the harried teacher trying just to find a way to get through the day. Michael Apple and Susan Jungck (Apple & Jungck, 1990) have described the intensification process and how it contributes to teachers' willingness to employ an utterly routinized and vapid computer curriculum, simply because it was already prepared (freeing them from having to write one) and kept the kids busy (freeing the teacher to complete other tasks). Again, this has nothing to do with the technical capabilities of computers, and every-thing to do with pre-existing power relations at the site of use.

Thus far I have only considered situations in which administrators initiated the pur-chase of computers. However, sometimes it is a teacher who pushes for computer pur-chases. What dynamics are at work then? One key factor is the effort of teachers to acquire the status of "professionals." Randall Collins, drawing on the social theory of Max Weber, analyzes the process of professionalization as a struggle among informal-ly constituted groups for positions of power (Collins, 1979); new technologies are often a resource in this struggle. In a context of organizational politics, the most desirable position to be in is to control an area of uncertainty that is crucial for other organiza-tion members. Given the aura of mystery surrounding computers for the uninitiated, and the incredible popular valorization of the pertinent skills, they seem to qualify as "a crucial area of uncertainty." A teacher, then, who can manage the introduction of computers to his or her school, become the local expert, and control their use, has made an excellent move in the struggle over positions of power.

This interpretation is supported by an interesting survey result: Early in the decade of rapid growth in computer use, single teachers often initiated use in their schools, and when they did instruction was often about computer programming; later, administrators were more often the initiators, and instructional use less often emphasized knowledge about computers per se (Becker, 1983–1984). This pattern supports Collins' focus on posi-tional politics, for in his story, the initiating teacher would certainly have the most to gain if instruction emphasized scarce knowledge about computers. Administrators would fare better if the innovation amounted to instruction of traditional material through a new—and highly controllable—technique. Yet again we see that what gets done with the com-puters may have less to do with their intrinsic properties than with social dynamics.

Collins can also help with understanding the parental pressure for computer pur-chases. The training in job skills that figures so prominently in much public rhetoric he considers a fiction; what happens in school is irrelevant to on-the-job productivity (a claim he supports in his book). But he does see technical change as a source of new forms of "cultural currency." Once we have computers, before long we have a new market in credentials certifying computer expertise. Parental demands on schools to begin credentialing their children won't be far behind. From this perspective, all the talk about the need for job-related technical training is a response to the current crisis in the credentials market. The older credentials have become badly inflated: Everyone has them and they no longer guarantee a cushy sinecure. Alert players of positional poli-tics react by creating a new credential. Initially, of course, no one has it, so the first few to acquire it are now distinguished from the crowd that has inflated the old credentials, and stand to benefit substantially. But one cannot announce the true purpose of the new credential, whence the wholly unsubstantiated rhetoric about job training.

Once the computer credential catches on, a mad rush for it is likely to ensue, yielding the exponential growth we have observed. But not everyone is in a strong enough position to obtain access to the new credential. The computer-intensive classroom is a very expensive innovation, out of reach for the many communities that cannot afford it (or lack the clout to force their school officials to find a way to afford it). This barrier brings us back to the notion of redifferentiation, and the discussion I promised of how computer-based education fits into that process.

I referred above to a division between instruction about computers, and instruction in traditional subjects via computer (typically through drill-and-practice programs), which corresponded to whether the initiating staff member was a teacher or an administrator. The same division also tends to hold according to student's race (white students program; others drill), student's rated ability ("high-ability"; "low-ability"), and community socioeconomic status (wealthier; poorer) (Becker, 1983–1984, 1986–1987). We may be seeing here the seeds of the two-tier society that some fear. The differentiation process that once reserved certain privileges for wealthy white men through, for instance, college attendance, may be breaking down because of demographic and economic changes, but it may also be re-established through preferential provision of computer-based education. Some students will learn how to direct the new technology, whereas others will learn—if they can afford any exposure at all—how to be directed by it.

One final comment on this matter of redifferentiation: Whereas I am asserting a tendency for class and racial disparities to be reproduced by the different kinds of computer education children of different backgrounds receive, I am not claiming that is necessarily an intended result. It may not be that privileged groups push for introduction of certain kinds of computer education *specifically in order* to distance themselves from other groups. That may be the farthest thing from their minds when they lobby for computer purchases; perhaps a benign initiative is colonized by the dynamics of a pre-existing social structure, telling us nothing about why the computers are first introduced. But that is exactly my point—regardless of why they are introduced into the educational setting, computers become part of the pre-existing social dynamic of that setting. And the effect of their presence, their impact, depends on how they may be recruited into ongoing conflicts. If you drop an artifact like the computer into a setting where some people are more powerful than others, it should come as no surprise that the computer ends up perpetuating the advantage of the more powerful, for they are most able to reap the benefits of its presence.

THE TECHNOLOGICAL SOCIETY:
PREDISPOSITIONS OF COMPUTING TECHNOLOGY

The previous part of this chapter, "The Site of Use," explored the impact of social context—the school environment—on the classroom use of computers. How the new technology gets swept up into its users' pursuit of their pre-existing goals is critically important, and often overlooked by proponents of educational computing, but it is only part of the story. The technology, although responsive to the social dynamics of the school setting, is not completely malleable. Certain stubborn tendencies seem to reappear, no matter where computers are used. To understand these tendencies I've had to turn my attention back to the technology itself. Or, more precisely, to the social environments of the past in which the technology was developed. As I said in the introduction, the propensities now built into the computer reflect the goals and assumptions of the people who created it. Those social relations of the past are now embodied in the technology and constrain its use in the present. This part of the chapter will consider what predispositions the technology carries with it into any context, and explore where they come from, that is, what historical social relations they are the residue of.

To begin with, just what are the "stubborn tendencies" that recur wherever schools use computers? Following is a list of characteristics that seem to crop up frequently in descriptions (both by teachers and other observers) of computer-oriented classrooms. There is nothing inevitable about these tendencies: They merely indicate what will happen in the absence of positive action to make something else happen instead. Many teachers do manage to avoid these outcomes, but overriding the propensities of the technology takes a special effort.

individualism	Computers are most readily used in ways that reinforce the attitude that each student benefits only from work done in isolation from others. I'll suggest in the following that this tendency derives from our culture's ideology of progress, which has been built into computers.
technical fixes	The same ideology also implies that all problems, including social ones, have technical solutions. Consequently computers are turned to in hopes of remedying all manner of shortcomings in schools. Unless, again, a special effort is made to the contrary, computer use reinforces this bias toward reliance on technical, rather than social, interventions.
domination of nature	The tendency is for computer use—with its emphasis on commands and preprogrammed behavior—to persuade students that the outside world is best dealt with through attempts to control it. Other, more cooperative, modes of interaction among humans, or between humans and nature, are harder to model with computers.
efficiency	Computer use reinforces our overemphasis on efficiency as the sole criterion for the appropriateness of an action. Such considerations as ethical, spiritual, esthetic, and emotional ones are very difficult to address through computing.

"instructional systems" thought	In computer-based classrooms, students are often treated as components of an "instructional system." As one element of a system, their particular needs are subordinated to the overall goal of establishing an ideal "learning environment." In this role, they are addressed exclusively in terms of their information processing capabilities, not as autonomous, whole human beings. I will suggest below that this tendency derives from the origin of instructional computing in military training programs.
quantitative fixation	Computers deal most easily with quantified entities, and with precisely specified interactions. Unless special efforts to the contrary are taken, qualitative information and ambiguous concepts tend to be shunted aside.
top-down thinking	Computers also lend themselves to a top-down style of thinking, where all problems are approached in a divide-and-conquer manner. More exploratory or holistic methods are excluded.
positivism	The intellectual tradition behind computing presumes that cognition is a matter of representing and manipulating what already exists "out there" beyond the person doing the thinking. This reified conception of the origins of knowledge denies the dynamic, socially constructed nature of what we know. Accordingly, computer use most often reinforces passive acceptance of what the facts are, with decisions to be made on the basis of fixed data.
centralization	Although in the abstract it might seem that computers enable greater independence and variety in individual students' activities, in practice they rarely do. That possibility is overridden by a powerful leaning towards centralized control.
infectiousness	Computers have a penchant for taking over whatever process they're a part of, so that even when used as an means to some other end, they somehow become an end in themselves, monopolizing people's attention and subverting other agenda.

If these are the tendencies computers carry with them into all contexts, the next question is where those tendencies come from. What aspects of the social environment in which computers were developed are responsible for passing on these predispositions? I will explore, in turn, three sources of this inheritance: the ideology of progress that underlay the development of the modern conception of science in the seventeenth century; the military setting of the computer's creation during this century; and the intellectual orientation some have called the "rationalistic tradition."

Progress and Technology: The Long View

Tracing the origins of the cultural baggage carried by computers involves the sort of large-scale history of forms of thought that Michel Foucault is known for. Thomas Popkewitz has concentrated for some years now on analyzing the history of education from a perspective like Foucault's (see e.g., Popkewitz, 1991). Typical concerns of his are how we view ourselves as individuals and as members of society, how we conceive of time and of space, and what we find intrinsically valuable. For each of these questions, what is at issue is what the unspoken boundaries of our mental universe are, what unconscious presuppositions constrain our conscious thoughts. These boundaries shift slowly, over considerable lengths of time. In any given period, their current configuration is what makes any public policy initiative (or private action, for that matter) plausible or sensible.

The story that has emerged from ponderings like Popkewitz's is a striking portrait of the evolution of Western society over the last few centuries. The main feature has been the appearance, and eventual dominance, of the notion of progress. The value of progress is now such a fundamental component of our world view that it is very difficult to question it, to imagine a world in which it is not an obvious truth. But "progress," however ascendant at present, does have a history. It appeared sometime, and may eventually disappear. I don't mean to suggest that before a certain date nothing ever changed, nothing happened that we would recognize as progress, nor that after some future date our civilization will again cease to change. New things have, of course, always happened and will continue to happen. But what's unique about the current period is how we conceptualize "new things that happen": We value their *newness* per se. We maintain progress as a conscious goal. It is assumed that whatever is newer is not just different but somehow better. Over the long term, so it is believed, our society does not merely repeat itself but somehow improves.

These assumptions are deeply embedded in our culture, and are so pervasive as to be virtually invisible. But their impact becomes apparent when the sales of a breakfast cereal or laundry detergent are boosted simply by stamping "new, improved" on the box in a bright color, or when the evolution of species is referred to as the development of "higher" forms of life.

Another shift that has occurred over the last few centuries has been a change in the relationship between humans and the rest of nature. Traditionally, nature was to be appeased, admired, understood, or otherwise adjusted to. More recently, nature has been seen as there to be controlled. Rather than engaging in a delicate coexistence with nature, stretching indefinitely into the past and future, "man" now exercises continually increasing dominion over nature. And "man" is meant literally in this context. The fact that most statements commending the conquest of nature use gender-specific language is no accident, no innocent byproduct of habitual use of male pronouns. Human control of nature is described in male-over-female terms, some have argued, because male control of women provided the model on which the drive to control nature was based. (See Merchant, 1980, or the shorter summary in Merchant, 1983, especially pp. 113–116, or Schweickart, 1983, pp. 201–304.)

Technology has been central to both shifts, the ascendancy of progress and the sub-jugation of nature. Its connection to the first shift is that progress in general is taken to be synonymous with progress in technique. As a consequence, we seek technological solutions to social problems of any kind, even those better addressed through other means.[2] As for the shift to dominion over nature, technology has been the means through which dominion has been established. In fact, furthering that dominion has been identified by some as the very definition of technology, and the very purpose of science. Consider, for instance, this from Francis Bacon, who helped form the modern conception of science in the seventeenth century: "I am come in very truth leading you to Nature with all her children to bind her to your service and make her your slave" (cited in Bowers, 1988, p. 130). (Note again the gendered language in which dominion over nature is described. the link between scientific control of nature and masculine control of women continues to the present; "the current forms of both technology and eroticism emphasize relations of dominance, control and submission" [Hacker, 1989, p. 50].)

Related to these two changes was a new development in political philosophy: the rise of liberal individualism. Whereas dominion over nature was advocated as "freeing" humanity from the demands of the rest of nature, liberal individualism "freed" individuals from the demands of the rest of humanity. The same sort of progress urged for society—bold development beyond the constricting shackles of the past—was prescribed for individuals as well. Political philosophers posited natural rights that guaranteed each individual complete self-determination except as limited in an implicit social contract. (Of course only white, male property owners possessed these "natural" rights.[3] Nature is apparently a little eccentric.) A moral basis was thus provided for immoderate pursuit of personal ambition.

These trends all add up to a vision of progress through individual, technologically oriented action. And, in some sense, the vision's promise has been fulfilled. This peculiar manner of action has brought all sorts of benefits, from the availability of answering machines to the eradication of smallpox. But at what cost? Freedom from the past, from the claims of nature, and from the claims of other persons, also means isolation from those entities: To the extent this modernist mindset has come to dominate, we are cut off from the lessons of the past, denied an intimate connection with nature, and isolated from fellow humans.

That mindset has not come to dominate entirely; alternatives do exist, albeit largely in subsidiary roles. Single-minded pursuit of progress has spawned a cult of effi-

---

[2] An important contemporary example of this same inclination was the original SDI ("Star Wars") proposal offered by President Reagan in 1983. Given the dangers posed by massive stockpiles of nuclear weapons, rather than defuse the geopolitical tensions that might precipitate a nuclear attack, Reagan called for an antiballistic missile system to fend off whatever attacks might occur, rendering ICBMs "impotent and obsolete." His technological fantasy was, however, unrealizable, and only hindered more useful (nontechnological) measures to reduce the danger of nuclear war.

[3] At least in the eyes of most commentators. These restrictions were contested from the beginning by a minority faction, arguing for inclusion of women, people of color, and poor folks. This oppositional tradition can trace its roots at least as far back as J. S. Mill.

ciency (see Callahan, 1962), which tends to exclude all other criteria for the appropriateness of an action. Ethical considerations, spiritual, esthetic, and emotional considerations—all are on the defensive. If some act can be shown to foster efficiency, usually nothing else need be said to justify it. It is simply common sense (or has become so) that the most efficient is the best thing to do. Being esthetically advantageous, or spiritually beneficial, is itself enough to justify an act only in certain subcultures. In public discourse for the broadest audiences, such concerns rarely carry much weight on their own, especially if opposed by the dictates of efficiency.

Let us now turn to the postwar conduct of science and see how this underlying mindset is expressed in the particular institutional setting that bred the modern computer.

The Federal Government and Post-World War II Science

The development of the computer is rooted in the close collaboration since World War II of the federal government, major research universities, and industrial corporations. During and immediately after the war, the federal apparatus for funding scientific research expanded dramatically, transforming the relationship of the federal government to American universities and corporations. The key figures form a single community of people who move freely among institutions in all three areas, with something of a shared culture connecting them all.

Members are distinguished by assumptions about the special status of science which may not pertain outside the community: Science is held to take place, unlike other social endeavors, in an abstract realm, governed by objective reason and divorced from the messiness of human desires. Since scientists are engaged in disinterested pursuit of the truth, it is safe to grant their community complete self-determination, unencumbered by interference from nonscientists. The universal benefits of scientific progress justify this privilege (along with generous public support); the nature of the scientific enterprise necessitates it.

Other policymakers, not surprisingly, may take exception to this view. That it has prevailed despite their opposition, and despite obvious shortcomings, demonstrates the power of the implicit mindset described in the previous section. Our fixations on progress through technological advancement, on individual initiative, and on technical fixes for social problems, render practically unchallengeable any appeal for public support of scientific research, particularly if the appeal utilizes a romanticized image of the lone scientist exercising brilliance in splendid seclusion from worldly affairs.

I will resist the temptation to digress into a full recounting of the history of the relationship between science and the federal government; it's a fascinating story. Here's a quick summary (see Kevles, 1978 for a fuller account): federal support of science on a large scale began during World War II, with the intent of aiding the war effort. Military implications were clearly foremost. After the war, a political battle ensued over how civilian government agencies would continue to fund corporate and university laboratories. There were two competing proposals, one backed by Harley Kilgore, a populist senator, and one backed by Vannevar Bush, a science administrator. Kilgore's proposal was the more democratic of the two, insisting that the public should receive the benefits of any work sponsored by the government, and that scientists funded by the government should be accountable to the political process. Bush's proposal, however, prevailed, establishing access for scientists to public money, with little public accountability. Meanwhile, the military has remained a major federal sponsor of scientific research. In particular, the development of the computer has been driven almost entirely by military money.

The history demonstrates how false the common assumptions about the special status of science are. Science does not take place in some abstract realm, remote from ordinary human concerns—and frailties. Scientific activities, both in industry and in universities, have patently been greatly influenced by federal funding. But I must reemphasize what some observers have neglected: The federal government is not some external entity, forcibly overruling the wishes of the technical establishment. The people awarding grants and making policy belong to the same community as the scientists themselves. It is meaningful neither to say the federal government determines scientific activities nor that science takes control of federal policy. Technical objectives, through association with the fundamental cultural imperative of progress, do somehow swallow up federal policy, yet at the same time are themselves influenced by the interaction. The results of government action, intended or otherwise, derive from the assumptions about science and its relation to society shared by all members of the scientific community. So those assumptions, that shared culture, which is itself shaped by the underlying imperative of progress, in turn shapes both technical objectives and federal policy, and htereby indirectly shapes the resulting technology.

Now let's return to the question of to what extent, and how, current technological artifacts reflect their military heritage. One response is provided by Douglas Noble, who has written on the military origins of instructional technology systems and the continuing evidence of their command-and-control lineage (Noble, 1991).

Noble's historical investigation led him to conclude that military research in training and human factors has had overwhelming influence on the development of educational technologies since World War II.[4] Training technologies developed by or for the military were subsequently disseminated into public education, actively promoted by educators, psychologists, and policymakers with extensive military research backgrounds. The technologies transferred in this manner express their military heritage through their adherence to the doctrine of the "man-machine system," the core concept of modern weaponry. Noble identifies two key characteristics of man-machine thought: People are seen as components of large systems, typically computer-based, and all components (both persons and machines) are reduced to their information processing functions. Such systems are desired in the military context because of their amenability to a centralized com-

---

[4] I should note that at other times, the influence often ran in the opposite direction. In the 1910s and 1920s, it was educational psychologists who brought to the military such innovations as IQ tests and behavioristic instructional techniques.

mand structure. But when transferred to the classroom, man-machine ideology is plainly destructive of traditional educational goals. It is designed to produce human components to meet the needs of weapons systems, whereas schools—one would hope—aim rather to meet human needs, and are concerned with people as more than information processors.

For Noble, then, instructional computing reflects its military origins quite directly: the same technology used for training soldiers—that is, the physical system, the accompanying practices, *and* the man-machine ideology both embody—is sold to schools, despite being a technology devised to meet military requirements. (Why schools would nonetheless welcome the merchandise is another story. Noble lists among possible reasons: pressure for "productivity," a drive to modernize and professionalize, corporate marketing, and, not least, successful proselytizing by the researchers/educators he studied.) Some advocates of educational computing, although recognizing the limitations of current software, believe those limitations can potentially be overcome. Noble thinks not. He believes a hardened agenda is "built into" such uses of the computer in education, one with a long history not easily reversed, an agenda for converting all of society into one great man-machine system.

Noble's work reveals one item of the cultural baggage carried by the computer. Unconscious assumptions are built into the machine, and then transmit certain ways of thinking. In the case of Noble's work, the pertinent unconscious assumptions would include that people ought to adjust to social conditions (rather than the opposite), and that nothing crucial is excluded if we treat people as information processors only. Those, like myself, who find these assumptions erroneous and dangerous are consequently dismayed by the presence in classrooms of instructional technologies based on them.

Knowledge Representation

Another example of a predisposition of computing technology derives from the fact that in preparation for use by computers, knowledge is formalized, converted into a form suitable for symbolic manipulation. Let me illustrate what this would mean in a classroom.

One computable form of knowledge is that contained in rule-based expert systems: if-then rules, or "productions," asserting conclusions to be drawn (or actions to be taken) when the specified conditions hold. An expert system designed to identify animals from their characteristics might include rules like "if an animal has feathers, then it is a bird," and "if an animal is a bird, does not fly, swims, and is black and white, then it is a penguin."[5]

---

[5] Borrowed from Winston, 1977, pp. 145–147. Of course, the animal identifier is a simplistic illustration. The following rule is a more realistic example, from a working program (MYCIN, an expert system which advises physicians on bacterial infections): "if the infection type is primary-bacteremia, and the suspected entry point is the gastrointestinal tract, and the site of the culture is one of the sterile sites, then there is evidence that the organism is bacteroides" (Winston, 1977, p. 243).

Now consider a high school history class that has discussed the life cycles of several empires. The class might attempt to generate "rules for preserving an empire." The effort to produce a production-like representation of the relevant considerations (essentially an imperial advisor expert system) would entail identifying similarities in the several cases and abstracting them, that is, identifying the key dynamics—an instructive exercise. But what are the implications of how the empire problem was formulated? What social goals are implicitly favored? To begin with, one might have analyzed the same historical material by generating "rules for toppling an empire." It depends on whose side you're on and what you're hoping to accomplish.

A deeper set of assumptions, beyond which side you're on, is also embedded in the formulation of the problem. Here *representation* comes to the fore. Representing a set of events as the "fall" of an empire (and this is equally true of the underdog representation of those events as the successful toppling of an empire) imposes a particular ordering on the events. There are impermeable divisions drawn between "during the empire" and "after the empire," between "the former rulers" and "the later rulers." But what is usually described as the fall of the Roman Empire to eternal invaders (leaving aside the import of labeling those invaders "barbarians") could also be thought of as a gradual transformation due to a fairly peaceful migration of cultural forms (due, in turn, to population migrations, commercial transactions, etc.). The representation as "conquest" is, of course, no less present in the standard form of history as a textual narrative. What the computable form does, however, is fix that representation in a particularly powerful way, and one that threatens to more effectively blot out awareness of alternative representations. The point is not the "accuracy" of any one representation, but the need to be conscious of the ordering imposed by *any* representation and the relative difficulty of perceiving that imposition.

Here's another example. Not long ago the publisher of a directory of households in the city where I live sent us a blank form, with a request that we fill in information pertaining to our household and return the form. The first line on the form was marked "husband," the second was marked "wife," and the rest were designated for "other occupants over 18 years of age." My household at the time happened to consist of five unrelated adults. We had no husbands and no wives. I called the publisher to complain about their apparent assumption that all households contain a married couple. The person who answered the phone was pleasant but not particularly helpful. She suggested I cross out the labels "husband" and "wife," and fill in our names in any order. I asked how the information would then be entered into their database. She said that was no problem, whoever happened to be on the first line would be labeled head of the household, and we would be listed in the directory under their name. Which is to say I could cross out whatever I liked, but it would have no effect on what got into their database. I told her our household had no head, and we would not be returning the form.

Had their listings not been standardized into a fixed format with everything stuffed into an abstract set of categories, had their final product simply been a large sheaf of cards users could flip through, then I could have scribbled any sort of explanation on our card and it would remain there for users to see. But in formalizing the information, they conclusively imposed an ordering on it, and one whose exclusions will not necessarily be obvious to users of the directory, who will just see a tidy list of households, organized "naturally" by name of household head.

Dog-Wagging Tails and Misleading Metaphors

Another propensity of computer systems is that when used as a means to some end, then tend to subvert the end they purportedly serve and become an end in themselves.

> Often, the information system is treated as a component in the larger system, whose objectives it is expected to serve.... In cases like this, a curious kind of subversion has often been observed. The information system, displaying the ingestive propensities of a snake, swallows up the whole enterprise. What may start out to be the design of a system of health, criminal justice, or land usage becomes a frenetic hunt for information, with a data bank the primary, and perhaps only, result. The larger objectives of the system are obscured if not obliterated; the resources devoured; the total effort begins and ends with the data-gathering and manipulation stage. (Hoos, 1983, p. 12)

I wish to mention briefly one final aspect of the cultural heritage conveyed by the computer: specialized usage altering the meaning of common sense terms. Assigning specialized meanings to common terms is, in itself, not necessarily bad—many fields have technical vocabularies that do exactly that. What's dangerous is when the two meanings become confused, when the distinction between the two kinds of use is not clearly maintained.

As an example, some computer languages contain a module called an "evaluator." What it does resembles, in some loose metaphorical sense, the human activity also called evaluation. It involves assigning a value to something, but the value is a software construct rather than an ethical judgment; it is a value-free value. Allowing the distinction between the two activities to slide, in either direction, is badly misleading. On the one hand, by misreading computer evaluation as human evaluation, it is easy to attribute to the computer a capacity it does not have. On. the other hand, once the metaphor is established, it is easy to assume human evaluation consists of nothing more than what the computer performs.

A similar problem potentially exists around a number of other terms: read, listen, interpret, memory. In all cases the dual danger is that the language suggests machines have human-like capabilities or humans operate in a machine-like fashion. Acting on either of these assumptions can be disastrous, as has been argued by Joseph Weizenbaum, the most well-known insider critic of what computer scientists are up to. He believes that the most important question is not what computers *can* do, but what they *ought* to do. He focuses on the danger of attributing human-like judgment to computers.

There have been many debates on "Computers and Mind." What I conclude here is that the relevant issues are neither technological nor even mathematical; they are ethical. they cannot be settled by asking questions beginning with "can." The limits of the applicability of computers are ultimately statable only in terms of oughts. What emerges as the most elementary insight is that, since we do not now have any ways of making computers wise, we ought not now to give computers tasks that demand wisdom. (Weizenbaum, 1976, p. 227)

PULL THE PLUG?

I have tried to provide here what much literature on educational computing lacks, namely a broader and more critical sense of the likely consequences of introducing computers into classrooms, based on the social conflicts already in progress in schools, into which computers will be drafted as a resource serving one party or another, and the predispositions built into computing technology through the unstated assumptions of its designers. My conclusions have tended toward the ominous, emphasizing a variety of negative possible outcomes. What then do I recommend—should we just pull the plug and henceforth ban computers outright from public schools?

No, not at all. My goal is not to start a crusade against technology; it is rather to stimulate some of the thinking that must be done for us to make constructive use of technology. I hope to contribute in two ways.

First, the factors I have outlined create a bias: Some outcomes (and they're not pleasant) are more likely than others. But this bias can be overcome. If special efforts are taken, there's no reason people can't favor the less likely outcomes. The special efforts must, however, be taken, and if people are unaware of the bias, the effort won't be made. So I have tried to exhibit the bias, create awareness of it, in hopes that teachers will take steps to work around it.

Second, I would like to see the bias eventually eliminated. For that to happen, its sources must be understood. Many writers are critical of the current state of educational software; most of the criticism, however, looks in what I believe to be the wrong direction. It has the internalistic, technical, focus I described at the very beginning of this chapter. Making the software more sophisticated is not the answer, for such software will simply be a more sophisticated carrier of the same propensities, and a more sophisticated weapon in the same social conflicts. (That response itself betrays the faith in technical fixes that is part of the problem.) What is really needed in order to relieve individual teachers of responsibility for circumventing educational computing's tendency to reinforce the inequitable and dehumanizing aspect of our schools is to make changes at the source. Permanent improvements—fashioning a technology with a different set of propensities, and constructing a social context that will put the technology to different uses—will require transcending our culture's ideology of progress, and altering the terms of the social battles now raging through our schools.

REFERENCES

Apple, M. W. & Jungck, S. (1990), You don't have to be a teacher to teach this unit: Teaching, technology, and control in the classroom. *American Educational Research Journal 27:2* (Summer).

Becker, H. J. (1983–1984). *School uses of microcomputers* (series of six newsletters). Baltimore, MD: Center for Social Organization of Schools, The Johns Hopkins University.

Becker, H. J. (1986–1987). *Instructional uses of school computers* (series of six newsletters). Baltimore, MD: Center for Social Organization of Schools, The Johns Hopkins University.

Bowers, C. A. (1988). *The cultural dimensions of educational computing: Understanding the non-neutrality of technology.* New York: Teachers College Press.

Callahan, R. (1962). *Education and the cult of efficiency: A study of the social forces that have shaped the administration of the public schools.* Chicago: University of Chicago Press.

Collins, R. (1979). *The credential society: An historical sociology of education and stratification.* Orlando: Academic Press

Hacker, S. (1989). *Pleasure, power, & technology.* Boston: Unwin Hyman.

Hoos, I. (1983). *Systems analysis in public policy: A critique* (revised edition). Berkeley: University of California Press.

Kevles, D. (1978). *The physicists: The history of a scientific community in modern America.* New York: Knopf.

Merchant, C. (1980). *The death of nature: Women, ecology, and the scientific revolution.* San Francisco: Harper & Row.

Merchant, C. (1983). Mining the Earth's womb, in *Machina Ex Dea: Feminist Perspectives on Technology* in Rothschild, J., (Ed.), New York: Pergamon Press.

Noble, D. D. (1991). *The classroom arsenal: Military research, information technology, and public education.* London: Falmer.

Popkewitz, T. (1991). *A political sociology of educational reform.* New York: Teachers College Press.

Schweickart, P. (1983). What if… science and technology in feminist utopias, *Machina ex dea: Feminist perspectives on technology* in Rothschild, J. (Ed.), New York: Pergamon Press.

Weizenbaum, J. (1976). *Computer power and human reason: From judgment to calculation.* San Francisco: W. H. Freeman.

Winston, P. H. (1977). *Artificial intelligence.* Reading, MA: Addison-Wesley.

9

Artificial Intelligence at War: An Analysis of the Aegis System in Combat*

Chris Hables Gray

Oregon State University

Aegis (e' jis): The Shield of Zeus or his brainchild, Athena. Sometimes emblazoned with the head of Medusa, the gorgon. Also the skin of Amalthea, the goat that nursed Zeus as a babe. Also, goatskin.

INTRODUCTION

Well, to me Aegis is an expert system in many respects. In fact, it has overcome much of the propensity to make mistakes through expert system instrumentation. (Meyer 1988, p. 103)
                                            —Rear Admiral Meyer (Ret.) Aegis manager 1970–1983[1]

Aegis is truly Star Wars at Sea.

                                            —A US Navy Admiral (US 1988, p. 18)

---

* I wish to thank the DIAC reviewers of the chapter who made many detailed and insightful comments.

[1] Others argue that the Aegis, although "a giant step up the ladder of automation in combat systems"

The Aegis System is the US Navy's most advanced "shipboard defensive system against attacks from aircraft and sea skimming missiles" (US, 1988, p. 17).[2] It is probably the most advanced such system in the world and is almost certainly the most complex and advanced computer system that has seen significant military action.[3] In some respects it is an expert system, in others an autonomous weapon, in every case an information and weapon control network of great sophistication.

The actual system, according to Rear Admiral Jerome F. Smith consists of:

> the radar system (AN-SPY-ID) command and decision system (Mark 7 Mod O), weapon controls system (Mark 8 Mod 0), a fire control system (Mark 99 Mod 3), operational readiness and test system (Mark 7 Mod 0), logistic support equipment, combat support equipment, Aegis display system (Mark 2 Mod 0), and the Aegis Combat Training System... the inertial navigation system, the AN/WS-5, which is required to support it, global positioning system, Harpoon weapon system (AN/SWG-1 alpha), Phalanx Close In Weapons System Mark 15 Mod 12, a vertical launching system, the one in the CG-47 class complete with its subcomponents, the standard missile (SM-2 Block 2).[4]

The Aegis system takes in various kinds of electronic information (radio and radar signals from other sources, radar reflections from the ship's own radars, the ship's own position, target, and other information from humans) and distills it into information for

---

because of its self-testing, automated detecting, and total hands-off capabilities, is still "not an application of expert systems technology" in a full sense. (Keen, 1988, p. 98) Just exactly what counts as being artificial intelligence (AI) work is a matter of some debate and continual redefinition. I term the Aegis an artificial intelligence for several reasons. First, it fits most dictionary definitions of AI, as given for example by Chandor (1981, p. 28) and Beardon (1989, p. 12). Second, the military clearly thinks of it as an AI system, and that is a key reason it has had the effect it has. And, third, although the details of its programming are highly classified it seems to me that any system that coordinates so many complex subsystems, that integrates so much different data, that controls so many deadly weapons, and that has the independent ability to find a target, choose the target, and destroy that target as the Aegis does, qualifies as having artificial intelligence.

[2] Quoting Con. Bennet (D-FL) during hearings on selling the Aegis system to Japan. Fewer than twenty Aegis systems had been installed as of 1990 but more than 35 more were planned for various Ticonderoga-class cruisers and Arleigh Burke-class guided missile destroyers. Each Aegis system cost roughly $517 million, uninstalled, in 1987. (US, 1988, pp. 15, 17).

[3] For a survey of advanced computers in military development and deployment see Gray, 1988.

[4] This is actually a list of the components being sold to Japan, complete with model numbers (US, 1988, p. 10). But in its outline it covers the scope of the actual Aegis systems; except for the systems' crew, an integral (and often ignored) part of the complete weapon system.

The main contractors for the Aegis and related systems are RCA (integration), Raytheon (radar), Sperry Rand (computers), FMC (missile launchers), General Dynamics (Standard missiles, Phalanx system), Computer Sciences Corporation (computer software), General Electric (Vulcan machine guns), and Johns Hopkins University (technical advice). There are over 600 other lesser suppliers as well (Petty, 1987, p. 161).

the humans and the weapons through a system of 16 Unisys UYK-7 mainframe computers, 12 Unisys UYK-20 minicomputers, coordinated through 28 different computer programs. The weapons include ship-to-ship Harpoon missiles, ship-to-air Standard missiles (up to 122), and two six-ton, six-barreled Phalanx automatic machine guns that can spit out 50 20-mm uranium-core bullets a second. The humans can either choose the targets and tell the computer system to engage them or put Aegis on automatic and it will do it itself.[5]

What has this system done? It has performed tracking with a high level of accuracy in thousands of hours of actual combat conditions but it has never been attacked directly by air, therefore much about its effectiveness is unknown. However, there have been several minor cases, and one major one, that on closer examination reveal some significant tendencies.

The next two sections discuss the Aegis in combat. Then two sections discuss the implications of its performance so far and make predictions about its future operations.

THE TESTING SCANDALS AND OTHER INCIDENTS

Rear Admiral Wayne E. Meyer (Ret.), Aegis project manager from 1970 to 1983[6] estimated that 31% of Aegis expenses went into testing (Meyer, 1988). Yet, almost every major test of the Aegis System has been criticized.

Rep. Denny Smith (R–OR) reports that of the 22 targets fired at through 1984 only seven were hit. Responding to Smith and other critics the Navy arranged new tests in the spring of 1984 that resulted in 10 of 11 targets being hit. Unfortunately, according to the General Accounting Office, the Aegis operators were told how many targets were coming and from where, and the attackers were limited to two at a time (Hilts & Moore, 1988).

Major "operational" tests of the tracking systems were done near Exit 4 of the New Jersey Turnpike to monitor civilian air traffic over New York airports (Cockburn & Silverstein, 1988), and in a cornfield in the Midwest (Biddle, 1986), even through radar and other electronics respond quite differently at sea than over land.

According to Captain P. T. Deutermann, commander of Destroyer Squadron 25 off Lebanon in late 1983, a small "Cessna type" aircraft was flying directly toward his destroyer, the *USS Tattnall,* clearly visible to himself and many others on the ship. But the *USS Ticonderoga*'s Aegis system repeatedly failed to spot the plane. Finally, as the plane closed, the destroyer trained its guns on it and it left. Deutermann notes, "I have the clear impression that there remained considerable doubt out on the flagship that

---

[5] Most of these details are from Pretty 1987, pp. 160–161; and Editors of Time-Life books, 1988, pp. 94–96.

[6] He's called "Mr. Aegis" in the interview cited here.

we had a valid contact simply because [*Ticonderoga*] did not see it...."[7] There is the real possibility that the plane was not seen because the Aegis was programmed to ignore targets of its profile (Friedman, 1989).

In March of 1986 the *USS Yorktown* fired two Harpoon ship-to-ship missiles at an unknown target in the Gulf of Sidra that the Aegis system identified as a missile-attack boat. Although at first claiming a sinking the Pentagon now admits that they can't confirm that any ship was seen or sunk (Hilts & Moore, 1988).[8]

The final incident worth considering is the attack on the *USS Stark*. Although the *Stark* was not defended by an Aegis system, certain key Aegis subcomponents were on board. It is significant that the Phalanx automatic gun system (20-mm machine guns that can shoot 3,000 rounds a minute with built-in targeting radar and autonomous firing abilities if put on automatic) failed to detect the incoming missiles, as did the *Stark's* Mark 92 fire control radar and the SLQ 032 radar sensor.[9] There were also reports that the Phalanx was not even operational at all, although the Pentagon denies this (Moore, 1987; US Government, 1987).

According to the crew, the system was off until just before the attack because it always broke down if it was left on for any significant length of time. They also claim that that day it needed a replacement part that was late in arriving. Crew members and officers testified under oath that even when operational the Phalanx radar system,

---

[7] From a letter he wrote to the *Proceedings—U.S. Naval Institute,* quoted in Hilts and Moore (1988). Admiral Meyer (Ret.) discusses this incident:

The charge was that there was a little bitty plane and the great Aegis didn't find it. Well, my reaction is la-de-da. Kamikaze! First of all, to the best of my knowledge, the plane never was in the radar's field of view. It has been my experience through hundreds of thousands of hours of operation of this system that every single object in the field of view of this radar has been detected. I do not know of any kinks that we did not anticipate. If this were the case here, it would certainly have been the extraordinary exception. (Meyer, 1988, p. 105)

[8] Some officers have told reporters that it may have been a "low-flying cloud" that was destroyed (Grier, 1986, p. 5). That it was a small commercial or pleasure boat that was "Harpooned" is also possible. Admiral meyer (Ret.) comments

Now let's take the one associated with *Yorktown*—some inane thing about the ship's Aegis radar having targeted something that the press reported was actually a cloud. Was it a cloud? I don't know. I've never seen the data: I only know what was printed. The captain, whom I consider to have been one of our top-drawer captains, determined that there was a surface target. And he determined that the target ought to be engaged with Harpoons, with the approval of proper authority. I believe I'm correct that the press reported that the target then disappeared. Well, what else can we expect the captain to do? Are you going to walk into a dark room having heard rattling in the middle of the night, and not take some action for your protection? What else did we expect? It doesn't matter whether they were clouds. What matters is the action. And by the way, *Yorktown* performed marvelously in guiding our interceptors to the Egyptian airliner carrying the *Archille Lauro* hijackers. (Meyer, 1988, p. 105)

[9] There was no chance of the Phalanx shooting down the Exocet missile because the Phalanx system was not on automatic, but it should have picked up the missile on its targeting radar and given off a loud alarm. Some analysis claim it did not because the missile came from the "blind side" of the *Stark* (Moore, 1987).

which should have warned the crew of the incoming missiles, often failed to detect targets. Although official reports state that the Phalanx was never turned on and that the Exocet missiles approached the ship from its blind spot bow-on, crew members disputed both claims in legal proceedings after the incident (Webb, 1991).

In those same proceedings, soon dismissed on grounds of national security by judges in Texas and Connecticut, engineers and technicians from General Dynamics (the Phalanx manufacturer), Navy experts, and a former Secretary of the Navy (James H. Webb, Jr.), all offered critical testimony on the Phalanx. Among their charges were admissions by key personnel that the Phalanx was tested using "outlaw" software that allowed faulty circuit boards to pass the Navy's tests, that there were failures on "virtually all of the circuit cards" used in Phalanx at one time or another, that on the average Phalanx systems could only operate a few hours without breaking down, and that the overall reliability of the Phalanx was "extraordinarily low" (Webb, 1991). Another critic, who had helped train the *Stark's* air defense officers, revealed that not one officer had ever failed the course and that in many respects training was incredibly inadequate (Freeman, 1992). The *Stark's* captain blamed these technical failures for the death of his 37 crewmen (AP, 1987; Moore, 1987). Yet, he knew of these problems and still placed incredible faith in the technology. This misplaced faith, plus mistaken judgments about the competence of the Iraqi military, were the responsibility of the captain and he paid with his career.

And this was something on the mind of every USN captain in the Persian Gulf from then on, especially Capt. William Rogers III of the Aegis Cruiser *USS Vincennes.* Later he wrote of the *Stark's* effect on himself and the crew: "Vivid memories of a blackened hulk and flag-draped coffins were never far from our minds" (Rogers & Rogers, 1992, p. 4).

THE *USS VINCENNES* AND FLIGHT 655

My guess is that in Vincennes' situation no admiral would ever have given any other ship the right to open fire.

— Rear Admiral Meyer (Ret.), Aegis manager 1970–1983
(Meyer, 1988, p. 103).

In understanding the destruction of flight 655, the cause most emphasized by the Navy in its investigation and analysis was the context the *Vincennes* was operating in. The very reason the Aegis cruiser had been sent to the Gulf was intelligence information that the Iranians were considering using Chinese Silkworm missiles to attack the US military in the Gulf.[10] Other intelligence information indicated that Iran was planning to strike a

---

[10] To quote Admiral Kelly in his congressional testimony.

In fact, the decision was made to send her because we did not know which direction Iran was going to go in at that time and, of course, we had evidence that they had continued construction on the

major blow against the United States (the "Great Satan") around July 4th. There was also official speculation that the Iranians might arm F-14s with air-to-sea missiles (instead of the iron bombs that they normally might carry) or use a commercial airliner for a kamikaze attack. Despite these concerns, the Navy did not supply air cover to the Persian Gulf units so that direct identification of air threats by carrier aircraft could not take place.[11]

The Navy did not consider that the Aegis is a system specifically for confronting massive Soviet air assaults. It is supposed to be able to track 280 targets at once and attack them with 20 or so standard missiles at any one time. So committed is the Navy to managing the target-rich environment of general war that it has ignored a number of support systems that would prove invaluable in target recognition under the much more likely conditions of low-intensity conflict. Any one of them could have prevented the tragedy of Flight 655.[12]

And finally, in terms of the general context, there was the wounding of the *Stark*.

The immediate situation of the *Vincennes* was also crucial. She was several miles inside Iranian territorial waters engaged, along with the frigate *USS Elmer Montgomery*, in a surface action against a number of small Iranian patrol craft, one or more of which may have been sunk. Despite initial US claims that this "battle" took place in international waters, later admissions by the US Government in the World Court, where Iran sued over the incident, and by Admiral Crowe (who was serving as Chairman of the Joint Chiefs in 1988) on national television on July 1, 1992, make it clear that this was not so. There is even strong evidence that the United States was involved in a conscious attempt to provoke the Iranians into an attack on the US units (Barry & Charles, 1992). This surface action was just starting when the seven minutes of Flight 655 were tracked by the *Vincennes*, which was no doubt justifiably concerned that the Iranian Air Force might try and defend its territory while it was trying to shoot some tiny boats in rough seas. To make matters more confusing, one of the automatic 5-inch guns on the ship was jammed and so, in attempts to free it, the ship was

---

Silkworm sites.

And in fact she was pulled out early of a fleet exercise and given very short notice to deploy over there. So the specific reason that the Chairman decided to deploy her in this case was to counter the Silkworm threat (US 1989, p. 32).

[11] Glenn Goodman Jr. (1989) claims that the Navy has increased deployments without air cover since the early 1980s and a similar accident is very possible in the Caribbean or some other site.

[12] Goodman has a very good discussion of these systems. First there is the ARTIS (Aircraft Radar Target Identification System) that uses pattern-recognition software to determine characteristic aircraft signatures from existing radar returns. The program's development was discontinued in 1988 because it could only identify one plane at a time but it has been renewed since the destruction of the Iranian airliner. The Navy is also considering installing electro-optical systems that use long-range TV and infrared sensors to identify approaching aircraft. Such systems that use long-range TV and infrared sensors to identify approaching aircraft. Such systems are already used on F-14s, for example. Goodman has also advocated putting the commercial airliner schedules into a computer data base on ships such as the *Vincennes* but the Navy, unbelievably, says it doesn't have the computer space (Goodman, 1989, pp. 79, 80, 83).

"maneuvering radically" (US, 1989, p. 5).[13] As Capt. Rogers put it in a note during the official inquiry into the incident: "We were like a blind-folded bear fighting off rats!" (Rogers & Rogers, 1992, p. 135).

There was also an Iranian P-3 aircraft flying nearby in a pattern it could well use if it were directing an attack on the *Vincennes,* although it did change its course when asked by the *Vincennes.*

Relying mainly on official and semiofficial military accounts (Friedman, 1989; US, 1989; Barry & Charles, 1992), it is possible to set out in a rough chronological order the mistaken assumptions and judgments that led to the downing of #655:[14]

1. One minute into the flight of 655, the Identification (ID) Supervisor decides that the target blip wasn't #655 because it is 27 minutes past the scheduled departure time or because he doesn't see it on the Navy's list of commercial flights. On the Aegis display Flight 655 is indicated at this time by a symbol that means unidentified, assumed hostile, aircraft.

2. The ID Supervisor sees a military Mode II IFF signal. Aegis data shows no record of this "squawk." The best theory of its origin is that as Flight 655 moved away from Bandar Abbas airport the IFF operator failed to move the gate that searched for IFF signals with it right away. So it accidentally picked up a stray Mode II signal[15] instead of the Mode III civilian-military signal that #655 was broadcasting and that was

---

[13] All of which "certainly raised the pucker factor" according to Admiral Fogarty in his testimony to Congress (US, 1989, p. 5).

The violent maneuvers may have also been to bring the rear 5-inch gun to bear on the Iranian small boats that were close enough to put a few bullets into the Vincennes' bow (Friedman, 1989, p. 74; Rogers & Rogers, 1992, p. 13).

[14] When categorical statements are made about what Aegis noted or didn't note they are based on the Nay's replaying of the *Vincennes* Aegis tapes in a simulated Combat Information Center at the Aegis Combat System Center at Wallops Island, VA. I am assuming in this case that there were no recording errors and that the information was not tampered with, although both are certainly technically possible. That maps released to the public were doctored and that the government and Capt. Rogers have seriously misstated what they know happened, is now beyond question (Barry & Charles, 1992).

Some of the reviewers of this article have complained on the use of journalistic sources instead of official government information, as if the government was more reliable, and disinterested, than journalists. Such naivete is not only poor scholarship but reveals a dangerous ideological bias. All sources have their weaknesses and strengths but all things being equal I'd trust *Newsweek* over the US Navy. For example, the Barry and Charles article is based on filmed (and broadcast on ABC's *Nightline*) interviews with Admiral Crowe, Captain Rogers, and other Naval personnel as well as on the proceedings of the World Court. Charles Barry is a retired Marine colonel and military intelligence officer. The few public denials there have been of the *Newsweek–Nightline* reports have been very unconvincing. Capt. Rogers' account of the incident (in Rogers & Rogers, 1992) on the other hand, is so replete with obvious omissions and misstatements of fact as to be embarrassing.

[15] Probably from Bandar Abbas airport, which had military as well as civilian functions and where F-14s were stationed.

picked up by many others, including the *USS Sides,* a frigate operating nearby.

3. Aegis picks up flight 655's specific IFF signal of 6760, the human operator reads it as 6675. Someone says its an F-14. The civilian IFF signals aren't known to the crew of the *Vincennes* anyway.

4. Responding to an unknown voice on the internal communication system an operator tags #655 as a F-14 on the tactical display. From now on flight 655 has a small notation "F-14" next to its symbol.

5. The Combat Information office says that the target is possibly a commercial plane but at the same time the anti-aircraft officer, Golf Whiskey, is reporting that the target is descending and accelerating (faster than a commercial airliner could go) toward the ship. Even though the Aegis record and the observations of all other ships show that flight #655 was ascending and at a moderate speed, at least two other *Vincennes'* crewmen also claim they saw information that #655 was descending and accelerating at more than one instance (US, 1989, p. 30).

6. Even though the *Sides* had correctly identified flight 655 as a nonthreatening commercial airliner her captain did not argue with the *Vincennes'* labeling of the target as an F-14. In explaining why, Lt. Richard Thomas of the *Sides* commented about the *Vincennes,* "We called her Robocruiser, she always seemed to have a picture…. She always seemed to be telling everybody to get on or off the link as though her picture was better" (Rogers & Rogers, 1992, p. 133). Admiral Fogarty also commented on why neither Captain Carlson of the *Sides* did not dispute the *Vincennes'* identification.

His ship was not being threatened, which it was not, and that the *Vincennes,* being very capable AAW ship, if they call an F-14, then they are probably right (US, 1989, p. 21).

This reasoning also explains why Capt. Rogers' superior, Admiral Smith on the aircraft carrier the *USS Forrestal,* did not dispute the *Vincennes'* identification, even though his team had also correctly judged flight 655 as a commercial airliner.

During this time there was "growing excitement and yelling" of "com air" in the Combat Information Center of the *Sides,* which indicates to me that at least some of her crew realized that the *Vincennes* had made a mistaken identification and was about to shoot down a civilian airliner, which is what they claimed during the official inquiry (Rogers & Rogers, 1992, p. 133; US, 1989, p. 45).

7. Because of the data analysis Aegis performs automatically there was no way for the operators on the *Vincennes* to evaluate the radar blip directly that might have allowed an experienced radar operator to deduce that it was not an F-14.[16]

---

[16] Friedman pointed out that "the shape of a raw video blip is a poor indicator of target size and shape" but at least it is some indicator that is superior to the Aegis displays of #655, which were symbols indicating an unidentified, assumed hostile, aircraft and then an F-14, assumed hostile, aircraft (Friedman, 1989, p. 78, fn. 2; and US, 1989 'pictures of recreated *Vincennes'* Aegis displays, complete with errors, are in Barry and Charles, p. 38).

8. Because of their need for enough distance to allow for full acceleration, the Standard missiles had to be used before the airliner came too close (the exact distance is classified) or the *Vincennes* would have had to rely on the one Phalanx automatic machine gun that was working.[17]

There were also some significant errors and failures that didn't contribute to the downing of flight 655 but could, under other circumstances, lead to equally serious mistakes.

The failure of one of the two automatic 5-inch guns.

There was a 1.5-mile error in the plot of the civilian air flight path zone centerline on the Aegis tactical displays.

The failure for 28 seconds of the "Link-11" interface that is the "tactical data link used to automatically exchange information between other units" (US, 1989, p. 5).[18]

In the two minutes prior to the launching of the antiaircraft missiles the *Vincennes* failed to illuminate flight 655 with its fire control radar because the operator was pushing the buttons in the wrong sequence (US, 1989, p. 28). The Standard missile follows the reflected signals of this radar to its target. No illumination, no kill.

From the turning of the captain's firing key it was fourteen seconds until the launch sequence began. Three seconds later the first missile was fired followed by the other after one second (US, 1989, p. 28).[19]

PERFORMANCE

Clearly, many scientists, military officers, politicians, and bureaucrats believed the Aegis Weapon System would be effective in combat. However, some outside critics, especially computer scientists, had warned that such highly automated defense systems would be far more trouble-prone than their proponents anticipated. In this section their pre-

---

[17] The other one was apparently out of commission (Friedman, 1989, p. 74). Considering what the crew of the *Stark* claimed about their Phalanx system (see the preceding) and that two of the *Vincennes'* close-in weapons, both automatic systems, were not working during combat it is not a good showing for automatic gun subsystems.

[18] Incidentally, this is a subsystem that has failed totally in at least one training simulation (Johns, 1988, p. 48).

[19] Although the Navy doesn't consider this a failure I find 14 seconds a long time to begin firing when the target has been tracked for seven minutes. Perhaps this delay was related to the failure of the fire control radar to fix #655 in the minutes before the missiles were launched. Barry and Charles (1992) claim outright that Lt. Zocher hit the wrong keys 23 times in a row and the actual firing had to be performed by a veteran petty officer. This is hinted at by Freeman (1992) as well.

dictions and arguments will be compared to the system's performance. One important distinction must be stressed—*Aegis is a man-machine weapon system.* That the human parts of this system committed most of the crucial errors is interesting, but not an argument that the system didn't fail.

As we go through the reasons for the failures of the Aegis system so far in combat we can see that all of these failures were expected.

The failure of training or modeling simulations to predict the combination of decisions that led to the downing of flight 655.[20]

The impossibility of predicting how a complex computer system will react.[21]

The breakdown of human-machine communication.[22]

That human perceptions of computer systems can lead directly to human error.

This last point deserves special discussion. The most significant single cause of the shooting down of flight 655 seems to be that in the stress of their combat situation the crew of the *Vincennes* interpreted all information as confirmation that flight 655 was a threat, even when that involved directly misreading the data supplied by the Aegis subsystems. As noted, Aegis itself provided the rationale for sending the *Vincennes* into the Persian Gulf and because of Aegis she was given very liberal rules of engagement. Because the *Vincennes* had the Aegis, the *Sides* did not challenge its identification of flight 655 as an F-14. Having the Aegis gave the captain and crew of the *Vincennes* the confidence, and ability, to shoot down the Iranian airliner; but the ability to see it was actually nonthreatening, nor the confidence to risk that it was hostile.

---

[20] Brian Cantwell Smith describes this as the fallacy of using models to describe "Full-blooded Action" (Smith, 1985). Christine Floyd stresses that "All models of reality anchored in a program are, by their very nature, reductionistic..." (Floyd, 1985). David Lorge Parnas, who has years of experience with military computing, points out that "Practical software must deal with so many distinct situations (or states) that complete testing is impossible" (Parnas, 1987, p. 222). See also Gary Chapman's article (1987b), whose case against the AirLand Battle manager being developed by DARPA and the US Army certainly applies to Aegis and to using expert systems for battle management in general. Ornstein and Suchman (1985) raise the same concerns in their article, which cites numerous examples of computer failures.

[21] See all of the articles cited in footnote 20. Smith (1985) has an especially good discussion of the limits of correctness and the proliferation of levels of failure. Note that the Aegis system had hardware, software, interface, and human errors during its processing of flight 655. Parnas, in both his articles, makes a number of practical comments on the limits of military computing including the important observation that enemy actions and battlefield modifications greatly add to the complexity and uncertainty of all computer weapon systems.

[22] Floyd (1985) has put it most strongly. "Here we must make it clear that between human beings and machines there can be no communication in the proper sense of the word...." Smith (1985) makes some arguments that are certainly applicable to the Aegis system. Because of the inherent instability of the human-machine interface Pullum argues that only nonvital tasks be performed that rely on good human-machine communication.

That computers can change human decision making has been ignored by many analysts, although there is a growing understanding of its importance. (See Winograd & Flores, 1987 for an extended discussion.) In military terms it has already led to a number of significant errors (Gray, 1988).[23] Although the military has recognized this problem it has clearly failed to overcome it.[24]

The Aegis gave the *Vincennes'* captain and crew the illusion that they knew more than they did. And when that was added to the general context (especially the fate of the *Stark* and the intelligence warnings of possible Iranian attacks), the specific context (the surface battle inside Iranian territorial waters, the nearby Iranian P-3), and the way humans make judgments under stress, it is not surprising that a number of coincidences became a general attack. As Admiral Fogarty remarked on Capt. Rogers' thinking:

> He was in combat at time, and, as he has said and testified he thought everything was related on that day. (US, 1989, p. 20)

What this means for the near future, as more Aegis systems, and even more complex systems, are deployed,[25] is more "accidents" such as this. Nothing has happened to disprove the predictions of the critics of military computing. The evidence is mounting that the limitations of advanced systems in combat are very much as expected.

The problem isn't that the systems are not perfect, no mechanical or organic system

---

[23] The philosopher John Ladd has explained how this happens on a policy level in terms that are very applicable to all the Aegis deployments discussed in the chapter.

At the risk of exaggeration, the preoccupation with computerization dominates military technology, which in turn dominates military thinking, which itself dominates foreign policy, i.e., international politics. This is because our political leaders, our government bureaucracies, and much of the general public take for granted that superior computer technology guarantees superior military technology. In turn it is assumed that superior military technology guarantees superior military power, and that superior military power guarantees political effectiveness on the international scene n the pursuit and protection of our national interests. (Ladd, 1987, pp. 298–299)

[24] One of the best discussions is by Lt. Commander Eric Johns (1988). However, his advocacy of better trainings and simulations and of a more coherent career path for surface warfare officers does not begin to address the more fundamental problems raised by the computer scientists and linguists cited above.

Clement Urban, a retired navy officer and currently a researcher for the Navy, has a good article that emphasizes better human factors research in designing weapon systems. But in its detailed argumentation it ends up making a strong case that human-machine communication is inherently so difficult that the failures that have plagued the deployed Aegis systems are inevitable. He points out, for example, that "one researcher catalogued 27 different, but not necessarily independent, human information-handling biases" (Urban, 1988, p. 58). At another point he notes that "at least 50% of major systems failures" were caused by human error according to an 1981 GAO study (US, 1981). Human factors is not the problem. The differences between humans and machines is the problem.

[25] The role of computers has grown so central that the traditional organizing categories of C3I are being changed in many cases to C4I so as to include computers along with command, control, and communication. (See also Chapman, 1987a.)

is. The problem is that more is expected from the system than it can deliver. This can be explained as technophilia, an irrational faith in technology, a veritable ideology of technology. Yes, the Aegis system is a remarkable collection of computers and other machines, but its ability to enhance human performance of tactical tasks (such as tracking and destroying aircraft) doesn't mean it necessarily improves human judgment in complex military situations and it certainly offers no solution to difficult political problems that are intractable to people alone. But from the high government officials who rushed to send the *Vincennes* to the Gulf to the crew of the *Sides* who deferred to the Robocruiser's identification of flight 655, to her crew itself, the belief in this wondrous technology was too seductive to resist.[26]

RESPONSIBILITY

But one thing is clear: The USS Vincennes *acted in self-defense.*
—US Vice-President George Bush (Bush, 1988)

It is clear that the policy of the US government is that it is better to kill hundreds of civilians than risk US military men and women.[27] The US now has a shoot-first policy, largely because of high technology (UP, 1989).

And it is disturbing that the United States has refused to accept any responsibility for the shooting down of flight 655. In a speech before the UN Security Council, then Vice President Bush not only claimed the *Vincennes* was acting in self-defense, but also

---

[26] At one point earlier in the day, a Capt. McKenna in the onshore command center in Bahrain had to order Capt. Rogers out of Omani territorial waters, something the Omanis had already done. Rogers resisted but eventually complied. "Aegis arrogance" is how Capt. McKenna described the *Vincennes'* aggressiveness (Barry & Charles, 1992, p. 32). Complex and impressive high technology weapon systems change human behavior in many different ways, from geostrategic thinking to the rules-of-battle individual soldiers follow. For an extensive discussion of this phenomena see Gray, 1994.

[27] As Capt. Rogers explains in his book any "aircraft or surface ship" that moved into a position where it might be able to "fire a missile, drop a bomb, or use gunfire" against a US ship was considered "hostile" and could be attacked. He remarks that, " 'Don't take the first round' was engraved in the decision-making procedure of all American ships in the Gulf" (Rogers & Rogers, 1992, pp. 10–11).

Admiral Crowe defended Capt. Rogers' action by stating, "The number one obligation of the commanding officer of a ship or of a unit is the protection of his own people" (quoted in Rogers & Rogers, 1992, p. 45).

And Vice President Bush said that Capt. Rogers:

did what he had to do to protect his ship and the lives of his crew. As a military commander, his first duty and responsibility is to protect his men and his ship. (Bush, 1988, p. 2)

This justification comes up in almost all of the official accounts. Saving US lives certainly rates higher than the official "mission" in this case, since the mission was to preserve freedom of passage in the Gulf, which was denied to flight #655 most emphatically. This fear of having military people killed is a major force behind the military's computerization in general (Gray, 1988; Keen, 1988).

that it was Iran's "irresponsible and… tragic error" that led to the destruction of Iran Air 655 for which they must "bear a substantial measure of responsibility" because they allowed flight 655 to fly over an active combat zone.[28]

Some of the recommendations made by the United States to the Council of the International Civil Aviation Organization and certain of the reforms by the US Navy represent implicit criticisms of the US actions. For example, the Navy plans to redesign the Aegis large display screens and make other technical improvements, review certain training procedures, install VHF radios that can tune into commercial frequencies, monitor civilian ATC frequencies, and obtain IFF civilian codes and flight plan information.[29]

But no moral, or legal, responsibility has been admitted. This, too, has been predicted:

> As warfare becomes more and more technological and technology becomes more com-
> puter controlled, accountability becomes less and less possible. Accountability and com-
> puter technology mix like oil and water. For accountability is essentially a human and

---

[28] Because of the state of Iranian command and control the airport official probably had no idea there was a naval action in the Gulf at that time. Anyway, the flight was nearly on time, within its flight plan, flying a civilian profile, and broadcasting its specific civilian identification code. The *Vincennes* just mishandled all of this information.

Among Bush's other inaccurate claims is that the information available to the *Vincennes* indicated that "an Iranian military aircraft was approaching… With hostile intentions." It is now clear that that was merely the interpretation of information that indicated otherwise (Bush, 1988).

[29] Specifically, the Navy plans to

- Redesign the Aegis large screens to show aircraft altitude information.
- Consider slaving the RCI gate to a hooked track.
- Introduce military/civilian interaction scenarios into training.
- Review Aegis IFF operator training.
- Install VHF radios that can be turned to commercial frequencies.
- Implement new voice challenge procedures.
- Encourage civilian aircraft to use weather radar more.
- Encourage civilian aircraft to monitor emergency frequencies.
- Encourage civilian aircraft to fly higher.
- Get the IFF civilian codes.
- Monitor civilian ATC frequencies.
- Get civilian flight plan information.
- Have the *Vincennes* CO strengthen the anti-aircraft co-ordinator position (US, 1989, pp. 17–18).

As of 1989 the Navy had already installed additional VHF radios on ships in the Gulf, reviewed a redesigned large display screen by Hughes Aircraft's Ground System's Group (which supplies the Aegis CIC large screens), restarted the ARTIS program, tested mast-mounted electro-optical systems, and continued research on central IFF, a multiple sensor identification system (Goodman, 1989).

social response to one's fellows when the going is rough. (Ladd, 1987, p. 313)

Ethically and practically, this turning over of responsibility to machines has been strongly criticized, yet it is accelerating.[30] Some authorities even talk of humans giving up all of their responsibilities, even those of a ship's captain. During the Congressional hearings investigating the "downing" of flight 655, Sen. Warner wondered out loud whither or not the doctrine that "a captain is responsible for the ship" should be, or even was, changing:

> In view of the technological nature of warfare today, and the complexity of the instruments of offence and defence that are under the command of a captain of a modern ship?" (US, 1989, p. 3)

But then, who is responsible?

REFERENCES

Associated Press (1987). Stark captain blames deficient radar for frigate's failure to defend itself. *San Jose Mercury News,* Nov. 15, p. 8C.

Barry, J. & Charles, R. (1992). Sea of lies. *Newsweek,* July 12, pp. 29–39.

Beardon, C. (Ed.). (1989). *Artificial intelligence terminology: A reference guide.* Wiley.

Beusmans, J. & Wieckert, K. (1987). Computing, Research, and War: If 'Knowledge is Power,' Where is Responsibility? In Proceedings of Directions and Implications of Advanced Computing (DIAC-87) Symposium. Seattle, WA, July 12, 1987. Palo Alto, CA: Computer Professionals for Social Responsibility.

Biddle, W. (1986). How much bang for the buck? *Discover,* September, pp. 50–66.

Bush, G. (1988). The Persian Gulf conflict and Iran Air 655, an address before the UN Security Council, July 14, 1988. Published by the US Department of State, Bureau of Public Affairs as Current Policy No. 1093.

Chandor, A. et al. (Eds.). (1981). *The Penguin dictionary of computers.* New York: Penguin.

Chapman, G. (1987a). The new generation of high technology weapons, *Computers in Battle,* Jovanovich, New York: Harcourt Brace (pp. 61–100).

Chapman, G. (1987b). Thinking about 'autonomous' weapons. *The CPSR Newsletter,* (3), Fall, pp. 1, 11–14.

---

[30] In addition to the critiques already cited see also Beusmans and Wieckert (1987) and Landau (1987).

Gary Chapman points out that there are related moral problems with computer weapon systems as well, especially as they become more autonomous:

> The moral problems of such machines are immediately obvious. In fact... They may be illegal under the agreements concerning war crime law that the United States has signed. There are three pillars of international war crime law, all three of which are toppled by the deployment of autonomous weapons: war may not be waged outside of "military necessity"; no harm should come to noncombatants, as far as is possible under the circumstances; and war cannot be wedged so that the enemy is given no chance to surrender. It is impossible to build a machine which can comply wit these requirements concerning the just use of force. (Chapman, 1987b, p. 14)

Cockburn, A. & Silverstein, K. (1988). The system that brought down flight 655. *Harper's*, September, pp. 64–65.

Editors of Time-Life Books (1988). *Understanding computers: The military frontier.* New York: Time-Life Books.

Floyd, C. (1985). The responsible use of computers: Where do we draw the line? *The CPSR Newsletter,* June.

Freeman, D. (1992). Let's avoid another Stark. *Proceedings—U.S. Naval Institute,* June, Vol. 119/6, pp. 34–39.

Friedman, N. (1989). The *Vincennes* incident. *Proceedings—U.S. Naval Institute,* May, *115* (5) 72–77.

Goodman, G. W., Jr. (1989). *Vincennes* tragedy could be repeated closer to home. *Armed Forces Journal International,* July, 79, 80, 83.

Gray, C. H. (1988). The strategic computing program at four years: Implications and intimations. *AI and Society—The Journal of Human and Machine Intelligence, 2* (2) Winter, pp. 142–149.

Gray, C. H. (1994). *Postmodern war: Computers as weapons and metaphors.* London: Free Association Press.

Grier, P. (1986). Aegis to put swagger in the Navy's step. *The Christian Science Monitor.* August 21, pp. 3–5.

Hilts, P. J. & Moore, M. (1988). The 'shield of the fleet' may have a few holes in it. *The Washington Post National Weekly Edition,* July 11–17, p. 8.

Johns, E. (1988). Perfect is the enemy of good enough. *Proceedings—U.S. Naval Institute,* October, (10) 37–48.

Keen, T. J., USN Retired (1988). Artificial intelligence and the 1,200-ship navy. *Proceedings—U.S. Naval Institute.* October, 114 (10) 96–100.

Ladd, J. (1987). Computers and war: Philosophical reflections on ends and means. *Computers in Battle* (pp. 302–314) Bellin, D. & Chapman, G., (Eds.). New York: Harcourt Brace Jovanovich.

Landau, S. (1987). The responsible use of 'expert systems', presented at DIAC-87 and printed in the *Symposium Proceedings,* pp. 167–182. Available from Computer Professionals for Social Responsibility.

Meyer, W. E. (1988). Interview. *Proceedings—U.S. Naval Institute,* October, *114* (10) 102–105.

Moore, M. (1987). Behind the failure of the U.S. frigate. *The San Francisco Chronicle,* May 25, pp. 13–14.

Ornstein, S. & Suchman, L. (1985). Reliability and responsibility. *Abacus, 3* (1) Fall, 57–61, 68.

Parnas, D. L. (1985). Software aspects of strategic defense systems. *American Scientist,* Sept.–Oct., 3, 28–31.

Parnas, D. L. (1987). Computers in weapons: The limits of confidence from Bellin and Chapman, eds., *Computers in Battle* (pp. 202–232) Bellin, D. & Chapman, G., (Eds.). New York: Harcourt Brace Jovanovich.

Pullum, G. K. (1987). Natural language interfaces and strategic computing. *AI & Society: The Journal of Human and machine Intelligence, 1* (1), July–September, pp. 47–58.

Rogers, W. & Rogers, S. (1992). *Storm center: The USS Vincennes and Iran Air Flight 655.* Annapolis: Naval Institute Press.

Smith, B. C. (1985). Limits of correctness, from the Center for the Study of Language and Information, report No. CSLI-85-36, Stanford University. Also available from Xerox Corporation.

United Press (1989). US permission to 'shoot first' biggest change, says admiral. *The Seattle Times*, Sept. 2, p. A4.

Urban, C. D. (1988). The human factor. *Proceedings—U.S. Naval Institute.* October, *114*, (10), 58–64.

US Government (1981). Effectiveness of U.S. Forces can be increased through improved weapon systems design. General Accounting Office Report to the Congress PSAD-81-17, January 29.

US Government (1987). Committee on armed services report on the staff investigation into the Iraqi attack on the USS *Stark.* June 14.

US Government (1988). Hearings on the sale of the aegis weapon system to Japan. By the Seapower and Strategic and Critical Materials Subcommittee of the Committee on Armed Services, House of Representatives, One Hundredth Congress, First and Second Sessions, held December 1, 1987, February 4, 11, and March 3, 1988.

US Government (1989). Investigation into the downing of an Iranian airliner by the U.S.S. *Vincennes*, by the Committee on Armed Services, United States Senate, on September 8, 1988, published in 1989.

Williamson, R. (1988). Iran Air 655: Steps to avert future tragedies. An address by the Assistant Secretary for International Organization Affairs to the Council of the International Civil Aviation Organization on July 13, 1988. Published by the U.S. Department of State, Bureau of Public Affairs, as Current Policy No. 1094.

Webb, G. (1991). U.S. Scuttles suits alleging naval gun doesn't work. *San Jose Mercury News*, February 21, pp. 1A, 10A.

Winograd, T. & Flores, F. (1987). *Understanding computers and cognition.* Reading, MA: Addison Wesley.

10

Mudding: Social Phenomena in Text-Based Virtual Realities

Pavel Curtis
Xerox PARC

INTRODUCTION

The Machine did not transmit nuances *of expression. It only gave a general idea of people—an idea that was good enough for all practical purposes.*

—E. M. Forster, 1973

A MUD is a software program that accepts "connections" from multiple users across some kind of network (e.g., telephone lines or the Internet) and provides to each user access to a shared database of "rooms," "exits," and other objects. Each user browses and manipulates this database from "inside" one of those rooms, seeing only those objects that are in the same room and moving from room to room, mostly via the exits

```
>look
Corridor
The corridor from the west continues to the east here, but
the way is blocked by a purple-velvet rope stretched across
the hall. There are doorways leading to the north and south.
You see a sign hanging from the middle of the rope here.
>read sign
This point marks the end of the currently-occupied portion of
the house. Guests proceed beyond this point at their own risk.
--The residents
>go east
You step disdainfully over the velvet rope and enter the dusty
darkness of the unused portion of the house.
```

Figure 10.1.   A typical MUD—database interaction.

that connect them. A MUD, therefore, is a kind of *virtual reality*, an electronically represented "place" that users can visit.

MUDs however, are not, like the kinds of virtual realities that one usually hears about, with fancy graphics and special hardware to sense the position and orientation of the user's real-world body. A MUD user's interface to the database is entirely text-based; all commands are typed in by the users and all feedback is printed as unformatted text on their terminal. The typical MUD user interface is most reminiscent of old computer games like Adventure and Zork (Raymond, 1991); a typical interaction is shown in Figure 10.1. Three major factors distinguish a MUD from an Adventure-style computer game, although

- A MUD is not goal-oriented; it has no beginning or end, no "score," and no notion of "winning" or "success." In short, even though users of MUDs are commonly called *players*, a MUD isn't really a game at all.

- A MUD is extensible from within; a user can add new objects to the database such as rooms, exits, "things," and notes. Certain MUDs, including the one I run, even support an embedded programming language in which a user can describe whole new kinds of behavior for the objects they create.

- A MUD generally has more than one user connected at a time. All of the connected users are browsing and manipulating the same database and can encounter the new objects created by others. The multiple users on a MUD can communicate with each other in real time.

This last factor has a profound effect on the ways in which users interact with the system; it transforms the activity from a solitary one into a social one.

Most interplayer communication on MUDs follows rules that fit within the framework of the virtual reality. If a player "says" something (using the **say** command), then every other player in the same room will "hear" them. For example, suppose that a player named Munchkin typed the command

```
say Can anyone hear me?
```

Then Munchkin would see the feedback

```
You say, "Can anyone hear me?"
```

and every other player in the same room would see

```
Munchkin says, "Can anyone hear me?"
```

Similarly, the `emote` command allows players to express various forms of "nonverbal" communication. If Munchkin types

```
emote smiles.
```

Then every player in the same room sees

```
Munchkin smiles.
```

Most interplayer communication relies entirely on these two commands.[1]

There are two circumstances in which the realistic limitations of `say` and `emote` have proved sufficiently annoying that new mechanisms were developed. It sometimes happens that one player wishes to speak to another player in the same room, but without anyone else in the room being aware of the communication. If Munchkin uses the `whisper` command

```
whisper "I wish he'd just go away…" to Frebble
```

then only Frebble will see

```
Munchkin whispers, "I wish he'd just go away…"
```

The other players in the room see nothing of this at all.

Finally, if one player wishes to say something to another who is connected to the MUD but currently in a different and perhaps "remote" room, the `page` command is

---

[1] In fact, these two commands are so frequently used that single-character abbreviations are provided for them. The two example commands would usually be typed as follows:

```
"Can anyone hear me?
:smiles.
```

appropriate. It is invoked with a syntax very like that of the `whisper` command and the recipient sees output like this.

```
You sense that Munchkin is looking for you in The Hall.
He pages, "Come see this clock, it's tres cool!"
```

Aside from conversation, MUD players can most directly express themselves in three ways: by their choice of player name, by their choice of gender, and by their self-description.

When a player first connects to a MUD, they choose a name by which the other players will know them. This choice, like almost all others in MUDs, is not cast in stone; any player can rename themself at any time, though not to a name currently in use by some other player. Typically, MUD names are single words, in contrast to the longer "full" names used in real life.

Initially, MUD players appear to be neuter; automatically generated messages that refer to such a player use the family of pronouns, including "it," "its," and so on. Players can choose to appear as a different gender, though, and not only male or female. On many MUDs, players can also choose to be plural (appearing to be a kind of "colony" creature: "ChupChups leave the room, closing the door behind them"), or to use one of several sets of gender-neutral pronouns (e.g., "s/he," "him/her," or "e," "em," and "eir").

Every object in a MUD optionally has a textual *description* that players can view with the `look` command. For example, the description of a room is automatically shown to a player when they enter that room and can be seen again just by typing "`look.`" To see another player's description, one might type "`look Bert.`" Players can set or change their descriptions at any time. The lengths of player descriptions typically vary from short one-liners to dozen-line paragraphs.

Aside from direct communication and responses to player commands, messages are printed to players when other players enter or leave the same room, when others connect or disconnect and are already in the same room, and when objects in the virtual reality have asynchronous behavior (e.g., a cuckoo clock chiming the hours).

MUD players typically spend their connected time socializing with each other, exploring the various rooms and other objects in the database, and adding new such objects of their own design. They vary widely in the amount of time they spend connected on each visit, ranging from only a minute to several hours; some players stay connected (and almost always idle) for days at a time, only occasionally actively participating.

This very brief description of the technical aspects of mudding suffices for the purposes of the chapter. It has been my experience, however, that it is quite difficult to properly convey the "sense" of the experience in words. Readers desiring more detailed information are advised to try mudding themselves, as described in the final section of this chapter.

SOCIAL PHENOMENA OBSERVED ON ONE MUD

Man is the measure.
—E. M. Forster

In October of 1990, I began running an Internet-accessible MUD server on my personal workstation here at PARC. Since then, it has been running continuously, with interruptions of only a few hours at most. In January of 1991, the existence of the MUD (called LambdaMOO[2]) was announced publicly, via the Usenet newsgroup `rec.games.mud`. As of this writing, well over 3,500 different players have connected to the server from over a dozen countries around the world and, at any given time, over 750 players have connected at least once in the last week. Recent statistics concerning the number of players connected at a given time of day (Pacific Standard Time) appear in Figure 10.2.

LambdaMOO is clearly a reasonably active place, with new and old players coming and going frequently throughout the day. This popularity has provided me with a position from which to observe the social patterns of a fairly large and diverse MUD clientele. I want to point out to the reader, however, that I have no formal

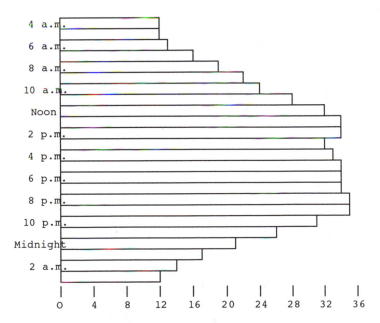

Figure 10.2. Average number of connected players on LambdaMOO, by time of day.

---

[2] The "MOO" in "LambdaMOO" stands for "MUD, Object-Oriented." The origin of the "Lambda" part is more obscure. Based on my years of experience with the Lisp programming language.

training in sociology, anthropology, or psychology, so I cannot make any claims about methodology or even my own objectivity. What I relate below is merely my personal observations made over a year of mudding. In most cases, my discussions of the motivations and feelings of individual players is based on in-MUD conversations with them; I have no means of checking the veracity of their statements concerning their real-life genders, identities, or (obviously) feelings. On the other hand, in most cases, I also have no reason to doubt them.

I have grouped my observations into three categories: phenomena related to the behavior and motivations of individual players, phenomena related to interactions between small groups of players (especially observations concerning MUD conversation), and phenomena related to the behavior of a MUD's community as a whole.

Cutting across all of these categories is a recurring theme to which I would like to draw the reader's attention in advance. Social behavior on MUDs is in some ways a direct mirror of behavior in real life, with mechanisms being drawn nearly unchanged from real-life, and in some ways very new and different, taking root in the new opportunities that MUDs provide over real life.

Observations about Individuals

The Mudding Population.   The people who have an opportunity to connect to LambdaMOO are not a representative sample of the world population; they all read and write English with at least passable proficiency and they have access to the Internet. Based on the names of their network hosts, I believe that well over 90% of them are affiliated with colleges and universities, mostly as students and, to a lesser extent, mostly undergraduates. Because they have Internet access, it might be supposed that the vast majority of players are involved in the computing field, but I do not believe that this is the case. It appears to me that no more than half (and probably less) of them are so employed; the increasing general availability of computing resources on college campuses and in industry appears to be having an effect, allowing a broader community to participate.

In any case, it appears that the educational background of the mudding community is generally above average and it is likely that the economic background is similarly above the norm. Based on my conversations with people and on the names of those who have asked to join a mailing list about programming in LambdaMoo, I would guess that over 70% of the players are male; it is very difficult to have any firm justification for this number, however.

Player Presentation.   As described in the Introduction, players have a number of choices about how to present themselves in the MUD; the first such decision is the name they will use. Figure 10.3 shows some of the names used by players on LambdaMOO. One can pick out a few common styles for names (e.g., names from or inspired by myth, fantasy, or other literature, common names from real life, names of

Toon	Gemba	Gary_Severn	Ford	Frand
li'ir	Maya	Rincewind	yduJ	funky
Grump	Foodslave	Arthur	EbbTide	Anathae
yrx	Satan	byte	Booga	tek
chupchups	waffle	Miranda	Gus	Merlin
Moonlight	MrNatural	Winger	Drazz'zt	Kendal
RedJack	Snooze	Shin	lostboy	foobar
Ted_Logan	Xephry	King_Claudius	Bruce	Puff
Dirque	Coyote	Vastin	Player	Cool
Amy	Thorgeir	Cyberhuman	Gandalf	blip
Jayhirazan	Firefoot	JoeFeedback	ZZZzzz...	Lyssa
Avatar	zipo	Blackwinter	viz	Kilik
Maelstorm	Love	Terryann	Chrystal	arkanoiv

Figure 10.3. A selection of player names from LambdaMOO.

concepts, animals, and everyday objects that have representative connotations, etc.), but it is clear that no such category includes a majority of the names. Note that a significant minority of the names are in lower case; this appears to be a stylistic choice (players with such names describe the practice as "cool") and not, as might be supposed, an indication of a depressed ego.

Players can be quite possessive about their names, resenting others who choose names that are similarly spelled or pronounced or even that are taken from the same mythology or work of literature. In one case, for example, a player named "ZigZag" complained to me about other players taking the names "ZigZag!" and "Zig."

The choice of a player's gender is, for some, one of great consequence and forethought; for other (mostly males), it is simple and without any questions. For all that this choice involves the fewest options for the player (unlike their name or description, which are limited only by their imagination), it is also the choice that can generate the greatest concern and interest on the part of other players.

As I've said before, it appears that the great majority of players are male and the vast majority of them choose to present themselves as such. Some males, however, taking advantages of the relative rarity of females in MUDs, present themselves as female and thus stand out to some degree. Some use this distinction just for the fun of deceiving others, some of these going so far as to try to entice male-presenting players into sexually explicit discussions and interactions. This is such a widely noticed phenomenon, in fact, that one is advised by the common wisdom to assume that any flirtatious female-presenting players are, in real life, males. Such players are often subject to ostracism based on this assumption.

Some MUD players have suggested to me that such transvestite flirts are perhaps acting out their own (latent or otherwise) homosexual urges or fantasies, taking advantage of the perfect safety of the MUD situation to see how it feels to approach other men. Although I have had no personal experience talking to such players, let alone the opportunity to delve into their motivations, the idea strikes me as plausible given the other ways in which MUD anonymity seems to free people from their inhibitions. (I say more about anonymity later on.)

Other males present themselves as female more out of curiosity than as an attempt at deception; to some degree, they are interested in seeing "how the other half lives," what it feels like to be perceived as female in a community. From what I can tell, they can be quite successful at this.

Female-presenting players report a number of problems. Many of them have told me that they are frequently subject both to harassment and to special treatment. One reported seeing two newcomers arrive at the same time, one male-presenting and one female-presenting. The other players in the room struck up conversations with the putative female and offered to show her around but completely ignored the putative male, who was left to his own devices.

In addition, probably owing mostly to the number of female-presenting males one hears about, many female players report that they are frequently (and sometimes quite aggressively) challenged to "prove" that they are, in fact, female. To the best of my knowledge, male-presenting players are rarely if ever so challenged.

Because of these problems, many players who are female in real life choose to present themselves as otherwise, choosing either male, neuter, or gender-neutral pronouns. As one might expect, the neuter and gender-neutral presenters are still subject to demands that they divulge their real gender.

Some players apparently find it quite difficult to interact with those whose true gender has been called into question; since this phenomenon is rarely manifest in real life, they have grown dependent on "knowing where they stand," on knowing what gender roles are "appropriate." Some players (and not only males) also feel that it is dishonest to present oneself as being a different gender than in real life; they report felling "mad" and "used" when they discover the deception.

Although I can spare no more space for this topic, I enthusiastically encourage the interested reader to look up Van Gelder's fascinating article (McLuhan, 1984) for many more examples and insights, as well as the story of a remarkable successful deception via "electronic transvestism."

The final part of a player's self-presentation, and the only part involving prose, is the player's *description*. This is where players can, and often do, establish the details of a persona or role they wish to play in the virtual reality. It is also a significant factor in other players' first impressions, since new players are commonly `look`ed at soon after entering a common room.

Some players use extremely short descriptions, either intending to be cryptic (e.g., "the possessor of the infinity gems.") or straightforward (e.g., "an average-sized dark elf with lavender eyes.") or often, just insufficiently motivated to create a more complex description for themselves. Other players go to great efforts in writing their descriptions; one moderately long example appears in Figure 10.4.

A large proportion of player descriptions contain a degree of wish fulfillment; I cannot count the number of "mysterious but unmistakably powerful" figures I have seen wandering around in LambdaMOO. Many players, it seems, are taking advantage of

You see a quiet, unassuming figure, wreathed in an oversized,
dull-green Army jacket which is pulled up to nearly conceal
his face. His long, unkempt blond hair blows back from his
face as he tosses his head to meet your gaze. Small round
gold-rimmed glasses, tinted slightly grey, rest on his nose.
On a shoulder strap he carries an acoustic guitar and he lugs
a backpack stuffed to overflowing with sheet music, sketches,
and computer printouts. Under the coat are faded jeans and a
T-Shirt reading 'Paranoid CyberPunks International'. He meets
your gaze and smiles faintly, but does not speak with you. As
you surmise him, you notice a glint of red at the rims of his
blue eyes, and realize that his canine teeth seem to protrude
slightly. He recoils from your look of horror and recedes back
into himself.

Figure 10.4. A moderately long player description.

the MUD to emulate various attractive characters from fiction.

Given the detail and content of so many player descriptions, one might expect
to find a significant amount of role-playing, players who adopt a coherent character with features distinct from their real-life personalities. Such is rarely the case,
however. Most players appear to tire of such an effort quickly and simply interact
with the others more or less straightforwardly, at least to the degree one does in
normal discourse. One factor might be that the roles chosen by players are usually taken from a particular creative work and are not particularly viable as characters outside of the context of that work; in short, the roles don't make sense in the
context of MUD.

A notable exception to this rule is one particular MUD I've heard of, called
"PernMUSH." This appears to be a rigidly maintained simulacrum of the world
described in Ann McCaffrey's celebrated "Dragon" books. All players there gave
names that fit the style of the books and all places built there are consistent with what
is shown in the series and in various fan materials devoted to it. PernMUSH apparently
holds frequent "hatchings" and other social events, also derived in great detail from
McCaffrey's works. This exception probably succeeds only because of its single-mind-
edness; with every player providing the correct context for every other, it is easier for
everyone to stay more-or-less "in character."

Player Anonymity. It seems to me that the most significant social factor in
MUDs is the perfect anonymity provided to the players. There are no commands available to the players to discover the real-life identity of each other and, indeed, technical
considerations make such commands either very difficult or impossible to implement.

It is this guarantee of privacy that makes players' self-presentation so important
and, in a sense, successful. Players can only be known by what they explicitly project and are not "locked into" any factors beyond their easy control, such as personal appearance, race, and so on. In the words of an old military recruiting

commercial, MUD players can "be all that your can be."[3]

This also contributes to what might be called a "shipboard syndrome," the feeling that since one will likely never meet anyone from the MUD in real life, there is less social risk involved and inhibitions can be lowered safely.

For example, many players report that they are much more willing to strike up conversations with strangers they encounter in the MUD than in real life. One obvious factor is that MUD visitors are implicitly assumed to be interested in conversing, unlike in most real-world contexts. Another deeper reason, though, is that players do not feel that very much is at risk. At worst, if a player feels that he's made utter fool or himself, he can always abandon the character and create a new one, losing only the name and the effort invested in socially establishing the old one. In effect, a "new lease on life" is always a ready option.

Players on most MUDs are also emboldened somewhat by the fact that they are immune from violence, both physical and virtual. The permissions systems of all MUDs (except those whose whole purpose revolves around adventuring and the slaying of monsters and other players) generally prevent any player from having any kind of permanent effect on any other player. Players can certainly annoy each other, but not in any lasting or even moderately long-lived manner.

This protective anonymity also encourages some players to behave irresponsibly, rudely, or even obnoxiously. We have had instances of severe and repeated sexual harassment, crudity, and deliberate offensiveness. In general, such cruelty seems to be supported by two causes: the offenders believe (usually correctly) that they cannot be held accountable for their actions in the real world, and the very same anonymity makes it easier for them to treat other players impersonally, as other than real people.

Wizards. Usually, as I understand it, societies cope with offensive behavior by various group mechanisms, such as ostracism, and I discuss this kind of effect in detail elsewhere in this chapter. In certain severe cases, however, it is left to the "authorities" or "police" of a society to take direct action, and MUDs are no different in this respect.

On MUDs, it is a special class of players, usually called *wizards* or (less frequently) *gods*, who fulfill both the "authority" and "police" roles. A wizard is a player who has special permissions and commands available, usually for the purpose of maintaining the MUD, much like a "system administrator" or "superuser" in real-life computing systems. Players can only be transformed into wizards by other wizards, with the maintainer of the actual MUD server computer program acting as the first such.

On most MUDs, the wizards' first approach to solving serious behavior problems is, as in the best real-life situations, to attempt a calm dialog with the offender. When this fails, as it usually does in the worst cases of irresponsibility, the customary response

---

[3] Kiesler and her colleagues (Kiesler et al., 1991) have investigated the effects of this kind of electronic anonymity on the decision-making and problem-solving processes in organizations: some of their observations parallel mine given here.

is to punish the offender with "toading." This involves (a) either severely restricting the kinds of actions the player can take or else preventing them from connecting at all, (b) changing the name and description of the player to present an unpleasant appearance (often literally that of a warty toad), and (c) moving the player to some very public place within the virtual reality. This public humiliation is often sufficient to discourage repeat visits by the player, even in a different guise.

On LambdaMOO, the wizards as a group decided on a more low-key approach to the problem; we have, in the handful of cases where such a severe course was dictated, simply "recycled" the offending player, removing them from the database of the MUD entirely. This is a more permanent solution than toading, but also lacks the public spectacle of toading, a practice none of us were comfortable with.

Wizards, in general, have a very different experience of mudding than other players. Because of their palpable and extensive extra powers over other players, and because of their special role in MUD society, they are frequently treated differently by other players.

Most players on LambdaMOO, for example, upon first encountering my wizard player, treat me with almost exaggerated deference and resect. I am frequently called "sir" and players often apologize for "wasting" my time. A significant minority, however, appear to go to great lengths to prove that they are *not* impressed by my office or power, speaking to me quite bluntly and making demands that I assist them with their problems using the system, sometimes to the point of rudeness.

Because of other demands on my time, I am almost always connected to the MUD but idle, located in a special room I built (my "den") that players require my permission to enter. This room is useful, for example, as a place in which to hold sensitive conversations without fear of interruption. This constant presence and unapproachability, however, has had significant and unanticipated side effects. I am told by players who get more circulation than I do that I am widely perceived as a kind of mythic figure, a mysterious wizard in his magical tower. Rumor and hearsay have spread word of my supposed opinions on matters of MUD policy. One effect is that players are often afraid to contact me for fear of capricious retaliation at their presumption.

Although I find this situation disturbing and wish that I had more time to spend out walking among the "mortal" members of the LambdaMOO community, I am told that player fears of wizardly caprice are justified on certain other MUDs. It is certainly easy to believe the stories I hear of MUD wizards who demand deference and severely punish those who transgress; there is a certain ego boost to those who wield even simple administrative power in virtual worlds and it would be remarkable indeed if no one had ever started a MUD for that reason alone.

In fact, one player sent me a copy of an article, written by a former MUD wizard, based on Machiavelli's "The Prince;" it details a wide variety of more-or-less creative ways for wizards to make ordinary MUD players miserable. If this wizard actually used these techniques, as he claims, then some players' desires to avoid wizards are quite understandable.

Observations about Small Groups

MUD Conversation.   The majority of player spend the majority of their active time on MUDs in conversation with other players. The mechanisms by which those conversations get started generally mirror those that operate in real life, although sometimes in interesting ways.

Chance encounters between players exploring the same parts of the database are common and almost always cause for conversation. As mentioned, the anonymity of MUDs tends to lower social barriers and to encourage players to be more outgoing than in real life. Strangers on MUDs greet each other with the same kinds of questions as in real life: "Are you new here? I don't think we've met." The very first greetings, however, are usually gestural rather than verbal: "Munchkin waves. Lorelei waves back."

The @who (or WHO) command on MUDs allows players to see who else is currently connected and, on some MUDs, where those people are. An example of the output of this command appears in Figure 10.5. This is, in a sense, the MUD analog of scanning the room in a real-life gathering to see who's present.

Players consult the @who list to see if their friends are connected and to see which areas, if any, seem to have a concentration of players in them. If more than a couple of players are in the same room, the presumption is that an interesting conversation may be in progress there; players are thus more attracted to more populated areas. I call this phenomenon "social gravity," it has a real-world analog in the tendency of people to be attracted to conspicuous crowds, such as two or more people at the door of a colleague's office.

It is sometimes the case on a MUD, as in real life, that one wishes to avoid getting into a conversation, either because of the particular other player involved or because of some other activity one does not wish to interrupt. In the real world, one can refrain

```
Player name         Connected    Idle time     Location
-----------         ---------    ---------     --------
Haakon (#2)         3 days       a second      Lambda's Den
Lynx (#8910)        a minute     2 seconds     Lynx's Abode
Garin (#23393)      an hour      2 seconds     Carnival Grounds
Gilmore (#19194)    an hour      10 seconds    Heart of Darkness
TamLin (#21864)     an hour      21 seconds    Heart of Darkness
Quimby (#23279)     3 minutes    2 minutes     Quimby's room
Koosh (#24639)      50 minutes   5 minutes     Corridor
Nosredna (#2487)    7 hours      36 minutes    Nosredna's Hideaway
yduJ (#68)          7 hours      47 minutes    Hackers' Heaven
Zachary (#4670)     an hour      an hour       Zachary's Workshop
Woodlock (#2520)    2 hours      2 hours       Woodlock's Room
```

Total: 11 players, 6 of whom have been active recently.

Figure 10.5.   Sample output from LambdaMOO's @ who ***command.***

from answering the phone, screen calls using an answering machine, or even, in cop-resent situations, pretend not to have heard the other party. In the latter case, with luck, the person will give up rather than repeat himself more loudly.

The mechanisms are both similar and interestingly different on MUDs. It is often the case that MUD players are connected but idle, perhaps because they have stepped away from their terminal for a while. Thus, it often happens that one receives no response to an utterance in a MUD simply because the other party wasn't really pre-sent to see it. This commonly understood fact of MUD life provides for the MUD equivalent of pretending not to hear. I know of players who take care after such a pre-tense not to type anything more to the MUD until the would-be conversant has left, thus preserving the apparent validity of their excuse.

Another mechanism for avoiding conversation is available to MUD players but, as far as I can see, not to people in real life situations. Most MUDs provide a mechanism by which each player can designate a set of other players as "gagged," the effect is that nothing will be printed to the gagging player if someone they've gagged speaks, moves, emotes, and so on. There is generally no mechanism by which the gagged player can tell *a priori* that someone is gagging them; indeed, unless the gagged player attempts to address the gagging player directly, the responses from the other players in the room (who may not be gagging the speaker) may cause the speaker never even to suspect that some are not hearing them.

We provide a gagging facility on LambdaMOO, but it is fairly rarely used; a recent check revealed only 45 players out of almost 3,000 who are gagging other players. The general feeling appears to be that gagging is quite rude and is only appropriate (if ever) when someone persists in annoying you in spite of polite requests to the contrary. It is not clear, though, quite how universal this feeling is. For example, I know of some play-ers who, on being told that some other players were offended by their speech, suggest-ed that gagging was the solution: "If they don't want to hear me, let them gag me; I won't be offended." Also, I am given to understand that gagging is much more com-monly employed on some other MUDs.

The course of a MUD conversation is remarkably like and unlike one in the real world. Participants in MUD conversations commonly use the emote command to make gestures, such as nodding to urge someone to continue, waving at player arrivals and departures, raising eyebrows, gagging to apologize or soothe, etc. As in electronic mail (though much more frequently), players employ standard "smiley-face" glyphs (e.g., ":-)," ":-(," and ":-|") to clarify the "tone" with which they say things. Utterances are also frequently addressed to specific participants, as opposed to the room as a whole (e.g., "Munchkin nods to Frebble. 'You tell 'em!'").

The most obvious difference between MUD conversations and those in real life is that the utterances must be typed rather than simply spoken. This introduces signifi-cant delays into the interaction and, like nature, MUD society abhors a vacuum.

Even when there are only two participants in a MUD conversation, it is very rare for there to be only one thread of discussion; during the pause while one player is typ-ing a response, the other player commonly thinks of something else to say and does so, introducing at least another level to the conversation, if not a completely new topic. These multitopic conversations are a bit disorienting and bewildering to the uninitiated, but it appears that most players quickly become accustomed to them and handle the multiple levels smoothly. Of course, when more than two players are involved, the opportunities for multiple levels are increased. It has been pointed out that a suitable punishment for truly heinous social offenders might be to strand them in a room with more than a dozen players actively conversing.

This kind of cognitive time-sharing also arises because of the existence of the page command. Recall from the Introduction that this command allows a player to send a message to another who is not in the same room. It is not uncommon (especially for wizards, whose advice is frequently sought by "distant" players) to be involved in one conversation "face-to-face" and one or two more conducted via **page**. Again, although this can be overwhelming at first, one can actually come to appreciate the relief from the tedious long pauses waiting for a fellow conversant to type.

Another effect of the typing delay (and of the low bandwidth of the MUD medium) is a tendency for players to abbreviate their communications, sometimes past the point of ambiguity. For example, some players often greet others with "hugs" but the "meanings" of those hugs vary widely from recipient to recipient. In one case the hug might be a simple friendly greeting, in another it might be intended to convey a very special affection. In both cases, the text typed by the hugger is the same (e.g., "Munchkin hugs Frebble."); it is considered too much trouble for the hugger to type a description of the act sufficient to distinguish the "kind" of hug intended. This leads to some MUD interactions having much more ambiguity than usually encountered in real life, a fact that some mudders consider useful.

The somewhat disjointed nature of MUD conversations, brought on by the typing pauses, tends to rob them of much of the coherence that makes real-life conversants resent interruptions. The addition of a new conversant to a MUD conversation is much less disruptive; the "flow" being disrupted was never very strong to begin with. Some players go so far as to say the interruptions are simply impossible on MUDs; I think that this is a minority impression, however. Interruptions do exist on MUDs; they are simply less significant than in real life.

Other Small-group Interactions.   I would not like to give the impression that conversation is the only social activity on MUDs. Indeed, MUD society appears to have most of the same social activities as real life, albeit often in a modified form.

As mentioned before, PernMUSH holds large-scale, organized social gatherings, such as "hatchings," and they are not alone. Most MUDs have at one time or another organized more or less elaborate parties, often to celebrate notable events in the MUD itself, such as an anniversary of its founding. We have so far had only one or two such parties on LambdaMOO, to celebrate the "opening" of some new area built by a player; if there were any other major parties, I certainly wasn't invited!

One of the more impressive examples of MUD social activity is the virtual wedding. There have been many of these on many different MUDs; we are in the process of planning our first on LambdaMOO, with me officiating in my role as archwizard.

I have never been present at such a ceremony, but I have read logs of the conversations at them. As I do not know any of the participants in the ceremonies I've read about, I cannot say much for certain about their emotional content. As in real life, they are usually very happy and celebratory occasions with an intriguing undercurrent of serious feelings. I do not know and cannot even speculate about whether or not the main participants in such ceremonies are usually serious or not, whether or not the MUD ceremony usually (or even ever) mirrors another ceremony in the real world, or even whether or not the bride and groom have ever met outside of virtual reality.

In the specific case of the upcoming LambdaMOO wedding, the participants first met on LambdaMOO, became quite friendly, and eventually decided to meet in real life. They have subsequently become romantically involved in the real world and are using the MUD wedding as a celebration of that fact. This phenomenon of couples meeting in virtual reality and then pursuing a real-life relationship, is not uncommon; in one notable case, they did this even though one of them lived in Australia and the other in Pittsburgh!

It is interesting to note that the virtual reality wedding is not specific to the kinds of MUDs I've been discussing; Van Gelder (1991) mentions an on-line reception on CompuServe and weddings are quite common on Habitat (Morningstar & Farmer, 1991), a half-graphical, half-textual virtual reality popular in Japan.

The very idea, however, brings up interesting and potentially important questions about the legal standing of commitments made only in virtual reality. Suppose, for example, that two people make a contract in virtual reality. Is the contract binding? Under which state's (or country's) laws? Is it a written or verbal contract? What constitutes proof of signature in such a context? I suspect that our real-world society will have to face and resolve these issues in the not-too-distant future.

Those who frequent MUDs tend also to be interested in games and puzzles, so it is no surprise that many real-world examples have been implemented inside MUDs. What may be surprising, however, is the extent to which this is so.

On LambdaMOO alone, we have machine-mediated Scrabble, Monopoly, Mastermind, Backgammon, Ghost, Chess, Go, and Reversi boards. These attract small groups of players on occasion, with the Go players being the most committed; in fact, there are a number of Go players who come to LambdaMOO only for that purpose. I say more about these more specialized uses of social virtual realities later on. In many ways, though, such games so far have little, if anything, to offer over their real-world counterparts except perhaps a better chance of finding an opponent.

Perhaps more interesting are the other kinds of games imported into MUDs from real life, the ones that might be far less feasible in a nonvirtual reality. A player on LambdaMOO, for example, implemented a facility for holding food fights. Players throw food items at each other, attempt to duck oncoming items, and, if unsuccessful, are "splattered" with messes that cannot easily be removed. After a short interval, a semianimate "Mr. Clean" arrives and one-by-one removes the messes from the participants, turning them back into the food items from which they came, ready for the next fight. Although the game was rather simple to implement, it has remained enormously popular nearly a year later.

Another player on LambdaMOO created a trainable Frisbee™, which any player could teach to do tricks when they threw or caught it. Players who used the Frisbee seemed to take great pleasure in trying to out-do each other's trick descriptions. My catching description, for example, reads "Haakon stops the Frisbee dead in the air in front of himself and then daintily plucks it, like a flower." I have also heard of MUD versions of paint-ball combat and fantastical games of Capture the Flag.

Observations about the MUD Community as a Whole

MUD communities tend to be very large in comparison to the number of players actually active at any given time. On LambdaMOO, for example, we have between 700 and 800 players connecting in any week but rarely more than 40 simultaneously. A good real-world analog might be a bar with a large number of "regulars," all of whom are transients without fixed schedules.

The continuity of MUD society is thus somewhat tenuous; many pairs of active players exist who have never met each other. In spite of this, MUDs do become true communities after a time. The participants slowly come to consensus about a common (private) language, about appropriate standards of behavior, and about the social roles of various public areas (e.g., where big discussions usually happen, where certain "crowds" can be found, etc.).

Some people appear to thrive on the constant turnover of MUD players throughout a day, enjoying the novelty of always having someone new to talk to. In some cases, this enjoyment goes so far as to become a serious kind of addiction, with some players spending as much as 35 hours out of 48 constantly connected and conversing on MUDs. I know of many players who have taken more-or-less drastic steps to curtail their participation on MUDs, feeling that their habits had gotten significantly out of control.

One college-student player related to me his own particularly dramatic case of MUD addiction. It seems that he was supposed to go home for the Christmas holidays but missed the train by no less than five hours because he had been unable to tear himself away from his MUD conversations. After calling his parents to relieve their worrying by lying about the cause of his delay, he eventually boarded a train for home. However, on arrival there at 12:30 AM the next morning, he did not go directly to his parents' house but instead went to an open terminal room in the local university, where he spent another two and a half hours connected before finally going home. His parents, meanwhile, had called the police in fear for their son's safety in traveling.

It should not be supposed that this kind of problem is the now commonly understood phenomenon of "computer addiction"; the fact that there is a computer involved here is more-or-less irrelevant. These people are not addicted to computers, but to *communication;* the global scope of Internet MUDs implies not only a great variety in potential conversants, but also 24-hour access. As Figure 10.2 shows, the sun never really sets on LambdaMOO's community.

Although it is at the more macroscopic scale of whole MUD communities that I feel least qualified to make reliable observations, I do have one striking example of societal consensus having concrete results on LambdaMOO.

From time to time, we wizards are asked to arbitrate in disputes among players concerning what is or is not appropriate behavior. My approach generally has been to ask a number of other players for their opinions and to present the defendant in the complaint with a precis of the plaintiff's grievance, always looking for the common threads in their responses. After many such episodes, I was approached by a number of players asking that a written statement on LambdaMOO "manners" be prepared and made available to the community. I wrote up a list of those rules that seemed implied

- **Be polite. Avoid being rude.** The MOO is worth participating in because it is a pleasant place for people to be. When people are rude or nasty to ne another, it stops being so pleasant.

- **"Revenge is ours," sayeth the wizards.** If someone is nasty to you, please either ignore it or tell a wizard about it. Please *don't* try to take revenge on the person; this just escalates the level of rudeness and makes the MOO a less pleasant place for everyone involved.

- **Respect other player's sensibilities.** The participants on the MOO come from a wide range of cultures and backgrounds. Your ideas about what constitutes offensive speech or descriptions are likely to differ from those of other players. Please keep the text that players can casually run across as free of potentially offensive material as you can.

- **Don't spoof.** Spoofing is loosely defined as "causing misleading output to be printed to other players." For example, it would be spoofing for anyone but Munchkin to print out a message like "Munchkin sticks out his tongue at Potrzebie." This makes it look like Munchkin is unhappy with Potrzebie even though that may not be the case at all.

- **Don't shout.** It is easy to write a MOO command that prints a message to every connected player. Please don't.

- **Only teleport your own things.** By default, most objects (including other players) allow themselves to be moved freely from place to place. This fact makes it easier to build certain useful objects. Unfortunately, it also makes it easy to annoy people by moving them or their objects around without their permission. Please don't.

- **Don't teleport silently or obscurely.** It is easy to write MOO commands that move you instantly from place to place. Please remember in such programs to print a clear, understandable message to all players in both the place you're leaving and the place you're going to.

- **Don't hog the server.** The server is carefully shared among all of the connected players so that everyone gets a chance to execute their commands. This sharing is, by necessity, somewhat approximate. Please don't abuse it with tasks that run for a long time without pausing.

- **Don't waste object numbers.** Some people, in a quest to own objects with "interesting" numbers (e.g., #17000, #18181, etc.) have written MOO programs that loop forever creating and recycling objects until the "good" numbers come up. Please don't do this.

Figure 10.6.   The main points of LambdaMOO manners.

by the set of arbitrations we had performed and published them for public comment. Very little comment has ever been received, but the groups of players I've asked generally agree that the rules reflect their own understandings of the common will. For the curious, I have included our list of rules in Figure 10.6; the actual 'help manners' document goes into a bit more detail about each of these points.

It should be noted that different MUDs are truly different communities and have different societal agreements concerning appropriate behavior. There even exist a few MUDs where the only rule in the social contract is that *there is no social contract*. Such "anarchy" MUDs have appeared a few times in my experience and seem to be quite popular for a time before eventually fading away.

THE PROSPECTS FOR MUDDING IN THE FUTURE

The clumsy system of public gatherings had been long since abandoned; neither Vashti nor her audience stirred from their rooms. Seated in her arm-chair, she spoke, while they in their arm-chairs heard her, fairly well, and saw her, fairly well.

—E. M. Forster

A recent listing of Internet-accessible MUDs showed almost 200 active around the world, mostly in the United States and Scandinavia. A conservative guess that these MUDs average 100 active players each gives a total of 20,000 active mudders in the world today; this is almost certainly a significant undercount already and the numbers appear to be growing as more and more people gain Internet access.

In addition, at least one MUD-like area exists on the commercial CompuServe network in the United States and there are several more commercial MUDs active in the United Kingdom. Finally, there is Habitat (Morningstar & Farmer, 1991), a half-graphical, half-textual virtual reality in Japan, with well over 10,000 users.

I believe that text-based virtual realities and wide-area interactive "chat" facilities are becoming more and more common and will continue to do so for the foreseeable future. Like CB radios and telephone party lines before them, MUDs seem to provide a necessary social outlet.

The MUD model is also being extended in new ways for new audiences. For example, I am currently involved in adapting the LambdaMOO server for use as an international teleconferencing and image database system for astronomers. Our plans include allowing scientists to give on-line presentations to their colleagues around the world, complete with "slides" and illustrations automatically displayed on the participants' workstations. The same approach could be used to create on-line meeting places for workers in other disciplines, as well as for other nonscientific communities. I do not believe that we are the only researchers planning such facilities. In the near future (a few years at most), I expect such specialized virtual realities to be commonplace, an accepted part of at least the academic community.

On another front, I am engaged with some colleagues in the design of a MUD for general use here a Xerox PARC. The idea here is to use virtual reality to help break down the geographical barriers of a large building, of people increasingly working from their homes, and of having a sister research laboratory in Cambridge, England. In this context, we intend to investigate the addition of digital voice to MUDs, with the conventions of the virtual reality providing a simple and intuitive style of connection management: If two people are in the same virtual room, then their audio channels are connected. Some virtual rooms may even overlap real-world room, such as those in which talks or other meetings are held.

Of course, one can expect a number of important differences in the social phenomena on MUDs in a professional setting. In particular, I would guess that anonymity might well be frowned upon in such places, though it may have some interesting special uses, for example in the area of refereeing papers.

Some of my colleagues have suggested that the term "text-based virtual reality" is an oxymoron, that "virtual reality" refers only to the fancy graphical and motion-sensing environments being worked on in many places. They go on to predict that these more physically involving systems will supplant the text-based variety as soon as the special equipment becomes a bit more widely and cheaply available. I do not believe that this is the case.

Although I agree that the fancier systems are likely to become very popular for certain applications and among those who can afford them, I believe that MUDs have certain enduring advantages that will save them from obsolescence.

The equipment necessary to participate fully in a MUD is significantly cheaper, more widely available, and more generally useful than that for the fancy systems; this is likely to remain the case for a long time to come. For example, it is already possible to purchase palm-sized portable computers with network connectivity and text displays, making it possible to use MUDs even while riding the bus, and so on. Is similarly flexible hardware for fancy virtual realities even on the horizon?

It is substantially easier for players to give themselves vivid, detailed, and interesting descriptions (and to do the same for the descriptions and behavior of the new objects they create) in a text-based system than in a graphics-based one. In McLuhan's (1964) terminology, this is because MUDs are a "cold" medium, whereas ore graphically based media are "hot;" that is, the sensorial parsimony of plain text tends to entice users into engaging their imaginations to fill in missing details, whereas, comparatively speaking, the richness of stimuli in fancy virtual realities has an opposite tendency, pushing users' imaginations into a more passive role. I also find it difficult to believe that a graphics-based system will be able to compete with text for average users on the metric of believable detail per unit of effort expended; this is certainly the case now and I see little reason to believe it will change in the near future.

Finally, one of the great strengths of MUDs lies in the users' ability to customize them, to extend them, and to specialize them to the users' particular needs. The ease with which this can be done in MUDs is directly related to the fact that they are purely text-based; in a graphic-based system, the overhead of creating new moderate-quality graphic would put the task beyond the inclinations of the average user. Whereas with MUDs, it is easy to imagine an almost arbitrarily small community investing in the creation of a virtual reality that was truly customized for that community, it seems very unlikely that any but the largest communities would invest the greatly increased effort required for a fancier system.

CONCLUSIONS

Vashti was seized with the terrors of direct experience. She shrank back into her room, and the wall closed up again.

—E. M. Forster

The emergence of MUDs has created a new kind of social sphere, both like and radically unlike the environments that have existed before. As they become more and more popular and more widely accessible, it appears likely that an increasingly significant proportions of the population will at least become familiar with mudding and perhaps become frequent participants in text-based virtual realities.

It thus behooves us to begin to try to understand these new societies, to make sense of these electronic places where we'll be spending increasing amounts of our time, both doing business and seeking pleasure. I would hope that social scientists will be at least intrigued by my amateur observations and perhaps inspired to more properly study MUDs and their players. In particular, as MUDs become more widespread, ever more people are likely to be susceptible to the kind of addiction I discuss in an earlier section; we must, as a society, begin to wrestle with the social and ethical issues brought out by such cases.

Those readers interested in trying out MUDs for themselves are encouraged to do so. The Usenet news group `rec.games.mud` periodically carries comprehensive lists of publicly available, Internet-accessible MUDs, including their detailed network addresses. My own MUD, LambdaMOO, can be reached via the standard Internet `telenet` protocol at the host `lambda.parc.xerox.com` (the numeric address is 13.2.116.36), port 8888. On a UNIX machine, for example, the command:

```
telenet lambda.parc.xerox.com 8888
```

will suffice to make a connection. Once connected, feel free to page me; I connect under the names "Haakon" and "Lambda."

ACKNOWLEDGMENTS

I was originally prodded into writing down my mudding experiences by Eric Roberts. In trying to get a better handle on an organization for the material, I was aided immeasurably by my conversations with Françoise Brun-Cottan; she consistently brought to my attention phenomena that I had become too familiar with to notice. Susan Irwin and

David Nichols have been instrumental in helping me to understand some of the issues that might arise as MUDs become more sophisticated and widespread. The reviewers of the chapter provided several pointers to important related work that I might otherwise never have encountered. Finally, I must also give credit to the LambdaMOO players who participated in my on-line brainstorming session; their ideas, experiences, and perceptions provided a necessary perspective to my own understanding.

REFERENCES

Forster, E. M. (1973). The machine stops. In *The Science Fiction Hall of Fame*, Vol. IIB, (B. Bova, Ed.) Avon, 1973. Originally in Forster, E. M. (1928). *The eternal moment and other stories*. Harcourt Brace Jovanovich.

Kiesler, S. Et al. (1991). Social psychological aspects of computer-mediated communication, in *Computerization and controversy* Dunlop, C. & Kling, R., (Eds.). Academic Press.

McLuhan, M. (1964). *Understanding media*. New York: McGraw-Hill.

Morningstar, C. & Farmer, F. R. (1991). The lessons of Lucasfilm's habitat, in *Cyberspace*, Benedikt, M., (Ed.). MIT Press.

Raymond, E. S. (Ed.) (1991). *The new hacker's dictionary.* Cambridge, MA: MIT Press.

Reid, E. M. (1992). Electropolis: communication and community on internet relay chat. *Intertek*, v. 3.3, Winter.

Van Gelder, L. (1991). The strange case of the electronic lover, in Dunlop, C. & Kling, R., (Eds.). *Computerization and Controversy*, Academic Press.

11

Cyberspace Innkeeping: Building Online Community

John Coate
The Gate, San Francisco, CA

SOMETHING OLD, SOMETHING NEW

When you log into an online service, you use new tools for an ancient activity. Even with all the screens and wires and chips and lines it still comes down to people talking to each other. The immense potential of this partnership of computer technology and human language is in this blending of the old and the new.

Language is so ancient a currency of communication that people of the Northern Hemisphere, from Europe to India, know of their common tribal roots mostly just by the remnant commonalities of the languages. Through all these thousands of years (sign language excepted), language has been either spoken or written. But online conversation is a new hybrid that is both talking and writing yet isn't completely either one. It's talking by writing. It's writing because you type it on a keyboard and people read it. But because of the ephemeral nature of luminescent letters on a screen, and because it has such a quick—sometimes instant—turnaround, it's more like talking. And this is where the online scene is such an adventure. The act of conversing over computers is such a new twist that the lasting term for what it is has not yet been coined.

The new with the old. It is also new because you often feel a real sense of place while logged in, although it exists "virtually" in each person's imagination while they stare into a CRT screen. It's old because even if the village is virtual, when it's working right it fulfills for people their need for a commons, a neutral space away from work or home where they can conduct their personal and professional affairs.

My work with online services such as the WELL in Sausalito and 101 Online in SF, is about building an online version of what Ray Oldenburg calls "the Third Place." In *The Great Good Place* he calls home the First Place and work the Second Place.

> Third places exist on neutral ground and serve to level their guests to a condition of social equality. Within these places, conversation is the primary activity and the major vehicle for the display and appreciation of human personality and individuality. Third places are taken for granted and most have a low profile. Since the formal institutions of society make stronger claims on the individual, third places are normally open in the off hours, as well as at other times. Though a radically different kind of setting from the home, the third place is remarkable similar to a good home in the psychological comfort and support that it extends.

I'll say right up front that my love for online interaction is because it brings people together. At the personal level it helps people find their kindred spirits and at the larger social level it serves as a conduit for the horizontal flow of information through the population.

In this chapter, I will first describe some of the elements that can combine to create a village-like quality in an electronic environment along with some of the social dynamics at play in there. I'll go into some of the basic constitutional and legal issues that confront us and then I'll offer a little advice for anyone who is, or wants to be, the innkeeper, so to speak, of their own online service. And, finally, I'll reflect a bit on some of my concerns for the future.

THE VIRTUAL VILLAGE

Whom Does It Attract?

Online systems attract independent-minded people. People who think for themselves and many people who work for themselves. Logging in is like a social coffee break for home office workers. Freelancers, contractors, entrepreneurs, and others who, because they are always looking ahead to that next job, need to have their shingle hung out. With so much "downsizing" happening in the corporate world and so many people moving from one job to another, online public forums are good places to run into others who may lead you to your next work opportunity.

Electronic mail is especially useful for maintaining and enlarging a personal network because, in practical terms, it allows you to conduct a larger volume of personal correspondence over a given period of time than any other medium such as writing paper letters and talking on the telephone.

The text display that still dominates online systems appeals to people who love wordplay, language and writing. And it appeals to people with active minds. The classic couch potato just isn't going to be that interested. Good conversation can be a hard commodity to find these days. If you love stimulating conversation—what I like to call an "intellectual massage"—where would you go, say, after work, to find some people to do it with, especially if they weren't already your friends? So many people have commented on how they haven't been able to enjoy such great conversation in so long. Often not since their days of hanging out at the college coffee shop, talking till the wee hours about anything that came to mind. A place to debate, joke, schmooze, argue, and gossip.

Many people have fairly specialized interests, and to find people with similar interests you often need the opportunity to interact with a larger base of people rather than just the few in your physical neighborhood. And online systems appeal to people who have numerous interests because you don't have to go from club to club all over town to hang out and talk with people interested in specific things like boating or books. You can get around town without getting up.

And of course online systems are used by private groups to conduct ongoing meetings. It's an efficient way for a group to stay in touch, collaborate on documents, or plan other meetings and events. One of the great strengths of online conferencing is how you can switch from a relaxing and playful kind of conversation to something serious or businesslike with just a few keystrokes.

And then there are people who just have unfulfilled social needs and want to meet some people.

Expensive Toy, Cheap Tool

Some people sign up, look around, decide a system isn't for them, and cancel their account after a few months. But many stay on for years. What keeps them logging in as a regular part of their routine? There is a benefit to the person that makes a real difference in their lives. Otherwise it wouldn't be worth the money. If you are just finding a degree of entertainment in the various conversations, then it could fascinate you for a long time or it might get old pretty soon at two or more bucks an hour. But if it helps you find your next job, or connects you with a new friend, or fulfills that need to have hood conversation with a bunch of bright people, then it becomes a real bargain. And that is the method behind the madness, so to speak. Behind all the screens of sentences are real people making real connections that make a real difference to them.

The Mind Pool

Ask a question about almost anything and you'll likely get an answer or a reference to an answer very quickly. It's a bit like fishing. Throw in your line and see what you catch. Everyone picks each other's brains. The informal nature of online conversation encourages people's amazing generosity in sharing the things that they know. It's a potluck for the mind.

However, you may not have time or inclination for this rather serendipitious method of gathering information. Cruising around the various topics looking for this or that nugget of information can be like panning for gold: you have to move a lot of rock. Sometimes you just want to go in there, find what you need and get out.

Good search tools are essential to a fully realized conferencing package. A challenge in designing online systems is making it easy to use the system either way. The truly successful design accommodates both approaches so that they may not only coexist, but are interchangeable at any time. Hang out and shoot the breeze over in this forum, then go over to another area and quickly zero in on the info you need.

Related to this is the need to have a simple beginner's interface that allows you to self-graduate to a command-driven "power user mode" at any time. Beginners aren't dumb, they're busy. Usually they don't have the time to deal with yet another learning curve. This is why most people don't learn to program their VCRs. Also essential is some kind of "bookmark" function that allows you to automatically see new comments since the last time you logged in.

The sysops don't create the information and sell it to everyone so much as the people themselves create the information and share it with each other. In a way we who manage online services are like operators of a picnic ground. We provide the tables and the people bring the food.

Unlike network TV or mass market magazines or even parts of other large online services, the information doesn't flow in a top-down manner, but rather horizontally among the peer groups of the participants. I like to call it a People's Think Tank. People join online systems because they are useful personal tools. The horizontal information flow is really a byproduct of this, but it has, I believe, a deep and abiding importance to all of us. Because the free flow of information among the people is essential to the health of a democratic society.

The Sense of Place

However, something more is going on here. Dry terms like "think tank," "information exchange," and "conferencing network" are too flat, too monodimensional. They don't convey the reality that although you and the other people logged in are separated by miles of phone lines looking at CRT screens that just display written words, it feels like a real place in there. And those terms don't show that it's just about the easiest, lowest risk way to meet new people that there is. Nor do they describe how, via all this online talk, people form and sustain relationships. This is when it crosses over into something else, something fuller, something more like a community. In attempts to accurately describe this we conjure up familiar images like village, town, neighborhood, saloon, salon, coffee shop, inn. It's as if it is all of these things, yet isn't really any of them because it's a new kind of gathering. It just helps to hang something familiar onto it so we can picture it.

The Tangible and the Intangible

The tangible part is the hardware and the software—the physical network. Obviously you have to have that, and it has to work reliably. The intangible—the people part—is just as important because a system is as much defined and shaped by everyone's collective imagination as it is by the computers, discs, and software tools.

All of this descriptive imagining about community comes from real people meeting there. But it goes much farther than that because traveling through the chips and wires, as a kind of subcarrier to the words themselves, is real human emotion and feeling. The spectrum of the "vibes" is just about as wide as it is when people meet face to face. It's sometimes harder to interpret them because there isn't any facial expression or body English, but they are there just the same and people feel them and react to them. Furthermore, the quality of the vibes—the atmosphere, the ambience—largely determines whether or not the people involved will develop any affection for the system at all.

Forums and Hosts

It's important for public forums to have hosts who welcome the newcomers, try to keep the conversations reasonably on track, and do basic housekeeping so there isn't too much clutter and confusion. They are responsible for maintaining some civilized degree of order in the conference. Old extinct discussions are pruned out like tree branches. When people argue too heatedly and start tossing out the ad hominems, the host blows the whistle.

Every host has his or her own style and some forums allow a lot more tumbling than others.

Conferencing is, by its very nature, a mix of organization and chaos. This hybrid of talking by writing presents some interesting new challenges. Both talking and writing have their unique strengths. With writing, organization, and a high concentration of useable information are desired. Online it's very useful to have labels for each discussion so you can get to the information you seek with efficiency. It's pretty difficult at a party to stand at the doorway of a crowded room where everyone is talking and determine which conversation is most interesting to you. In such cases, the benefits of the written word are strong. When talking, the whims of the people take the discussion off on any number of tangents. We have come to call this process of meandering "topic drift" and it often leads to the most delightful illuminations. So much so that many people find this to be one of the most appealing aspects of the whole online scene. But it can conflict with other peoples' expectations that a conversation will consist of material that is truly in keeping with the theme of the topic. Once again, this is where good searching tools are necessary so that finding information isn't like something out of Where's Waldo?

Seeing Who Else Is Logged In

Typing a command that shows you who else is logged in at the same time lets you get off quick e-mail to someone or engage them in a real-time conversation. But beyond that, it enhances the sense of "usness." Seeing who is logged in at the same time as you is like opening the window and looking out to see who's on the street. Some people check to see who else is around as soon as they log in.

Anonymity or Your Real Name?

Both approaches are valid and both *can* coexist. But they don't mix well.

If people don't have to take responsibility for what they say, then some of them will say a lot of irresponsible things. My problem with this is that, in an open group discussion, the signal-to-noise ratio develops a poor balance. Fortunately, it doesn't really behoove most people to use false names anyway, since that would defeat their networking goals.

However, I'm speaking here about the public arenas. I recently worked with a French-designed system. I configured it so you can't be anonymous in the open public forums but the live chat lines and e-mail can be anonymous or not, depending on how you prefer to do it. It can be a way of playing games, or it can be a form of personal protection.

A Wide Variety of Topics

It's important to have variety. If you don't see a topic covering what you want to talk about, you should be able to open up your own line of conversation. What happens then is that you see the same people in different places and in different contexts, and fuller pictures of the people emerge as they reveal more dimensions of themselves.

The Relationship of Public and Private Conversation

Being able to converse privately in e-mail or in a live chat with someone alongside a public discussion helps people form all kinds of relationships. It often starts with something like, "Hey, I liked what you said over in that discussion and I have a similar interest. Maybe we could talk more about it on the side." In the heat of debate, people use e-mail to form alliances, and when people are moved by a touching story or feel agreement with a particular statement, they use e-mail to lend support.

A variation on this private–public dynamic is the special-interest private conference. In a private forum or meeting, e-mail messages are like going into the hallway for a more personal caucus.

An online system should be designed so that it is easy to move between one form of conversation and another, and then back again. It shouldn't require a lot of keystrokes, (which is the computer's equivalent of walking) to, for example, read a public comment then quickly send that person a private message or see if they are online at that moment to be engaged in a real-time chat.

Encouragement of Free Speech

Although system managers or hosts usually have the ability to remove or "censor" a given comment, I generally discourage it as a practice. And I especially dislike the approach where there are paid censors who prescreen everything to make sure it conforms to their standards. Better for people to speak freely and frankly to each other because if each individual knows that he or she may speak freely and that they in fact take full responsibility for what they say, then it improves the content of the system. When it's working right, people wrestle with tough questions, and that corner of the larger society evolves that much more.

I encourage all online systems to be places where controversial subjects may be discussed in a civilized way. Of course, how you define "civilized" determines what you will allow. I frown on ad hominems, personal harassment, and threats but otherwise give wide berth to the variety of tastes and styles found wherever individuals gather.

The Face-to-Face Factor

Members of many online services like to see each other socially. A lot of online services host parties and get-togethers. The WELL has sponsored an open house pot luck party every month for over six years. Sometimes there is a special event like a picnic or a beach party. A few times we had some real big blowout bashes over in a big loft in San Francisco. We even entertained at a couple of them with a band formed from WELL members. Once we organized a group visit to the local art museum to view a special exhibit of Tibetan painting and sculpture. We collected $10 in advance from everyone and they opened up the museum for us an hour early.

On a smaller scale you can encounter someone online, start something up in e-mail, and then take them to lunch, get up a card game, go to a movie, or meet them about a business project.

When a number of the participants in a discussion have met offline, the overall sense of familiarity in the online atmosphere increases. And this increases the sense of place for everyone, including those who either can't or don't want to meet anyone outside the online environment.

Professional and Personal Interactions Overlap

This is where things really get interesting. Ultimately, any network is about relationships. I like to say that, rather than being in the computer business, I am in the relationship business. Some are ad hoc, some are long-term, some are for business, and some are social. Get online for business or for pleasure. Although you can just do one or the other, many people use it for both. I know people who got online just for fun but made contacts that led to a new job. I also know people who joined for business reasons such as getting help on a computer application or doing research and made some new friends through conversing in other nontechnical forums. Or maybe you are thinking of hiring someone you met online because of their technical expertise and by seeing their comments in other conferences you find that you also like their sense of humor. Or perhaps you don't care for their dogmatic attitude and that influences your decision the other way. The variations are endless.

One person who comes to mind is the radio producer who uses the WELL to talk shop with others in his field all around the country. When his two-year-old daughter became deathly ill, he would log in from way out on Cape Cod and would report, diary style, in the WELL Parents Conference about what they were going through. He would give the details and describe his emotional state and people would lend their support. It comforted him and it touched all of us who read it. And I doubt that this man has ever met any of the other people face to face. Furthermore, this experience greatly increased his enthusiasm for what this kind of network can do and that spread to his business related activities online. Another described, over the course of a few years, his search for his biological parents. When he finally found them many of us rejoiced with him after reading his eloquent account. This guy works the same online crowd for his consulting business.

For the term "village" (as in "electronic village" or "virtual village") to be applied to an online scene with any accuracy at all, this blending of business and pleasure must be present. Because that's what a village is: a place where you go down to the butcher or the blacksmith and transact your business, and at night meet those same neighbors down at the local tavern or the Friday night dance.

SOCIAL DYNAMICS

Making Communities Out of Individuals

A lot of why the online realm is characterized with the image of the frontier comes from trying to forge a community out of people who are not, by their nature, team players. Back in the pioneer days, the rugged individuals went west. These days the uncharted, unsettled territory is the realm of electronic group communications that is becoming known as the "virtual world" or "cyberspace."

Here online we have people with a new sort of pioneer outlook. Let me give you my thumbnail impression of what they have in common: Many work for themselves at home or in a private office. They possess great awareness and concern about their rights as individuals. They are often outspoken and articulate. And, on top of this, they are now doing a lot of relating to other people compared to what they were doing before, and in some cases compared to what they have ever done, certainly since their college or military days. This is all the more intensified by most people not really knowing each other before they got involved. So this pioneer image also comes to mind because it isn't just new technology, it's new for those involved at the personal–social level.

Use of the word "community" here doesn't imply that an online scene is one mono-lithic community. Rather, I use the word to suggest a commons that is made up of a bundle of smaller "communities of interest" that also have a common interest in the health of the overall system.

Commonalities and Differences

One of life's great paradoxes is that we are all the same and we are all different. One of the ironies of online interaction both public and private is that, in developing rela-tionships, people seek commonalities while displaying and discussing their differences. When people gather, much of what takes place as they develop these relationships and bonds, is a process of mutual discovery. This discovery produces a lot of the "aha!" moments that give online life its kick. These moments, in which many talk back to the computer screen, can range from empathetic tears to "I feel like that too" to "oh, neat!" to "what a bozo" to "if he says that again I'm gonna scream!"

The Level Playing Field

The great equalizing factor, of course, is that nobody can see each other online so the ideas are what really matter. You can't discern age, race, complexion, hair color, body shape, vocal tone, or any of the other attributes that we all incorporate into our impressions of people. This, of course, will change as audio and video become com-mon along with the written word. But, even then, a lot of people will play their sounds and show their video but won't show themselves.

If the balance tips to anyone's advantage, it's in favor of those who are better at articulating their views. Some people are amazingly skilled at debating. Other people feel shyness around their own forensic or expressive skills. Posting a comment is "step-ping out," so to speak, putting yourself "out there" to people you might not know. Therefore many of them are just "lurking" (reading without participating).

Still, the demographic makeup of the online population is one area that needs improvement, in my view. Every PC-based online net I know of has 80% or more men. And most of these are white men. PC systems are not exclusionary, but most of the population don't have the necessary equipment. Few people buy a PC and modem just to join an online service. And many who would otherwise enjoy the interaction can't hack the still engineer-oriented design of most computer systems.

The Meeting Place

I said earlier that an online community is one of the easiest ways to meet new people. Certainly it is very low-risk. I think this is mainly owing to the essential informality of online conversation. Rather than being required to sustain a single conversation with one or more people, relationships usually form out of numerous, often short exchanges. In a way, it reminds me of commuters who take the bus or ferry. They see each other frequently but each encounter is of a fairly short duration. In situations like this the pressure is minimal. If you'd rather read the paper than chat then you just do it and don't worry about it. But, over time, many people form enduring relationships this way.

The "Hot" Medium

In the online environment, just like any other social situation, the basic currency is human attention. In the public forums, you communicate with groups that may have as many as several hundred people involved—even if they don't all make comments.

Nobody comments on everything (although some people can be quite verbose!), but many people don't say anything at all. In fact, most people who use online services don't post any comments. They lurk. In the World of online services theory the lurker: poster ratio is one of the indicators. Ten or more lurkers for every poster is common. Many people who do post comments are aware of this fact and orate at times as if they are addressing the Roman Senate, the online Continental Congress, or the lunchtime crowd at Hyde Park. I have heard online discussion called "writing as a performing art." It sometimes reminds me of Amateur Night at the Apollo or the Gong Show, because you don't know what reaction people may have to the comment you make. Maybe you won't get any reaction. Maybe you'll get e-mail voicing support or dissent, maybe someone will take you on in the discussion, or maybe you will have said something good enough to warrant a string of online "amens." At any rate, many are reticent to say anything at all because of this version of stage fright, whereas others take to it like Vaudeville troupers. An online system is a place where you have to give yourself permission to step out and participate. Of course if you talk too much people may tend to ignore your comments after awhile.

Most services charge by the hour like a parking meter. Combining this expense with the cost of the phone call can add up to real money for extended participation in the scene. There are ways to cut the time spent online by "downloading" the material and reading it offline through your word processor. You can compose your responses and then "upload" them to the appropriate topics. But there are some people who don't want to do this, even though it saves them money, because the medium feels "hotter" to them if they are interacting directly online. It's as if being online in the moment is reading the magazine and the downloads are like reading photocopies of the articles. It just isn't as appealing to some people, even if it is cheaper.

The Personality You Project

Each person holds his or her own mental image of what the online society is and how it is structured. The corollary to this is the personality each person projects to everyone else. What you find here is that some people, viewing this as just another communication tool or social environment, try to make their online personality be as similar as possible to their personality everywhere else.

Other people change their personalities once they get online. This may come from the sense of safety and empowerment they feel in the sanctity of their room or office talking with people that they know can't deck them if they say the wrong thing. The online world might be where words can break your bones but sticks and stones can never hurt you.

Others may be self-conscious about their appearance or some handicap and, knowing that it isn't a factor in the interactions, simply feel more confident than they do elsewhere. For some others, the online environment seems to promote in them a certain kind of functional schizophrenia as if logging in was like Clark Kent stepping into the phone booth. Having an alternate persona is part of the game and much of what makes it fun for them.

I know some people who are much more bristly online than they are in person. And they enjoy the contentious nature of many of the conversations. They sometimes even agitate it to be more that way, as if it was a kind of "sport hassling." They like the ferment for its own sake.

Ferment

By its very nature, online discussion is going to involve disagreement. In our reach for analogies we often ask "is it a salon or is it a saloon?" Once again it's a hybrid. It's a salon, certainly, in the classic image of gathering for spirited, bright conversation where people of different backgrounds and disciplines come together for that intellectual massage that feels so good. But it's also like the Wild West saloon where you never know who's going to come in the swinging doors and try out their stuff on everybody. Somewhere on the system at all times there is some sort of ferment going on. Ferment is a necessary part of the recipe. Part of the scene will always be in flux. At times it will be argumentative and contentious. To a host or a manager this is a given, you accept that, and work with it.

There is concern among some participants that a topic or a forum won't feel "safe" to them. This elusive quality of safety depends on a few factors. The size of the group, the nature of the subject matter, the personalities of the people who happen to be in there talking, and the way that forum is hosted.

A forum environment that has a hostile atmosphere will discourage participation by those who have less aggressive tendencies. The hosting is important because in over-seeing the discussion, you don't want things to sink down too far but setting too high of a standard for "niceness" can also kill off a discussion before anything worthwhile gets figured out. That means that some temperatures will rise some of the time. There will always be some rough spots whenever a group works to define itself. Without any fer-ment at all, the "brew" will quickly go flat.

"Flaming," in Net Talk, means to torch someone with your verbal flame thrower. One gets the feeling that flaming gets to be even more of a sport over in the Unix net world than it does on a place like the WELL. They even have social protocols for it, like saying <Flame On> before you launch your missiles. In my view, it is easy enough to misunderstand someone online without having to lay it on even thicker.

Some of the arguments and debates we've had over the years have been pointless personal hassles, but many have led us to a fuller understanding of what we were as an entity, or what we thought we ought to be. It is important to note that policy and cus-tom has been shaped at times by arguments and hassles that were often quite person-al in nature. Like everything else in a scene there is a lot of blending of different elements. Disagreement about a point or a matter of principle can get complicated when mixed in with dislike for the other person's style or personality.

On the other hand, people often lend affirmation and support to others. This may be something as simple as complimenting them on something they said or wishing them good luck in one way or another. It's like sending an electronic "get well" card.

Newcomers

Many of the regulars and old-timers know each other pretty well. To a newcomer it can seem, as Alice Kahn once described it, like being a new kid in a high school.

When the face-to-face factor comes into the picture, things can get thicker still. People who haven't or don't see others "in person" may wonder if in-group tendencies get reinforced at social gatherings. In reality, the opposite is true for many people such as Carol Gould. She says

> My own experience at the WELL parties has been very positive. I was somewhat ner-
> vous about walking up to the group of people, none of whom I know, but I was able
> to enter a conversation or two and before long I felt fairly at ease. People were curious
> as to who I was and, surprisingly, claimed they'd "seen me around" on the WELL. At
> any rate, my sense was that people were curious and friendly, and it encouraged me to

come to the next event. And I would have to say that I have never felt excluded or rebuffed by anyone.

Perhaps it's just a clique in which everyone is a member. As SF Chronicle columnist Jon Carroll observed

> I had a great experience at Howard's book-signing, which was my first Well event. I met all these folks for the first time, and the air was filled with, "You mean you're onezie" and "I think that's rabor over there" and glad cries and furious conversation and the other people in the bookstore were like, "Who are these people?" In other words, I was member of a clique totally composed of people I had never met before.

There is, however, always a challenge for the regulars to remember what it is like for a newcomer.

It must be remembered by all that newcomers are essential to the survival of the group because they refresh the place, strengthen its vitality, and replace the people who move on. Without new viewpoints and personalities the place becomes stagnant.

Opting Out

I like to say that if you think you are in a community you probably are, and if you don't, you aren't. Online, this sense of community is far less obvious than it would be in a small town or a church community. In fact, it only exists as a commonly held, ongoing agreement of the participants who make it be true *for them*. Ultimately, all communities are a set of agreements among the people and in any community (and especially these days when many neighbors hardly know each other), one can always have strong or weak involvement with the group. But the online environment lends itself well to a person who wants to interact online, follow rules, observe protocol and etiquette, and still being completely disengaged from any sense of belonging to a community.

There will always be people who will say, "uh-uh, not me. I'm just here for the info. I'm not part of any community, thank you very much." And I think that's healthy. Indeed, some of these people speak up at times when there seems to be an excess of "groupthink" taking place.

RIGHTS, RESPONSIBILITY, AND THE CONSTITUTION

These Are the Early Days

The image of the online community as a kind of Continental Congress isn't really too far-fetched because the many discussions regarding rules, policies, and customs of this new online environment are pioneering in nature. Nobody really knows what the future holds, except that electronic communication will be a lot more common and ways of interacting in virtual space will have a lot more variety. But it isn't known what social conventions, if any, people will observe as they try to get along with each other and conduct business in the electronic environment. It's all being debated and figured out as we go along. Things determined now will surely have long-term influence in the future, when they are more common to the whole population.

So that the best minds may be applied to the task of figuring out the social and legal issues of electronic interaction, we need as open a forum as we can put together. Without the goal of improved communication throughout the citizenry, regardless of their opinion or station in life, writers and sociologists who express the fear that electronic technology will widen the gap between the rich and poor—rather than narrow it—may be proved right. Allowing maximum freedom of expression for each person or institution represented is the only way that enough collective intelligence can be gathered so that these matters can be figured out for the common good.

Crackers and Law Enforcement

There are those who view their words as strict intellectual property and those who regard their online writing as so much ephemeral conversation and give it away as soon as they type it out. Then there's the phone company and those who would bypass the phone company. There are software companies and independent programmers. There are those who believe in uninhibited free speech and those who seek a degree of control over what can and can't be said and to whom you can say it, especially regarding minors. And all are really necessary in this widening national debate, because freedom in the electronic meeting space have to be established by the people actually using the services. Outside lawmakers or groups shouldn't be the ones to determine what happens in the virtual world. If we don't establish the rules and customs for ourselves, then larger, more impersonal institutions with far less sensitivity to the subtler elements of this endeavor will have their way and we will be compelled to play by their rules.

As it is now, there isn't much case law regarding these various issues, lending still more credence to the image of the "electronic frontier." In a small system like the WELL or a huge one like Prodigy, issues are worked out by making some rules and then seeing what happens. Some things work and some don't.

In a way, it's hard to make many generalizations because the electronic meeting places are very much a bundle of individuals. Every case is unique.

Larger patterns will emerge producing more clarity over time. Still, there are a few general categories into which most of these issues fall.

Free Speech

Is electronic conversation talking or writing? Or is it a hybrid of these two that is unique and new? And is this activity protected by the United States Constitution just like freedom of speech? If this is a kind of meeting place, is it then an assembly of people that is also protected by the First Amendment? I say that these are rights that must be protected. But if it isn't in writing anywhere, are the safeguards actually in place? In 1987 a bill was introduced in the California State Assembly to amend the California Constitution to include electronic speech in the guaranteed protections of the First Amendment. The bill died in committee because it was felt that the protection was built into the existing wording. I hope that it is true.

Privacy

Do your electronic files have the same Fourth Amendment protections from unreasonable search and seizure as your personal effects in your home? Is your private e-mail on a subscription-based service truly private? What rights do you have, what are the responsibilities of the operators of a system, and what are the limits placed on the government if they should want to look through your electronic files and correspondence?

In 1986, Congress passed the Electronics Communication Privacy Act (ECPA) which provides for some protection for the individual and defines the responsibilities of the system administrators. Recent history (especially in regard to the Jackson Games case where government agents seized and kept a company's files and records without making an arrest, or more recently the seized "Amateur Action" BBS in San Jose that had downloadable risque graphical files that were apparently available to clever minors who somehow would be more corrupted by them than a copy of *Playboy* hidden under their mattress) shows that the government is testing its powers. And the placement of limits on those powers is in dispute right now in the courts. The Electronic Frontier Foundation (EFF) has been created by concerned individuals to help shape these policies and to help protect and defend people that they feel were treated unjustly by the government.

The ECPA made it a crime for someone to gain unauthorized entrance into an online system. It also requires system operators to inform their customers about how much privacy they should expect and then insure that that privacy is not invaded. Most system operators have unlimited "root" privileges that include the ability to examine anyone's mail. On the WELL, and on 101 Online, we let people know that our system administrator has that power, but they do not read anyone's mail without their permission. If an operator surreptitiously examined someone's mail outside the regular stated duties of system maintenance, then it would be a violation of the ECPA and hence, a federal crime. But what if the FBI came to our office and ordered us to give them a copy of everyone's e-mail? Would we have to do it? What if they wanted to confiscate our equipment so they could comb through the files? Could they do it? According to the ECPA the answer is yes if they have a search warrant, but only if the material is more recent than six months. If it's been on a system longer than six months, then only a subpoena is required.

What this means in terms of government power is that although they are limited by certain procedures, if they really want to, they can shut down an operation, possibly throw the system administrators in jail, and otherwise wreak havoc.

This balance between the user, the system operator, and the government is one that is being defined a little more every day. My feeling is that unchecked and unopposed power will seek to extend that power into areas whenever they appear.

Ownership of Words and Intellectual Property

Is it publishing or is it just conversation that happens to be writing? The WELL User Agreement says "You own your own words." This simple phrase gets to the heart of the matter of intellectual property as applied in the online world, but, like all of these other issues, is fraught with ambiguity and is subject to myriad personal interpretation. "You own your own words" was intended to mean that you, and not the system operators or management, are responsible for what you say. You take the heat, but you get the credit. But does getting the credit mean that your every utterance is a standalone piece of copyrighted intellectual property that requires your express permission for reproduction? Does the fact that anything you say in an online system can be downloaded and printed out by anyone who happens to read it create a different class of reproduction than quoting without permission for a commercial publication? If a journalist quotes something from an online system and they don't obtain permission, did they steal it, or did they overhear it in a conversation? We can't lose sight of the concept of fair use here. Like a publishing agent told me once, "if you think it's fair use, then it probably is."

Although I don't like to see people get too maniacal about what happens to things they type into a system because actual control is already just about impossible, and getting worse, I do think that good manners and consideration of others' wishes are critically important, even into the far reaches of cyberspace.

Censorship

If a system is privately owned, what are the rights of the individual versus the right of the owner to remove someone's comment? Does a user of an online system waive certain absolute rights when they join a given network? Are the owners of a system responsible to their customers and the right of those customers to express themselves freely, or is the system responsible for making sure that some kind of community standards must apply to the electronic dialogue? Some of it is easy to answer because certain activities such as posting an illegally obtained credit card number or offering to sell controlled substances are clearly illegal and must be removed.

But what about "community standards?" Current obscenity law refers to "local community standards" having jurisdiction in deciding what constitutes obscenity. But in the online world, where people meet in virtual space even though the participants may be located anywhere in the world, are there any local standards that even can apply? Does the physical location of the system matter? If the WELL were located in Dothan, Alabama instead of Sausalito, California, would it have to alter its method of managing the online society? The question can be posed: do you bring the service to them (in which case their local community standards would apply) or did they come to you to get it (in which case your community standards would apply)? To me, the latter of these makes more sense.

101 Online bills its customers through the Pacific Bell phone bill. This gives them more say regarding content than I think they ought to have, but recent California law won't allow them to bill if public access areas qualify as "obscene." Obscenity is defined as appealing to prurient interests with no redeeming social, political, scientific, or artistic merit. Before we launched 101, I got Pac Bell to agree to a standard similar to an "R" rated movie. I can live with that because you can get away with quite a lot at the R rating these days. Anything past that and you can take it to a private area.

Whenever it is possible, I advocate giving access controls to the parents themselves, as we did at 101 Online where a parent can create a sub-ID for their kid and then control where the kid goes on the system. If you don't want your kid to go into the chat area then you can shut off access. Same with the Forum. I feel this is far better than trying to make everything conform to a so-called "family" standard maintained by paid censors, as on Prodigy.

KEEPING IT RUNNING

An Online Service Manager's Primary Job

Everything you do boils down to one thing: Keep the dialogue going.

In this sense it's like running a railroad or a cruise ship. In those kinds of businesses there is the need to keep the motors running or, in our case, the modems running. But the customers must also be pleased aesthetically as well as other ways that are not so tangible as making schedules and keeping the restrooms clean. We have to have good quality conversations and the atmosphere has to be warm enough that it encourages people to open up. You can't have just one of these things going for you; it has to run right *and* people have to like it.

Being a service business means that success brings increased pressure to deliver a high standard to the growing number of people. A service business isn't like doing a painting or making a record. It's more like an airline that upgrades its planes as the technology moves forward. The basic product needs to be constantly refined and made more efficient. Furthermore, large numbers of people involved in the same conversation changes the dynamics of the conversation. Growth means the potential for more good minds and hearts meeting and relating and sharing what they know. But size could cause the conversation to deteriorate by becoming cumbersome and complicated.

The real fuel that drives the engine of online interaction is enthusiasm. And you work to build and preserve that just as much as you work to keep the equipment together.

An Informal Atmosphere

You need to have rules and policies, but leave a lot of room for judgment calls. I like to run it similar to the way they referee NBA basketball games. There actually is a certain amount of body contact that goes on, but at some point you decide to blow the whistle and call a foul.

Although I believe that it is important to have wide acceptance of various personal codes of conduct, I do like to cultivate a social atmosphere where it's basically not OK to be a jerk. What that means in practical terms is rightfully a hot, ongoing discussion topic that helps a group arrive at its social equilibrium.

My feeling is that informality is essential to the healthy growth of an online community. According to Ray Oldenburg in *The Great Good Place*

> The activity that goes on in third places is largely unplanned, unscheduled, unorganized and unstructured. Here, however, is the charm. It is just these deviations from the middle-class penchant for organization that give the third place much of its character and allure and that allow it to offer a radical departure from the routines of home and work.

Hence, I favor just enough rules to get us by and no more.

Whoever's There: Those Are Your People

You can target and you can recruit and you can bring in your friends, but a lot of the population of the scene is self-selected. And these people whom you, too, will be meeting for the first time are going to be your customers and, hopefully, your allies, especially if they are part of your host group. The trick is to make your alliances with the best qualities in a person. Then, help introduce that good part of someone to the good part of someone else.

They aren't going to all agree and you don't want them to all agree. If everyone agreed on everything, the place would get dull fast. And they aren't going to all like each other either. Although it would be lovely if everyone got along, even if they disagree about a lot of things, it's a pretty unrealistic expectation. So, you have to be diplomatic. You will have to perform all sorts of little mediations between people, even if it's just to say, "Aw, he's not so bad, really."

On the flip side, when someone really special comes along, find a place for them so that the whole scene will benefit.

The Big Suggestion Box

Suggestions and advice happen at one time or another in just about every area of a system. In that sense the whole thing is like one huge suggestion box. While you don't have to do everything that everyone tells you, and ultimately you make the decisions, it is essential that people know that you are listening and that you not only listen to advice and suggestion, you welcome it.

You Need a Long Fuse

If you want to manage an online system that is devoted to the free exchange of ideas and opinions, then you need to have your tolerances set very high so that you don't melt down when the disagreement gets too thick.

There will always be people who disagree with your views or your approach and sometimes they may even be right. This is your opportunity to show what you mean by tolerance, because you have to expect a certain amount of criticism and you can't freak out when you get it.

Use a Light Touch

Computers and other high-tech gadgets call to mind images of Orwell's *1984* and other scary visions of people droning away at terminals while Big Brother determines their destiny and even their everyday actions. Ironically, among those most concerned about such possibilities are computer professionals themselves. As manager of an online environment you have a lot of clout, should you choose to wield it, so you need to be almost reassuring to people that you aren't interested in such heavy-haded control practices. Try to use a light touch in your actions and in the way you communicate to people both publicly and privately, even if you are refusing to take a suggested action. People like to know that their views are respected and considered and that they won't be treated in an arbitrary manner as if they were a number instead of a person.

"Innkeeping" for an online scene is a balance between setting policy rules based on your own vision of things and finding the "sense of the group" so that you can incorporate it into whatever decision you make. Different online systems deal with these matters in different ways. Some won't allow any real controversy at all, to the point that they kick you off the system if you try to continue talking about controversial things. Another has a set of words that, if included in a posting, automatically gets that posting censored. Some just knock out all the irrelevant comments as if they were a butcher whacking the fat off the edge of the steak.

Just about anything that smacks of heavy-handed administration has a kind of chilling effect on a scene that is based on the free flow of ideas. People won't stick around if it isn't any fun or if they feel they are being squelched.

Dealing with the Dark Side

The upbeat tone of this chapter is not intended to deny the reality that there is a dark side to online interaction. This is an arena of real life, as valid and dynamic as any other. This means that there is both opportunity and risk. Especially now in these early days when there is so much excitement about this wonderful new meeting place, a newcomer can have the illusion that the intentions of everyone they encounter in the online population are as good as they may appear from their works or tone of their conversation. It isn't always so.

Some aspects of how much privacy you have and how much control you have over what people know or can find out about you varies according to the design of each online system and some are common to all systems.

Common dangers to all include: "Cracking" (breaking into someone's account, usually by guessing or obtaining their password); the system operator's ability to read your e-mail and files without being detected; e-mail that moves through the Internet which can be read by the postmaster of every site it passes through; material you have erased and believe to be gone but that may be stored and retrieved on backup tapes at the system location.

Some Unix-based systems, like the WELL, provide abundant opportunity for someone to check on the doings of others. You can see if someone is online, you can find out what they are doing, you can sometimes read their files and you can see when they log in and log out. It's a double-edged sword because the tools that allow people a lot of freedom and variety in how they communicate also provide better opportunity to snoop and harass.

As the manager of an online scene, you have a responsibility to inform people that there is danger and risk as well as opportunity. Think of yourself, perhaps, as the proprietor of a swimming pool or a beach resort. There is abundant opportunity for people to have fun, but if you aren't careful and aware, you could drown. Of course, you can't drown or get physically hurt from an online encounter or relationship, but you can get emotionally or economically hurt and those wounds are just as real online as they are anywhere else.

This is tricky stuff for everyone. How do you develop trust? Do you assume good intentions on someone's part unless they show you otherwise? Do you watch guardedly and only open up when someone earns it? The process of arriving at a sane balance is a journey that the group takes toward self-definition.

Censor, Ban, and Boot: The Heavy Artillery

The hosts of the conferences and forums have their own challenge in keeping things moving and energetic without it getting out of hand to the point that people feel intimidated or hurt. The atmosphere definitely varies from place to place based on how the host handles things. There are different tolerances for topic drift or what one person can say to another. Ad hominem statements are discouraged just about everywhere, but one host may, on reading a comment that attacks the person more than the statement, censor the comment outright. Another may just get into the conversation at that point and say something regarding ad hominem statements. Another may just let the fur fly.

The balance is tricky when you want to build traffic because some people will want things quite polite or they won't say anything at all, and some people won't participate if they think there's too much control going on.

My own preference for censoring or removing a comment is that if someone says something that is outright illegal such as, "hey everybody, I just found this credit card. Here's the number!" then you remove it. But if it's something controversial or personally offensive, then I prefer to let the comment stay there and perhaps make a comment after it, saying something like, "here is an example of a truly offensive comment which says a lot more about the person making it than the person to whom it is directed."

The second instrument of power available to a host is "banning." This means that a user can be denied the privilege of commenting in a given conference if that person has sufficiently violated the guidelines of that conference. This is a more serious action and one that engenders even more controversy and discussion than censoring.

Finally there is the most extreme action: booting someone off of the system. In the six years I was at the WELL, we did this only three times. I feel booting should be limited almost solely to deep and repeated harassment by one person to another. Harassment, which means "intent to annoy," does happen online. To keep it to a minimum and to let the one who feels harassed make the determination, online systems should have user controls in email and in real-time interaction (like chatting) that allow you to block incoming messages from any given person.

However, in each of these cases mentioned earlier, the boot wasn't permanent. Rather than treating it like being exiled from a country, never to return, it is more like being told to step outside of the saloon until you cool down. Because the point isn't to get rid of people. The point is to try to make it so everyone wants to stay and talk.

The Management as Part of the Community

For many years I have been the manager of an interactive online environment. The people, the discussions they have, and relationships that weave into the fabric of community are the main products of my business. But those of us who manage these products can also be a part of it. We too contribute to the discussions, joke and argue and tell stories about ourselves and the adventures we've had. We don't hold ourselves separate from the folks. We understand that it involves the heart as well as the mind. In that way we are akin to the innkeepers of old where the proprietor hangs out around the table and fireplace, sharing a cup with the guests. The whole place feels cozier because of it.

However, trust is not something easily granted by people; it has to be built. Particularly when the people involved are so independent minded. For a long time I had the very strong impression that if I acted too capriciously or with a heavy authoritarian hand that a bunch of people would sort of turn and say, "oh, gee I didn't know you were really the Brain Police. I guess I was wrong." That used to hang over me like a Sword of Damacles. Sometimes it still does, especially when there is some sort of crisis. And the trust has to be maintained; you can't ever take it for granted.

THE FUTURE

The Internet is growing so fast it can barely keep track of itself. Computerized communications reach more people all the time. Surveillance is refined now to the point that satellites can track individual vehicles from space. Photo images can be altered undetectably. Laptops are more powerful than computers that once filled entire rooms. Virtual reality. Genetic engineering.

We've been hearing it all our lives, but it still holds that never before has technology had the potential to do more harm. I might sound like someone back in the early part of the century when I say this but I'm going to say it anyway because it is the essence of everything I have learned about communication in cyberspace: humanity must dominate technology and never the other way around.

Above all else, I want these communication tools to help; to be part of the solution and not more of the problem.

To this end, I want to sound a warning about five areas of great concern to me.

First, the cost of the phone call to an online service is prohibitively expensive for people outside of the local urban calling areas. Even the big packet-switching nets don't go to cities with populations below about 100,000. This means that many of the people who could most benefit in touch online are priced right out of the market. And we all suffer from not having the input and views of people who live out in the country. I urge that we press for national information highways that are affordable to everyone.

Second, our society has computer users and computer non-users. Although hundreds of thousands of enthusiasts dial into online nets around the country, the general population is largely unaware that such systems even exist, let alone that they are as potentially important to them as their car or their TV. Still, millions of dollars have been and are being spent to bring online communications to the general public in the form of dedicated terminals such as Minitels and smart phones. Moreover, the phone companies and the cable TV companies are preparing to go to war over who will carry video signal to the nation. But for all the talk I have heard and all the reports I have read about hooking up the "global online community" little is happening to create systems where computer users and the general public can meet and talk on a common system. This is incredibly short-sighted, in my view. The real communication breakthrough will occur when those who use computers and those who don't can exchange openly and freely because access to the meeting place is not confined by the equipment that gets you there. The real system of the people will be one that combines these two worlds in a way that works for both.

Third, I feel great alarm at some of the recent raids on crackers and sysops who, in utter disregard of due process, have had their equipment and systems confiscated before any proof or conviction is forthcoming. This is nothing short of tyranny by law enforcement, especially in cases involving morality standards and not actual cracking or file theft. Moreover, I am concerned about some recent government proposals that would only allow encryption schemes that can be read by government authorities. There must be limits to government power in cyberspace.

Fourth, ownership of media is becoming more concentrated every day. Fewer corporations own more media outlets all the time. And it's getting worse. Right now the FCC wants to remove the limits on how many radio and TV stations a single corporation can own. Cable companies have almost complete vertical monopolies over the TV industry, from production to network to cable. We watch what they want us to watch. Now some cable companies and phone companies are merging, creating a new class of media giant. For freedom and democracy to survive, we must increase direct communication among ourselves—the people. But that will happen only if we, the people, demand that the structure of this new communications revolution be based on the "open platform" model. This model concedes that the private communication industry will prosper mightily, but demands that certain protections be thoroughly built-in. These protections include universal affordable service, free speech, privacy protection, widely available public service applications, and diversity of information sources. Let me pause on this final point for a moment. With this upcoming hybrid of telephone and television, let's make sure that the best of both are openly available to all so that, as in the printed word where everyone can be a writer and publisher as well as a reader, each person can be a broadcaster as well a consumer. If this happens there can be a communications renaissance. If it doesn't, then we may end up with another television "wasteland" with "five hundred channels and nothing on."

And finally, cyberspace is wonderful. It has the potential to hook us all up in ways that most of us didn't dream possible only a few decades ago. But the planet's wealth is increasingly concentrated in the hands of the few. And our planetary environment is deteriorating badly. Species are becoming extinct, global warming and ozone depletion aren't just theories anymore, and the planet's ability to sustain huge populations, while its resources are being plundered at unprecedented rates, is in peril.

What I don't want to see is that this virtual world will become a substitute reality that serves to placate a population that accepts a world where it's no longer safe to go outside because the air is too foul, the danger of skin cancer from the sun is too great or the social inequities of the real world are that much easier to ignore.

So I say that those of us who develop and use these tools in these still-early days have the responsibility to make sure that our work isn't co-opted into some huge techno-pacifier.

Rather, let us build into these networks a pervasive community spirit that invigorates our society at every level, from local to global, with a new democratic awareness. I don't think I was ever more inspired than when I learned that the failed coup in Russia was thwarted in great measure because the resisters, holding out in their various enclaves around Moscow and the rest of Russia, stayed in touch through an online network. Or more recently when the people of Thailand used cellular phones to stay in touch and organized after the military had cut off their phone lines. In both these cases, popular communication was a critical element in beating back military tyranny.

Big wheels are turning around the world right now. Let us make sure that we work to help, and not hinder, this great movement toward democracy and self-determination that may be the only hope for a world that, more than ever, needs to talk freely to itself.

APPENDIX A: JOHN COATE'S PRINCIPLES OF CYBERSPACE INNKEEPING

The currency is human attention. Work with it. Discourage abuse of it.

You are in the relationship business.

Welcome newcomers. Help them find their place.

Show by example.

Strive to influence and persuade.

Have a long fuse. Never let the bottom drop out.

Use a light touch. Don't be authoritarian.

Affirm people. Encourage them to open up.

Expect ferment. Allow some tumbling.

Leave room in the rules for judgment calls.

Think "tolerance."

Encourage personal and professional overlap.

Don't give in to tyranny by individual or group.

Encourage face-to-face encounters.

Help it be "woman-friendly."

It isn't just you: let the people help shape it.

Be part of the community.

APPENDIX B: GENERAL ADVICE FOR THE NEW ONLINE USER, BY HILARIE GARDNER

The benefits of being on-line far outweigh the risks, but being aware of the risks, the tools, and the support available better prepares the newcomer for the adventure:

Be aware:

1. That system footprints or tracks may be read to see

    • when and where your logins occurred

    • when and what commands you've executed

    • even information deleted may be retrieved from backups

2. That your account is only as secure as its password

3. That sysops or root-holders:

    • may read mail, files or directories without leaving footprints

- may undelete files you've erased
- may release your files, and so on under warrant

4. That default file protection may not be secure for newly created files

5. That mail:

- may be compromised by each forwarding site
- bounces may appear in entirety to the postmaster
- is owned by BOTH the sender and the receiver

6. That identifying biographies may be system searched or remotely fingered

7. That other users' identities:

- may not be what they appear
- may be falsely registered
- may have had their own account compromised

Be aware of the social dangers possible online:

1. Harassment, or frequent or unsolicited messages from another user, occasionally sent randomly to women's ids

2. Stalking, or being watched or followed online, occasionally coupled with physical confrontation

3. Flaming, or emotional verbal attacks

4. Addiction, or the need for support/feedback available online outweighing a reasonable budget of time or money.

Know how to protect yourself (privacy begins at home):

1. Protect your password:

- Choose a strong password (a combination of upper and lower case characters, and not a name or a dictionary word).
- Do not leave your terminal logged in unattended.
- Do not let anyone watch you log in.
- Log out cleanly.

2. Protect your files:

- Know the default for newly created files.
- Occasionally monitor your files.

3. Protect your information:

- Never send compromising information (your phone number, password, address, or vacation dates) by chat, sends, mail, or in your bio.

• See if encryption is available if necessary.

See what education–communication means are available:

1. Join a support group like the Santa Monica PEN's PEN Femmes, or the online groups BAWiT or SYSTERS.

2. Attend seminars, classes, or study groups.

3. Make use of private, special interest forums online.

4. Use peer pressure in public online to settle disputes.

5. Answer harassment and inappropriate behavior directly and unambiguously, and then post for comment and discussion.

6. Advocate for grievance procedures, tolerance guidelines, and the discouragement of false or anonymous user registrations.

7. Do not submit to unreasonable pressure.

8. Speak up for what you want.

12

*Community Networks: Building a New Participatory Medium**

Douglas Schuler

Seattle Community Network Association

I know of no safe depository of the ultimate power of the society but the people themselves, and if we think them not enlightened enough to exercise their control with a wholesome discretion, the remedy is not to take it from them, but to inform their discretion.

—Thomas Jefferson

COMMUNITY

The well-being of communities contributes to the well-being of the commonweal but the importance of community is no longer taken for granted. Communities are distinguished by lively interaction and engagement on issues of mutual concern but there is a growing view that the strands of community life are unraveling—violence, alcohol and drug use, crime, alienation, degradation of the political process, and ineffectual social institutions are increasingly accepted as inevitable "givens." Computers and communication technology are often touted as saviors of the modern age but the benefits of the "computer revolution" are unevenly distributed and the lack of access to communication technology contributes to the widening gulf between socioeconomic classes (Doctor, 1994).

Some advocates believe that computer technology in concert with other efforts, could play a role in rebuilding community by improving communication, economic opportunity, civic participation, and education. Whether these aims are realized will depend to a large degree on computer professionals whose experience and expertise make them vital participants in the development of future systems.

Community Networks

Community members and activists all over the world have developed and are developing community-oriented electronic bulletin boards or community networks with a local focus (see Figure 12-1 for a small sample). These community networks, some with user populations in the tens of thousands, are intended to advance social goals such as building community awareness, encouraging involvement in local decision making, or developing economic opportunities in disadvantaged communities. They're intended to provide "one-stop shopping" using community-oriented discussions, question and answer forums, electronic access to government employees and information, access to social services, e-mail, and in many cases, Internet access. These networks are also beginning to integrate services and information found on existing electronic bulletin board systems and on other remote systems. The most important aspect of community networks, however, is their immense potential for participation.

A Participatory Medium

Tom Grundner, the originator of the Cleveland Free-Net and the National Public Telecomputing Network (NPTN) describes computing networking as a "fourth media" (NPTN, 1991) "It's not radio, It's not television, It's not print, but it has characteristics of all three." He goes on to say that the main distinction is that community networks are interactive. People can interact with each and with the issues of the day. Community networks promote participation in the following ways.

Community-based. Since the systems are community based, the participants have aspirations, needs, and issues in common. The shared nature of the system promotes participation because everybody is involved. Reciprocal. Any potential "consumer" of information, commentary, issues, or questions is a potential "producer" as well. Compare this to television news programs where an

The Community Network Movement

An ad hoc alliance of librarians, educators, network, and bulletin board systems users, community activists, social service providers, government agencies, and concerned computer professionals is developing around the community network issue. Several web sites and distribution lists now exist on the Internet (Figure 12-2) providing active forums and sources of information on these issues. There are an increasing number of conferences and workshops on these topics including two influential round tables organized by Richard Civille for Computer Professionals for Social Responsibility and for the Center for Civic

Blacksburg Electronic Village—Montgomery County and the
Virginia Tech community, Virginia, US
  Cortney Martin
  540-231-4423
  fax 540-231-7413
  bev.office@bev.net
  Blacksburg Electronic Village, c/o Cortney Martin,
  1700 Pratt Drive, Blacksburg, VA 24060-6361
  Gopher: gopher.bev.net
  WWW: http://www.bev.net/

Big Sky Telegraph—Dillon, Montana, US
  Frank Odasz
  voice: 406-683-7338
  e-mail: franko@bigsky.dillon.mt.us
  Modem: 406-683-7680
  Telnet: 192.231.192.1
  Visitor login: bbs

Charlotte's Web—Charlotte, North Carolina, and vicinity, US
  Steve Snow
  shsnow@charweb.org
  704-336-8533
  c/o Public Library of Charlotte and Mecklenburg County
  310 N. Tryon St.
  Charlotte, NC 28202
  Login: webguest
  Modem: 704-336-8013
  Gopher: gopher.charweb.org
  Telnet: wilbur.charweb.org
  WWW: http://www.charweb.org

Chebucto Community Net—Halifax, Nova Scotia, Canada
  Login: guest
  Password: N/A
  Modem: 902-494-8006
  Telnet: ccn.cs.dal.ca
  WWW: http://www.ccn.cs.dal.ca
  e-mail:aa030@ccn.cs.dal.ca
  902-494-2449

Cleveland Free-Net—Cleveland, Ohio, US
  Jeff Gumpf
  voice: 216-368-2982
  e-mail: jag@po.cwru.edu
  Modem: 216-368-3888
  Telnet: freenet-in-a.cwru.edu
  Visitor login: Select #2 at first menu

Free-Net Finland—Finland's K-12 school (whole nation)
  Heikki Korpinen
  Login: visitor
  Password: no password

Figure 12-1. A Community Network Sampling

organization numbering in the hundreds dispenses its version of the news to people numbering in the tens of millions. In the United States this consumer-producer ratio is steadily shrinking. According to Ben Bagdikian (1992), "twenty-three corporations control most of the business in daily newspapers, magazines, television, books and motion pictures."

Contribution-based. Forums—both moderated and unmoderated—are based on contributions from participants. Any input to the forum becomes part of the forum itself—a record which can be printed, distributed further, or acted upon.

Unrestricted. Anyone can use the community network. Futhermore, users have maximal freedom from control on their postings. There are usually limitations on postings that are harassing, libelous, or criminal, however.

Accessible and Inexpensive. The systems are readily accessible from a variety of public as well as private locations. Further-more, the systems are free of charge or have a very low charge.

Modifiable. Since software is the substrate for community networks, they are (at least potentially) modifiable in several ways. Users can actually design or co-design new user interfaces or services. The openness of the Internet substrate, for example, has promoted the development of numerous wide area information servers such as gopher, WAIS, and WWW, while encouraging ongoing evolution.

Figure 12-1 continued—

Gopher: gopher.freenet.hut.fi
Telnet: freenet.hut.fi
WWW: http://www.freenet.hut.fi/
korpinen@freenet.hut.fi
358-0-4514007
Free-Net Finland, Helsinki
University of Technology, 02150 Espoo, Finland, Europe

Kyiv FreeNet—Ukraine
1 Klovskii Uzviz, Kyiv, 252010
Tel: 228-63-93
webmaster@freenet.kiev.ua
WWW: http://freelunch.freenet.kiev.ua/Project/freehome.html

La Plaza Telecommunity—Taos, New Mexico, US
Patrick Finn
505-758-1836
Fax 505-751-1812
info@laplaza.taos.nm.us
La Plaza Telecommunity Foundation
224 Cruz Alta
Taos NM 87571
Guest login: None available
Modem: (505) 758-2345
Gopher: gopher://laplaza.taos.nm.us
Telnet: laplaza.taos.nm.us
WWW: http://www.laplaza.taos.nm.us

National Capital Free-Net—Ottawa, Ontario, Canada
David Sutherland
voice: 613-788-2600 ext 3701
e-mail: aa001@freenet.carleton.ca
Modem: 613-564-3600
Telnet: freenet.carleton.ca
Visitor login: guest

Oregon Public Electronic Network (OPEN)—Oregon State Capitol Area—City of Salem/Marion
County, US
Ken Phillips
503-588-6355
Fax: 503 588-6369
kphillips@open.org
690 Ferry St SE, Salem OR 97301
WWW: http://www.open.org
Notes: OPEN is a community wide web based on the model of the world wide web.

Public Electronic Network (PEN)—Santa Monica, California, US
Keith A. Kurtz, PEN Project Manager
310-458-8383
fax: 310-395-2343
kkurtz@pen.ci.santa-monica.ca.us
The City of Santa Monica, 1685 Main Street, Santa Monica, CA 90401
Login: N/A

Figure 12-1 continued—

Password: N/A
Modem: 310-458-8989
Telnet: pen.ci.santa-monica.ca.us
WWW: http://pen.ci.santa-monica.ca.us

Prairienet—Central Illinois, US
e-mail: mmesseng or gbnewby
or ann @prairienet.org
voice: 217 244 1962
Login: visitor
Modem: 217-255-9000
Telnet: prairienet.org
www.prairienet.org

RCM—Rete Civica Milanese, MILANO, Italy
Information: +39 2 55006332
Modem: +39 2 55182133
fiorella_de_cindio@rcm.dsi.unimi.it
Login: curioso
Telnet: rcme.usr.dsi.unimi.it 3003
WWW: http://wrcm.usr.dsi.unimi.it

Seattle Community Network—Seattle, Washington, US
Randy Groves
voice: 206-865-3424
e-mail: randy@scn.org
Modem: 206-386-4140
Telnet: scn.org
Visitor login: visitor
WWW: http://www.scn.org/

Tallahassee Free-Net—Leon County Florida, US
e-mail: rousem@freenet.fsu.edu
voice: 904-487-2665
Tallahassee Free-Net 200
W. Park Ave, Tallahassee, FL 32301
Login: visitor
Modem: 904-488-5056
Telnet: freenet.fsu.edu
WWW: http://www.freenet.scri.fsu.edu

Wellington Citynet—Wellington, New Zealand
Richard Naylor
voice: +64-4-801-3303
e-mail: rich@tosh.wcc.govt.nz
Modem: +64-4-801-3060
Telnet: kosmos.wcc.govt.nz

WETA/CapAccess—Washington, DC and vicinity, US
Michael J. Strait
703-824-7300
Fax: 703-824-7350
info@weta.capaccess.org
PO Box 2626, Washington, DC 20013

Figure 12-1 continued—

> Guest Login: guest
> Password: visitor
> Modem: 202-785-1523
> Gopher: gopher.capaccess.org
> Telnet: capaccess.org
> WWW: http://www.capaccess.org

Youngstown Free-Net—Youngstown, Ohio, US
> Lou Anschuetz
> voice: 216-742-3075
> e-mail: lou@yfn.ysu.edu
> Modem: 216-742-3072
> Telnet: yfn2.ysu.edu
> Visitor login: visitor

Networking. Organizations increasingly are rallying around this issue (Figure 12-3).

In the "Apple Library of Tomorrow for 1993" call for proposals, Steve Cisler noted, "In 1992 it can honestly be called a movement. In many people's minds the model of a citizens-based, geographically delimited community information system has taken hold" (Cisler, 1992). As of this writing, community networks are planned or are in operation in over 100 locations in the United States.

A SAMPLING OF COMMUNITY NETWORKS

Several existing systems are briefly presented in the following to illustrate the wide-range of motivations, services, and approaches to community networking.

Community Memory—A Virtual People's Park

Community Memory of Berkeley, CA, created by Efrem Lipkin, Lee Felsenstein, and Ken Colstad, was the first community network (Levy, 1984). Initially started in the mid-1970s as a follow up to experiments conducted in 1972 and 1973 on unmediated two-way access to a message database through public computer terminals, Community Memory was conceived as a tool to help strengthen the Berkeley community. Their brochure states that "strong, free, nonhierarchical channels of communication—whether by computer and modem, pen and ink, telephone, or face-to-face—are the front line of reclaiming and revitalizing our communities." Their commitment to serving those without ready access to information technology is demonstrated by numerous training programs and their insistence that all Community Memory terminals be in public places: Terminals can be found in libraries and in laundromats but can't be reached via modem or from the Internet. Community Memory has adopted a creative approach to funding: They offer coin-operated terminals that are free to read, but require 25 cents to post an opinion and a dollar to start a new forum.

Community Memory has pushed its principles to their logical limits. Anonymity, for example, is possible because users are not required to use their own name or register to

Civic Nets (Reti Civiche e Freenets)
    WWW: http://vega.unive.it/contrib/audies/civicnet.html

Civic Practices Network
    WWW: http://cpn.journalism.wisc.edu/

Communet Distribution List
    Send mail to listproc@list.uvm.edu with message "subscribe communet firstname lastname"

Communications as Engagement
    WWW: http://www.cdinet.com/Millennium/

Community Computer Networks & Free-Net {R} Web Sites
    http://freenet.victoria.bc.ca/freenets.html

Community Network Movement
    WWW: http://www.scn.org/ip/commnet/home.html

Community Networking Resources
    WWW: http://www.sils.umich.edu/Community/Community.html

Community Networking Documents and Resources
    WWW: http://www.nlc-bnc.ca/ifla/services/commun.htm

Community Networks Surveys
    FTP: ftp://cs.washington.edu/research/community-networks/
    WWW: http://www.cs.washington.edu/research/community-networks/

Community Stories
    WWW: http://www.csn.net/anr/comindex.html

Freenet-admin distribution list
    Must be an NPTN affiliate to participate. Contact NPTN for more information.

Free-Nets & Community Networks
    WWW: http://hearld.usask.ca/~scottp/free.html

Intentional Community page
    WWW: http://www.well.com/www/cmty/

Neighborhoods Online
    WWW: http://libertynet.org/community/phila/natl.html

The Neighborhood Works
    WWW: http://www.cnt.org/tnw/tnwhome.htm

NCF Survey
    WWW: http://debra.dgbt.doc.ca/~andrew/survey.html

NPTN Cybercasting Catalog
    WWW: http://www.nptn.org/about.nptn/whois/jmk/catalog.html

Public Access Networks
    WWW: http://www.morino.org/

WWW Guide to Community Networking
    WWW: http://http2.sils.umich.edu/ILS/community.html

Figure 12-2. Online Resources

American Library Association
Peggy Barber
312-280-3217
50 East Huron Street
Chicago, IL 60611-2795

Association of Research Libraries (ARL)
Prue Adler
202-296-8656, prue@cni.org
21 Dupont Circle
Washington, DC 20036

Apple Library of Tomorrow
Steve Cisler
sac@apple.com
4 Infinite Loop MS 304 2A
Cupertino, CA 95014

Center for Civic Networking (CCN)
Miles Fidelman
617-241-9205, ccn@civicnet.org
91 Baldwin Street
Charlestown, MA 02129

Richard Civille
202-363-3831, rciville@civicnet.org
PO Box 65272
Washington, DC 20035

Center for Media Education (CME)
Jeff Chester
202-628-2620, cme@access.digex.net

1511 K Street, Suite 518
Washington, DC 20005

Computer Professionals for Social Responsbility
(CPSR)
Duane Fickeisan
415-322-3778, cpsr@csli.stanford.edu
P.O. Box 717
Palo Alto, CA 94301

Institute for Global Communications (IGC)
Jillaine Smith
415-442-0220, jillaine@igc.apc.org
18 de Boom Street
San Francisco, CA 94107

Libraries for the Future
Diantha Schull
800-542-1918
521 Fifth Ave., Suite 1612
New York, NY 10175-1699

National Public Telecomputing Network (NPTN)
216-247-5800
34555 Chagrin
Moreland Hills, OH 44022

Telecommunications Policy Roundtable
(A coalition of over 50 non-profit organizations)
For more information, contact Emily Littleton
at the Center for Media Education.

Figure 12-3. Supporting Organizations

use the system. Perhaps the most noteworthy of their convictions is that all of the information on the system is community-generated. This has two important implications. The first is that no central authority of any kind establishes what information is available. The other is that information (such as Internet newsgroups) is not imported from other sites. One of their most noteworthy projects is the "Alameda County War Memorial Project," in which information on every deceased veteran in Alameda County is stored on the system. According to their newsletter, "Friends and family can share their thoughts and reminscences at the memorial screen of their friend or relative. This unique capability enables the Alameda County Veteran's Memorial to become a growing piece of community history."

Cleveland (and other) Free-Nets—Electronic Infrastructure for the Twenty-First Century City

The Cleveland Free-Net, operating out of Case-Western University, has over 35,000 registered users and over 10,000 logins per day and is probably the largest community network in the world. It originated as "St. Silicon's Hospital and Dispensary" in 1986, in an electronic question and answer forum devoted to medical topics. This format still persists and is a major part of the system. Doctors, lawyers, automotive mechanics, and others answer questions on-line. The Free-Nets all use a "city" metaphor to orient users (Figure 12-4 and 12-5). One has to go to the appropriate "building" to find the desired information or services. Supreme Court decisions, for example, will be found in the Courthouse building. Free-Nets now exist in Peoria, Illinois, Denver, CO, Ottawa, Ontario, Canada, Youngstown, OH and many other locations, and are linked into a national Public Telecomputing Network (NPTN), which includes national as well as international sites.

Big Sky Telegraph—Western Ingenuity Overcoming Rural Long Distances

Frank Odasz of Western Montana University in Dillon started the Big Sky Telegraph (Odasz, 1991) in 1988 by electronically linking one- and two- room school houses across Montana. Now a fully distributed system consisting of "Big Skies" and "Little Skies," Big Sky Telegraph is an "action-oriented rural telecomputing testbed" designed to overcome some of the problems of the rural American West related to sparse population and long distances between communities. Big Sky Telegraph's approach is appropriate technology to demonstrate "low-cost, low-tech, high-imagination, scalable networking models." Education is the key and economic opportunity and sufficiency are the goals. Big Sky Telegraph offers 600 K–12 lesson plans and serves as a "telecurricular clearinghouse" for K–12 projects running on networks all over the world. It uses the telegraph metaphor, an approach reflecting the influential communication technology of the last century. As their brochure on "Homesteading the Educational Frontier" states

> Teachers in rural Montana serving as Circuit Riders, Community Telegraphers, and Teletutors have used modems to overcome time, distance, and economic limitations to empower rural education and community survival through the Big Sky Telegraph network.

Public Electronic Network (PEN)—A New Urban Polis

The Public Electronic Network (PEN) in Santa Monica, CA is a computer system designed to promote

National Public Telecomputing Network

After the success of the Free-Net model in Cleveland, people from all over the world began to make inquiries about establishing Free-Nets in their cities. Soon there were other Free-Net sites in the Midwest. The idea that Free-Nets could be established in a number of cities linked into a broader network became institutionalized into NPTN—the National Public Telecomputing Network—under the guidance of Tom Grundner, the orginator of the Cleveland Free-Net. NPTN is a non-profit organization that helps develop free, public-access community systems and helps to integrate them into a common network. NPTN also helps to develop and make available "network-quality" information and services via "cybercasting" to all NPTN affiliates. Currently there are over 20 NPTN affiliates who coordinate operational

Free-Nets and over 60 organizing committee" that intend to establish Free-Nets in their cities. The NPTN "Blue Book" (1993) is an excellent introduction to Free-Nets and describes the vision, the motivation, and the actual tasks involved in building a Free-Net.

The "Academy One" program designed to promote K-12 education using networking technology is an important example of an NPTN service. Academy One events have included "Kid Trek", for young science fiction writers, "Teleolympics" where scores of local athletes are compared with those from other locations using the network, and "Project Common Ground" "to improve the environment and to foster a student voice in the affairs of their communities."

community-oriented participatory democracy. Citizens can converse with public officials and city servants as well as with each other. It was established in 1989 and has over 3000 registered users and over 500 user logons per month. PEN provides access to city government information such as city council agendas, reports, public safety tips, and the library's on-line catalog and to government services such as obtaining permits. PEN also provides e-mail and conferences on a wide variety of local civic issues. PEN has served as an early testbed for may ideas related to "electronic democracy" and Pamela Verley (1992) has documented some of the problems that have surfaced using this medium.

Electronic Cafe International— Cultural Explorations with Video Technology

The Electronic Cafe in Santa Monica, CA, serves live multimedia cultural events with participants at remote sites as well as food. Using affordable technology

Figure 12-4. Welcome to the Cleveland Free-Net

```
                <<< CLEVELAND FREE-NET DIRECTORY >>>

 1 The Administration Building
 2 The Post Office
 3 Public Square
 4 The Courthouse & Government Center
 5 The Arts Building
 6 Science and Technology Center
 7 The Medical Arts Building
 8 The Schoolhouse (Academy One)
 9 The Community Center & Recreation Area
10 The Business and Industrial Park
11 The Library

Your Choice ==>
```

Figure 12-5.   Cleveland Free-Net Top Level Menu

such as slow-scan television over voice-grade telephone lines, Kit Galloway and Sherry Rabinowitz, have hosted a multitude of real-time encounters. Most notable, perhaps, was their 1984 linking of eight family-owned restaurants in the Los Angeles area into a shared video, audio, text, and "sketch" space. This cultural exploration was widely enjoyed by community residents and was a pioneer "groupware" application. Other cafes have been set up at the Telluride IDEAS festival (July, 1993) and at CPSR's annual meeting in Seattle (October, 1993). The Electronic Cafe's explorations into multimedia, cultural diversity, international communications, and aesthetics serve as excellent reminders of creative opportunities that transcend conventional text and discussion-based approaches.

A Clearinghouse of Community Networks Information

Assessing the size and scope of the Community Networking Movement is difficult because of the scarcity of data and the rapidly changing situation. This lack of data prevents researchers from adequately investigating the movement and inhibits communication between community network developers. To begin to address these needs I developed a survey that was sent to system administrators and electronic distribution lists (Figure 12-6). Of the over 100 systems that are either operational or planned, completed surveys on over 30 systems (in addition to the survey form and instructions) are available electronically (Figure 12-7). Each completed survey is dated and developers are encouraged to submit updated surveys when the system changes, so that an informal record of system evolution will be available.

From the limited data, some observations can be made. Approximately 63% of the systems are operational with the remainder in the planning or prototype stage. With the exception of the Big Sky Telegraph the systems serve urban or suburban populations and are distributed all over the United States and Canada. In the majority of cases (51%), a university is associated with the community network. Libraries have some sort of association with many of the systems (45%). Of the operational community networks the access methods vary: 1 (5%) relies on list servers in which e-mail is sent to the server and is distributed electronically to the list subscribers; 16 (76%) have Internet connections of some kind; 19 (90%) have dial-up connections, and two of these, the Boston Peace and Justice Hotline and RTK Net, contain audio information only and a touchtone telephone is the user terminal. Finally, Community Memory in Berkeley has public access, dedicated terminals only.

ADDRESSING COMMUNITY NEEDS

As Langdon Winner (1986) has pointed out, artifacts, being the result of human conscious and subconscious design, necessarily have "politics" that encourage certain attitudes and values and discourage others. As with other designed artifacts, input at early stages has stronger and more long-lasting influence on the system than input at later stages. As Winner explains, "Because choices tend to become strongly fixed in material equipment, economic investment, and social habit, the original flexibility vanishes for all practical purposes once the initial commitments are made." He goes on to say that, "The same careful attention one would give to the rules, roles, and relationships of politics must also be given to such things as the building of highways, the creation of television networks, and the tailoring of seemingly insignificant features on new machines." Community networks are no exception. In fact, the issue of attitudes and values—the politics of community networks—makes participation in community network development important.

The "politics" that are "designed-into" community networks must address community needs. In accordance with that philosophy the Seattle Community Network developed five interrelated needs and summary statements that apply to the community at large as well as smaller communities within the larger community:

Community Cohesion
> Communities need to be more cohesive, safer, healthier, and more caring.
> Opportunities for participation must be developed for all people, and disadvantaged neighborhoods need improved economic opportunity.

The community network survey contains information on
- Status
- Accessing the system
- Purposes
- Services
- User fees
- Information policy
- System affiliations
- Contacting system developers

Figure 12-6.   Community Network Survey Information

System (file) Name	*Location*
african-studies-bbs	Madison, WI
akron-regional-freenet	Akron, OH
arbornet	Ann Arbor, MI
big-sky-telegraph	Dillon, MT
blacksburg-village	Blacksburg, VA
boston-peace-and-justice-hotline	Brighton, MA
boulder-county-civic-network	Boulder, CO
CapAccess	Washington, DC
chippewa-valley-freenet	Eau Claire, WI
CIAO-trail-freenet	Vancouver, B.C., Canada
columbia-online-information-network	Columbia, MO
community-memory	Berkeley, CA
cruzio	Santa Cruz, CA
denver-freenet	Denver, CO
ecoline	Burlington, VT
eugene-community-network	Eugene, OR
FACTS	Fayetteville, NC
genesee-freenet	Flint, MI
heartland-freenet	Peoria, IL
IGC	San Francisco, CA
mt-view-community-network	Mountain View, CA
national-capital-freenet	Ottawa, Ontario, Canada
new-mexico-network	Albuquerque, NM
rtk	Washington, DC
santa-cruz-county-wan	Santa Cruz, CA
seattle-community-network	Seattle, WA
slo-county	San Luis Obispo, CA
SPACECON	Merritt Island, FL
suncoast-freenet	Tampa, FL
sustainable-development-info-network	Cambridge, MA
toronto-freenet	Toronto, Ontario, Canada
triangle-freenet	Triangle Park, NC
youngstown-freenet	Youngstown, OH

To obtain survey results, via anonymous ftp, the file transfer program on the Internet, ftp to atlas.ce.washington.edu. The survey results are in the pub/seattle-community-network/community-networks/surveys directory.

Figure 12-7.   Survey Respondants

The Informed Citizen

> People need and want to be well-informed. They need high quality, timely, and reliable information. They are interested in a wide range of opinions from a wide variety of sources.

Access to Education and Training

> People need training to use technology effectively. People need to be able to learn independently over the course of their lifetimes.

Strong Democracy
People need an inclusive, effective, ethical, and enlightened democracy.

An Effective Process
People need a process by which the described needs can be met.

For each need, the SCN group generated a specific measurable objective, a procedure for attaining the objective, an evaluation procedure, and a budget. This needs analysis can then be used as the basis of specific proposals. The SCN group also developed a set of principles (Figure 12-8) that would embody both their philosophy and their intentions over time.

The Seattle Community Network (SCN) is a free public-access computer network for exchanging and accessing information. Beyond that, however, it is a service conceived for community empowerment. Our principles are a series of commitments to help guide the ongoing development and management of the system for both the organizers and participating individuals and organizations.

Commitment to Access—
Access to the SCN will be free to all.
We will provide access to all groups of people particularly those without ready access to information technology.
We will provide access to people with diverse needs. This may include special-purpose interfaces.
We will make the SCN accessible from public places.

Commitment to Service—
The SCN will offer reliable and responsive service.
We will provide information that is timely and useful to the community.
We will provide access to databases and other services.

Commitment to Democracy—
The SCN will promote participation in government and public dialogue.
The community will be actively involved in the ongoing development of the SCN.
We will place high value in freedom of speech and expression and in the free exchange of ideas.
We will make every effort to ensure privacy of the system users.
We will support democratic use of electronic technology.

Commitment to the World Community—
In addition to serving the local community, we will become part of the regional, national and international community.
We will build a system that can serve as a model for other communities.

Commitment to the Future—
We will continue to evolve and improve the SCN.
We will explore the use of innovative applications such as electronic town halls for community governance, or electronic encyclopedias for enhanced access to information.
We will work with information providers and with groups involved in similar projects using other media.
We will solicit feedback on the technology as it is used, and make it as accessible and humane as possible.

Figure 12-8. Principles of the Seattle Community Network

Community Cohesion

Developers must work with community activists and community development organizations to design new projects and to support and extend existing services electronically. In Seattle, for example, an "electronic penpals" project to promote communication between school children in diverse neighborhoods has been proposed. In either case, Participatory Design principles and techniques of strong user participation in design are applicable (Schuler & Namioka, 1993).

To truly support community cohesion access must be universal. The barriers of cost, availability, literacy, and physical disabilities must be bridged. Connecting to community network services must be inexpensive and easy, and use open standards. No-cost minimal cost use from the home as well as publicly accessible terminals are required. Potential locations include already existing community locations such as libraries, schools, community and senior centers, and parks. Places where people traditionally congregate such as bars, coffeehouses, laundromats, bus stations, and shopping malls are also good candidates. Terminals must become as ubiquitous as telephones for use to become a natural, everyday occurrence.

Ray Oldenberg argues in *The Great Good Place* (Oldenbarg, 1989) that people need a "third place" away from their home—the "first place"—and away from the place of work—the "second place." Third places are characterized by their location on "neutral ground," a "leveling" tendency where social and economic standings (as well as physical characteristics) are greatly diminished, and as a place where "conversation is the main activity." Although Oldenberg's "third place" is a physical location such as a coffee house or a tavern many attributes of third places can be applied to community networks (Rheingold, 1993).

The Informed Citizen

As Paul Resnick and Mel King (1990) explained:

There is no such thing as a poor community. Even neighborhoods without much money have substantial human resources. Often, however, the human resources are not appreciated or utilized, partly because people do not have information about each other and about what their neighborhood has to offer. For example, a family whose oil heater is broken may go cold for lack of knowledge that someone just down the block knows how to fix it.

Community-oriented "want ads" could address this need. Other useful information includes calendars of events that are searchable by topic and date; bus schedules and routes; disaster preparation; carpool information; question and answer forums conducted by doctors, nurses, lawyers, recycling experts, and automotive mechanics; community maps; and community resources including social services, job banks, and after school activities for kids.

Access to Education and Training

Community networks can promote education in structured and unstructured ways. Providing access to community information and network resources helps people to pursue their own education. More structured approaches coordinated by professional educators are also possible. Curricula and network projects can be shared and both students and teachers can participate in forums. Big Sky Telegraph and NPTN's Academy One are involved in many innovative projects. Community networks can also provide a convenient initial access point for training the computer-naive as well as the computer-phobic.

Community networks provide important areas of research (Figure 12-9) but research need not be confined to universities. Community members themselves can propose and conduct meaningful research using Participatory Action Research (PAR) techniques. PAR (Foote Whyte, 1991) is an approach to scientific inquiry in which the scientific method is employed to conduct research while bringing about desired change, such as improving the quality of political dialogue in a forum. PAR explicitly acknowledges that the dictates of "normal science," such as repeatability, control variables, and closed-world assumptions, are irrelevant in real-world situations involving people (Baskerville & Wood-Harper). Findings, for example, which are related to schools in one community may not be applicable to schools in other communities. Users are full partners in PAR, making it particularly appropriate in the community network context.

Strong Democracy

Signs that the public is interested in pursuing "electronic democracy" include calls for "Electronic Town Meetings," e-mail to President Clinton, and the popularity of radio and television call-in shows. Community networks can increase public participa-

---

Community networks can be a focus for academic research. For example, in connection with a research proposal with faculty members from several schools and colleges at the University of Washington I identified six broad areas for research.

Developing collections of courseware, information, and services that can be made available electronically and effectively accessed and used by large numbers of community members.

Developing user interfaces and information retrieval methods that promote effective access to a wide variety of information types (including text, graphics, voice, video, and datasets) from remote sites.

Exploiting existing wide area information servers for sharing of information over a wide area as well as working with prototypes and next-generation information sharing applications.

Conducting research on usage patterns and individual and collective on-line behavior.

Developing and evaluating models for effective learning and collaboration over distances.

Developing policy frameworks and analysis methodologies.

Figure 12-9. Research Issues for Community Networks

tion by improving access to elected officials and agency employees through e-mail and electronic forums (Elgin, 1991). They can also improve access to government information and services and be the home of dozens of community-created forums on local issues. The technology by itself, however, can't ensure a more strongly democratic culture—thus the policies and processes that we create deserve critical attention.

Voting (Levine et al., 1988) and other types of democratic participation are practiced infrequently in the United States (Osborne & Gaebler, 1993). More disturbing is the common attitude that politics is inherently vile and all politicians are corrupt (Osborne & Gaebler, 1993). This polarization into "us" and "them" undermines democratic potential by discouraging participation. Sad, too, is the evidence that the media that are supposed to help citizens make informed decisions may actually be contributing to degradation of the political process. For example, network television's reliance on "sound bites" (averaging 8.5 seconds in 1992 according to *The New York Times* [10/31/92]) trivializes the process. A more serious charge is that of systematic bias. Some critics charge that the media is so structurally biased that democratic "consent" is actually "manufactured" (Herman and Chomsky, 1988). To counter these discouraging trends, increasing media diversity, citizen participation and access to communication channels is necessary. It is only then that the dream of a "strong democracy" (Barber, 1984) marked by the "pleasure of participation" and the "fellowship of civil association" can become realizable.

An Effective Process

As community networks are intended to be developed and maintained by citizens, developers must pay special attention to the process that institutionalizes them. The process must guide participation in three major ways: (1) network design and development; (2) the on-line community; and (3) governance.

Network Design and Development. The community network organization must develop a shared vision, a shared plan, and a shared voice. It must also establish how work will be organized, assigned, evaluated, and sanctioned. To this end, the Seattle Community Network (SCN) Project established five committees—hardware/software, policy, outreach, services, staff and facilities—and a steering committee. Communication approaches that are informative and inclusive are needed to support both internal development and community outreach.

Developing basic documents is another important responsibility. Documents include FAQs (Frequently asked questions), statement of purpose, principles, business plan, and budget. Other important documents include the policy statement that addresses a wide range of complex issues including censorship, privacy, dealing with grievances, establishing groups, and other areas, and the organization's by-laws that are legally required and form the basis for system governance over the years.

The On-Line Community. Participation in the on-line community can take forms. Basic participation means participating in forums, including those specifically devoted to discussing the system and how well it meets community needs. Extended use means modifying services, developing new services, or hosting forums.

Network Governance. Opportunities for participation extend to roles and responsibilities that transcend using the system. These will include (paid) staff roles, board members, advisory board members, and volunteers. Areas of responsibilities include users services such as training and documentation; system administration, including user accounts and software installation; outreach including publicity, fund-raising, and communication; and executive, including strategic planning, evaluating, and codesigning.

A MODEL FOR COMMUNITY NETWORKS

Community networks that address the described needs must be developed within existing social and technological contexts. Pertinent aspects of the contexts of community networks are reflected in a model consisting of two superimposed architectures. The first architecture (Figure 12-10) depicts the human context of community networks: how people interact and how social systems (including legal, political and economic) influence them. The second (Figure 12-11) depicts the system's technological infrastructure.

Social and Political Architecture

There are five components of the social and political architecture: the on-line community; individual and organizational participants; influencing organizations; the community network organization; and infrastructure providers.

On-Line Community. The group of people who use the community network constitutes the "on-line community." The on-line community is at the center of the social and political architecture—if this element is deficient the system is deficient. There are three main influences on the on-line community: The medium itself—essentially the technical specifications of the system including what information and services are available and the nature of the interaction approach (e.g., forums, "chat," or e-mail); the user population or demographics including number and characteristics of users as well as formal and informal roles assumed by users; and the resulting on-line community or society with its conventions, folkways, interaction patterns, and cast of characters.

John Coate, who worked for the WELL (The "Whole Earth 'Lectronic Link") for many years, compares a community network to an inn (Coate, 1992). While visiting an inn people may talk with people whom they know or with people that they encounter. To Coate, facilitating an on-line community is like "innkeeping"—the innkeeper encourages interchange between patrons but sometimes problems arise and order has to be restored. Much has been written about proper on-line interactions or "netiquette," but Henry Sedgewick's seven rules on the art of conversation may be the most succinct.

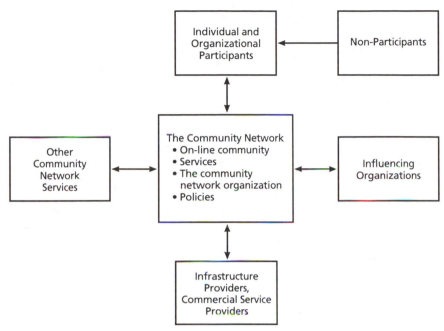

Figure 12-10. Social and Political Model

Individual and Organizational Participants.   Organizations, such as community associations, can provide information or services that further their goals. This may echo what they already disseminate in paper form. Lack of resources or technical expertise may inhibit their participation although the promise of increased penetration, reduced communication costs, and the desire to "computerize" their operations may promote participation. Furthermore, organizations that are considering making their information or services available electronically may reduce their costs considerably by not developing an independent system. An existing community network also makes it easier for potential clients by providing a common access point.

Influencing Organizations.   A wide range of organizations influence community network development and coordination. The government's potential for involvement is strongest—it can act as both regulator and supporter. Advocacy groups may include library or educational groups as well as other groups such as NPTN, CPSR, or the Center for Civic Networking. Recently the Corporation for Public Broadcasting has launched an initiative to help develop community networks. Other organizations may offer a competitive influence, including the telephone companies, cable television companies, and various other media and communica-

The Art of Conversation

1. Remain silent your share of the time (more rather than less).

2. Be attentive while others are talking.

3. Say what you think but be careful not to hurt other's feelings.

4. Avoid topics not of general interest.

tion companies. These companies are well-positioned to address community needs but have not prioritized it.

The Community Network Organization. The network organization is the primary mechanism that ensures that the community network is functioning well from technical and social points of view. It must see that the five needs are being adequately addressed. It must be involved with day-to-day operations, including system maintenance and administration, as well as community outreach, fundraising, and participation in the political process. The organization itself may be a nonprofit organization, a nonprofit–government cooperative venture, a governmental organization, or a (if certain guidelines are met) a for-profit organization. The network could also be allied in coalitions, cooperatives, or associations with other organizations. Each of these approaches carries with it a set of values, perogatives, and methods and with those a set of advantages and disadvantages for participatory community networking.

Infrastructure Providers. Infrastructure providers, including Internet providers, telephone companies, and cable television companies, influence individual community networks directly through their rates and policies. Their influence is more

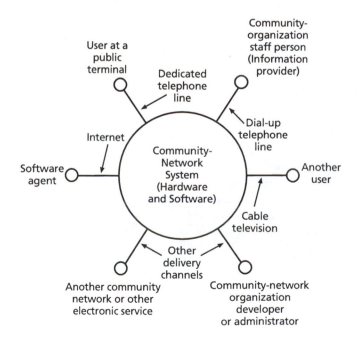

Figure 12-11. Technological Model

global, however, largely because of their strong role in public policy through lobbying and public relations work. The relations between companies of this magnitude have the potential to swamp issues of access and participation.

Technological Architecture

The technological architecture roughly parallels the social and political architecture. The computer system (including software, CPU's, memory, and interface devices) is at the core of the system, surrounded by different types of users—developers, participants, administrators, information providers, and other on-line information and services—which are connected through delivery channels and interfaces. A few of the most relevant aspects are listed in the following.

Hardware.   The hardware may be the least complicated component in the model. The community network computer needs to be an extremely reliable, multiprocessing machine whose main role will be gathering input from users, accessing data from disk, and presenting output back to users. The community network computer must also be configured to communicate with a potentially large number of devices. If e-mail and additional storage are offered to participants disk drives with gigabytes of storage will be required.

Software.   A community network at its current state of evolution essentially is a very large electronic bulletin board that ideally can accommodate hundreds of simultaneous users and a user base of tens of thousands. The software services that community networks often provide are forums (moderated and unmoderated); access to static information contained in files; e-mail; download-upload capabilities; chat; remote login; search capabilities; and database facilities. In addition, a simple menu structure with which to navigate information and services is often used. Furthermore, the system must easily incorporate new capabilities, such as search engines, multimedia applications, or wide area information servers, as they become available.

The user interface should be easy to use, consistent, and resistant to user input errors. The requirement that the system be accessible from a wide variety of terminals argues for a simple, text-based interface. The Cleveland Free-Net and other Free-Nets use a city metaphor to organize the contents (Figure 12-4). Placing the information into "buildings" is straightforward and users generally know where to look. One question is how far can or should the metaphor be taken. As the amount of information grows larger, say in the case of legal information, one might want to divide the buildings into "floors" and the floors into "rooms." As the system grows larger the metaphor by itself (i.e., without additional "directories") will fail. However, the city metaphor offers user portability: Users who are familiar with the city metaphor in his or her own community will be comfortable with it in another.

Delivery Channels.   The term "delivery channel" is applied loosely to the physical medium plus the protocol plus the interfaces that allow information to pass back and forth between the community network computer and users and other machines. It is important to think of delivery channels in a general sense because the physical substrate, protocols, and policies are currently in a state of flux. Because of this community network proponents must be active participants in all decisions concerning public uses of delivery channels including voice-grade telephone, ISDN, cable television, or radio transmissions.

NEAR TERM ISSUES AND DECISIONS

The community network movement is currently marked by strong interest and activity. Several issues, however, must be addressed in the short term if community networks will have an effective and long-lived influence. Identifying and addressing these issues is essential to determining what steps—including political action—must be taken to ensure the long-term health and survival of community networks. The following paragraphs offer glimpses of some of these issues.

Funding

Funding is needed for computer and communication equipment as well as office space and office expenses. Funding is also needed for administration, outreach, software development and maintenance. Volunteers and donated space and equipment can not meet the need for professional service over the long run. On the other hand, funding for community networks so far has been sporadic and unreliable. Equitable, reliable, and replicable funding approaches from indirect or direct participants (Figure 12-12) must be developed.

Access and Use

Community network developers speculate that community networks in the twenty-first century will become as common as public libraries are now. Currently they are available only in few locations and accessible to relatively few users. To promote universal use community networks must be easy to use, easy to access, and free of structural barriers to their use. In addition, the systems must be reliable and responsive; the user interface intuitive and nonintimidating; and special purpose interfaces must be developed for those with special needs.

Although public terminals are critical, penetration into the home also is important. People must be able to easily and inexpensively participate using one ore more delivery channels. Telephone, cable television, radio transmissions, or other approaches are all possible delivery channels and a certain percentage of the spectrum should be reserved for public use. Community networks must also be able to communicate with each other and with other electronic services using high-quality, low-cost technology.

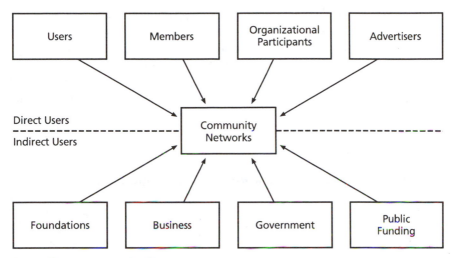

Figure 12-12. **Funding Possibilities**

Policy

An information policy must anticipate and address questions and issues like the following.

How private is my e-mail?

Can you ever deny me access to the community network?

Can I post "adult" material?

Do I have to use my real name?

How can I register a complaint against a moderator?

I'm receiving abusive e-mail. Can you put an end to it?

I'd like to use the network to advertise my product. Is that OK?

I have a commercial database service. Can you let people login to it?

The doctor in your question-and-answer forum gave bad advice. I'm suing you!

Someone reprinted my posting in a magazine without my permission!

Somebody on your network posted stolen credit card numbers. We're confiscating your equipment.

These types of issues reflect in large part the tension that exists between individual and community rights. They aren't unique to community networks, though its status as a new medium means that some community network issues are unresolved.

We can begin to devise policies based on other media but the analogy is often strained. Community networks like libraries must be champions of free speech. But disagreements in libraries are between library users and contents of books—not between two (or more) library users. Furthermore, libraries don't officially disallow material but the space limitations on their shelves provide implicit constraints unlike those of cyberspace. Community networks, like telephones, provide a medium for discourse—discourse that is sometimes acrimonious. Phone calls, however, are fleeting, private, and have few participants. Some "discussions" in public electronic forums are more like fist fights involving potentially large numbers of participants and spectators—and every spectator optionally can record the session that can be disseminated still further.

National Information Infrastructure (NII) and Political Action

The commercial sector is proposing a plethora of innovative programs that have become prominent in national media (see, e.g., *Time* magazine cover story on the "Information Superhighway" April 12, 1993). Nearly absent from this coverage is any mention of public-interest, truly interactive, participatory, civic, or community-owned and -operated networks. Large computer, telecommunications, and media companies are involved in formal and informal discussions on the future of the NII (e.g., in the Commerce Department's Information Infrastructure Task Force) but there is little effort to involve citizens in either education or consultation. Citizens are largely unfamiliar with the issues that their tax dollars helped create and critical decisions may be framed, debated, and resolved without their input. To redress this oversight the government should convene a series of local and regional meetings before critical and potentially irreversible actions are taken.

Encouraging public education and debate at all levels is paramount. This is probably addressed most easily by working with local or national groups (see Figure 12-3 and [Schuler, 1996] for a more extensive list) and by making your concerns known via individual correspondence and testimony. These groups and others are currently developing vision statements as well as policy recommendations on these issues. The development of free on-line services and information should accompany these efforts. Developing such services benefits community network participants directly while generally strengthening the community network movement. By providing high-quality, free services commercial information and service providers must increase the value of their products.

DIRECTIONS AND IMPLICATIONS

The world is emerging from a long cold war that has profoundly influenced the thinking and behavior of its leaders and citizens. To some degree the ending of the cold war has brought with it an unsureness of thought and of motivation (Chapman, present volume), which prevents us from tackling problems of national purpose to address current and future needs with compassion, confidence, and creativity. As with the section above this section can only offer glimpses of the issues facing us in the long term.

Universal Access and Equitable Participation

Universal access and equitable participation must not erode over time. We cannot rely on commercial interests to make the necessary guarantees. The overriding concern of profitability, responsibility to shareholders—not citizens—and a closed decision-making process argue strenuously against it. Furthermore, as Sandra Schickele has demonstrated (Schickele, 1993) the requirements of the free market mechanism are not met in the case of the Internet. She concludes that public subsidy is essential if network resources are to be made widely available. The need for accountability, public participation, and visibility clearly point to public ownership. Increasing the role of government, however, is viewed skeptically by many. Government can be corrupt, beholden to special interests, inefficient, unresponsive, or antagonistic to citizen participation and oversight. Lack of funds, technological expertise, and experience further limit government's effectiveness. Nevertheless, community networks in democratic societies must ultimately have a close relationship to a government, which in turn is controlled by citizens. Osborne and Gaebler's prescriptions for "reinventing government," (Osborne & Gaebler, 1993) particularly those involving "community-owned government," "mission-driven government," and "decentralized government" are particularly relevant in considering the potential role of government.

Consequences for Democracy

"Electronic democracy" can open new doors for participation but it is no panacea—nor is it impervious to abuse. Democracy is vulnerable to many threats and "electronic democracy" may be even more vulnerable. Democracy without democratic processes is just a word. New processes will need to be developed, say "Roberts Rules of Order—Revised for Electronic Participation," to ensure equity. With many systems, for example, a single individual or group can monopolize a discussion. A powerful group could possibly bombard the community network in a sustained, orchestrated, and persistent manner designed to overwhelm any opposition. In an even more paranoid scenario, powerful interests could attempt to shut down the entire community network if they objected to certain postings.

A Global Community

A global network is quickly becoming a reality. The Institute for Global Communications, awarded the Norbert Wiener award by CPSR for its work in developing network technology to empower previously disenfranchised individuals and groups working for progressive change, offers PeaceNet, EcoNet, ConflictNet, LaborNet, and access to several international partner organizations to subscribers in over 70 countries. With truly global networks impending, it's not too early to begin considering the prospects of a global community of communities. NPTN affiliates, for example, already are active in Canada, Mexico, Finland, and Germany. The Community Network Movement should welcome international partners. We should establish "sister networks," hold joint congresses, codevelop electronic services and generously share information. Reports of the birth of a golden age based on global networking are exaggerated but any relief from humankind's long history of suffering, intolerance, environmental degradation, and waste that can be promoted through global networking should be welcome.

New Technologies

New technologies including display devices, wireless, multimedia, and the like, coupled with new applications and modes of interacting such as MUDs (Curtis, 1992) and computational e-mail (Borenstein, 1992) have strong implications for usability, service providing, and participatory democracy. Technical innovations should be introduced into community networks when they will increase the ability to meet user needs; adopting new technology, however, will necessarily introduce some unfamiliarity or resistance. This translates into disruptions in the user community as prior conventions and patterns of interactions will require modification. Being cognizant of these implications will help alert network developers to the need for training, user preparation, usability testing, and participatory design.

The incorporation of new technology shouldn't dilute universal access. Low-cost text-based terminals must not, for example, be made obsolete with the introduction of new graphics technology. The solution probably will require multiple user interfaces, resulting in an "interface gap" but not sacrificing the basic level of universal access.

Control of Technology

We—in a collective sense—do have some control over technology and its effects on us. We attempt to influence the influence and direction of technology through its physical design and through policies surrounding its use. The idea of "controlling" community networks or other form of new communication technology, however, makes little sense. An interactive process of imagining, discussing, prescribing, monitoring, and evaluating is more in line with our aspirations, our limitations, and our habits.

CONCLUSIONS

The Community network movement with its great potential for renewed participation in community life is rapidly gaining momentum.[1] Although the potential is significant, the realization of this potential will depend on active, compassionate, creative, and persistent participation of computer professionals and others in technical, social, and political roles. With your help community networks will play a part in a revitalized, richer, and more inclusive future.

ACKNOWLEDGMENTS

This chapter appeared in Communications of the ACM (January, 1994) and is reprinted with permission. I'd like to thank Ray Alis, Alan Borning, Steve Cisler, Richard Civille, Andrew Clement, Carl Farrington, Miles Fidelman, Stephanie Fowler, Dave Levinger, Doug McLaren, Todd Newman, Helen Nissenbaum, Andy Oram, Evelyn Pine, David Tallan, and Terry Winograd for lots of helpful suggestions.

REFERENCES

Bagdikian, B. (1992). *The media monopoly.* Boston MA: Beacon Press.

Barber, B. (1984). *Strong democracy.* Berkeley, CA: University of California Press.

Baskerville, R., & Wood-Harper, T. (1993) A Critical Perspective on Action Research as a Method for Information Systems Research, Technical Report. Binghamton, NY: State University of New York.

Borenstein, N. (1992). Computational Mail as Network Infrastructure for Computer-Supported Cooperative Work, in *Proceedings of ACM Conference* on Computer-Supported Cooperative Work, Toronto, Canada.

Chapman, G. (1994, January). The National Forum on Science and Technology Goals: Building a Democratic Post-Cold War Science and Technology Policy. Communications of the ACM.

Cisler, S. (1992). *Apple library of tommorow proposal.* Cupertino, CA. Apple Computer Corporation.

Coate, J. (1992). Innkeeping in Cyberspace. In Proceedings of Directions and Implications of Advanced Computing (DIAC-92) Symposium. Berkely, CA, May 2–3. Computer Professionals for Social Responsibility, Palo Alto, CA. Also in this volume.

Curtis, P. MUDDING: Social Phenomena in Text-Based Virtual Reality. In Proceedings of Directions and Implications of Advanced Computing (DIAC-92) Symposium. Berkeley, CA, May 2–3, 1992. Computer Professionals for Social Responsibility, Palo Alto, CA.

Doctor, R. (1994, Oct.). Seeking equity in The National Information Infrastructure. Internet Research. 4 (3).

---

[1] Interest in community networks is exploding. As of early 1996 there were nearly 400 operational or planned systems (Doctor & Ankemi, 1996). Many of the themes of this chapter have been further developed in Schuler (1996).

Doctor, R., & Ankem, K. (1996). A Directory of computerized community Information Systems. Unpublished report. Tuscaloosa, AL: School of Library and Information Studies, University of Alabama.

Elgin, D. (1991). *Conscious democracy through electronic town meetings.* Whole Earth Review.

Foote, Whyte, W. (1991). *Participatory action research.* Sage Publications. Beverly Hills, CA.

Herman, E. & Chomsky, N. (1988). *Manufacturing consent—The political economy of the mass media.* New York: Pantheon Books.

Levine, M. et al., (1988). *The state and democracy: Revitalizing America's government.* New York: Routledge.

Levy, S. (1984). *Hackers: Heroes of the computer revolution.* New York: Dell.

NPTN (1991). Videotape, "If it plays in Peoria...," National Public Telecomputing Network, Moreland Hills, OH.

NPTN (1993). A Guide to the Development of Free-Net Community Computer Systems. Moreland Hills, OH: National Public Telecomputing Network.

Odasz, F. (1991). *Big Sky Telegraph.* Whole Earth Review.

Oldenberg, R. (1989). *The great good place.* New York: Paragon House.

Osborne, D., & Gaebler, T. (1993). *Reinventing government.* New York: Plume.

Resnick, P. & King, M. (1990). The Rainbow Pages—Building Community with Voice Technology. In Proceedings of Directions and Implications of Advanced Computing (DIAC-90) Symposium. Boston, MA, July 28. Computer Professionals for Social Responsibility, Palo Alto, CA. Also in this volume.

Rheingold, H. (1993). *The virtual community: Homesteading on the electronic frontier.* Reading, MA. Addison-Wesley.

Rheingold, H. (1991) *The great equalizer.* Whole Earth Review.

Schuler, D. (1996). *New community networks: Wired for change.* Reading, MA: Addison-Wesley.

Schuler, D., & Namioka, A. (Eds.). (1993). *Participatory design: Principles and practice.* Hillsdale, NJ: Erlbaum.

Schickele, S. (1993). The economic Case for Public Subsidy of the Internet. Distributed at the "Public Access to the Internet" conference held at the Kennedy School of Government, Harvard University, Cambridge, MA, May 26–27.

Verley, P. (1992). What's really happening in Santa Monica? BCS Impact!

Winner, L. (1986). *The whale and the reactor—A search for limits in an age of high technology.* Chicago, IL: University of Chicago Press.

13

Community Memory: A Case Study in Community Communication

Carl Farrington
Evelyn Pine

Community Memory Project

INTRODUCTION

In 1984, the Community Memory Project launched its community communications network by placing easy-to-use terminals in a Berkeley supermarket and a coffeehouse. Would ordinary people brave high tech tools to share information, conduct daily business, and enhance friendships? At the time, the idea seemed impossibly utopian.

Almost ten years after Community Memory began demonstrating the value of community-based telecommunications, there is a remarkable explosion of interest in public access community computer networks. Activists pushing for public access to the

National Information Infrastructure see local community networks as valuable "on-ramps" onto the electronic superhighway. The Internet now hosts several active community access mail lists. A number of community-based projects with strong public access components have emerged or are in the planning stages including networks in Seattle, in Washington DC, and in Victoria, British Columbia, as well as some of the Free-Nets. Santa Monica's Public Electronic Network has placed terminals in libraries and community centers. At the same time, businesses and government agencies have discovered the interactive computer kiosk as an effective delivery mechanism for government or commercial information. The articles about the Rainbow Pages, the WELL, and *mudding* attest to the vitality of experimentation in this area.

Despite growing interest and scattered activities, documentation of actual long-term operating history is scanty. Community Memory's track record in now a vital source of information about the potentials and pitfalls of public access community networks. This paper, first presented at DIAC '92, outlines the design decisions, experiences, and social implications of the Community Memory network.

The Community Memory Project is a small nonprofit corporation, whose purpose is to enhance and encourage full participation and free expression in society by providing and promoting tools through which individuals and groups can share knowledge, opinion, resources, and friendship.

One of the ways we meet our mandate is through projects demonstrating that easy-to-use local telecommunications networks can encourage participation by the entire community. Telecommunications technology has been explored extensively in business and academic settings, but applications to community settings have been almost nonexistent. This chapter discusses our experience with two such telecommunications networks.

BACKGROUND

We define a community as a group of people linked by a communications structure supporting discussion and collective action. The range of issues over which discussion and action are supported give some measure of the richness of a community.

By this measure, geographical groupings of people in urban society constitute poor communities. Channels for public discussion generally are limited to letters to the local newspaper or (generally poorly attended) political or governmental meetings. Most people have no input into formulating policy. Their role in most decisions about collective action is reduced from active participation to passive selection among predefined choices in polls, on ballots, and about personal expenditures.

The development of this situation was almost inevitable as relatively static communications structures faced issues of increasing population, increasing diversity, and an increasing range of problems for which no social consensus has developed. New communications technologies hold out some hope of improving this situation by cataloging the full range of community opinion, providing an open, public forum for discussion of issues, and allowing people to make contacts based on shared interests. To fulfill this role, a communications system must be both powerful and accessible.

Such a system must be powerful because human interest is so diverse. To appropriately handle such diversity, the system must support an elaborate degree of cross-indexing. This index must also be extensible to allow for initially unanticipated areas of concern. To handle more than cursory information on such a wide range of subjects, the system must have a large capacity, not only for storage, but for collection and dissemination.

Accessibility is an equally important requirement. As more people use such a system, the probability of useful connections multiplies. To take full advantage of this effect, the barriers that prevent people from using the technology must be addressed. These barriers can be economic, experiential, physical, or institutional.

Our conviction was that if such systems were to be widely accepted, they would have to be very inexpensive, and would have to include mechanisms for meeting their own costs. This conviction led us to the idea of using coin-operated, publicly located terminals. By placing terminals in public locations, a given number of people could be served with far less hardware than if each person required a terminal in their home or office. Making terminals coin-operated made it possible to recover some costs from user fees while avoiding the complexities of billing and giving anyone access on a pay-as-you-go basis without the need to establish credit or pay large deposits.

We also developed the conviction that community communications systems would be structured around a database model, rather than traditional conferencing or e-mail models. This conviction grew partially from the orientation toward helping people establish connections within the community, and partially from an orientation toward casual, "drop-in" use patterns, rather than consistent daily or weekly participation. Also, we wanted a single data model to support both organized database and individual contributions, to reduce the distinction between "producers" and "consumers" of information.

The Community Memory Project has worked to develop practical demonstrations of community communications systems that address the discussed requirements, and to test these systems in actual application in community settings. Our first major test of such a system ran from July of 1984 until November of 1988, and supported originally three, and later four public terminals. Our experience with that system, and significant changes in price and performance of desktop-class computers, prompted a significant revision in our designs. This revised system was deployed beginning in July of 1989, growing to ten terminals by February of 1990, and has been in operation up through the time of this writing (November, 1991).

THE FIRST SYSTEM

The first system was deployed as a test and public demonstration of our approach to a community communications tool. It ran on one of the early 68000-based UNIX systems, and supported four terminals running specially designed database and communications software.

Although the first system was designed to come as close as possible to the power and accessibility requirements outlined above, it was a compromise, primarily because of our limited resources. The biggest compromise was the small number of terminals supported, which limited the input and output capacity of the system. Also we were unable to include special hardware for coin operation, so access to the first system was free.

In most other respects, however, the first system was a reasonable test bed for our ideas. We chose to have the database consist of "messages" that were completely unstructured, arbitrarily long sections of text in order to let people say what they wanted to without undue formatting constraints. We chose to organize the database by allowing people to assign any number of self-chosen "index words" to a message, thus putting it under any subject headings where they thought others might look for such information. We spent seven months testing and revising the user interface, working with individuals who had never used computers before. This resulted in a system that was nonthreatening and easy to use. Finally, we chose an uncompromising policy of noncensorship of the information provided, both to reduce the cost of the system (since we didn't have to pay someone to review information) and to reduce the temptation to impose an institutional standard on what ideas and issues the system would address.

The first system began public operation on July 17, 1984, with a single terminal and a database consisting of about 600 messages we had entered ourselves, transcribed from traditional bulletin boards, and collected from people using earlier demonstration versions of the system. The original terminal was located in a cultural center and meeting space. Within two months, two more terminals were added, one at a grocery store and one at a department store. Several months later a fourth terminal was added at a second grocery store, near the most heavily used bulletin board (nonelectronic) in the city. The terminals remained in operation over four years.

The technical aspects of the first system functioned very well; most of our downtime was attributable to site sponsors physically moving the terminals around, power failures, and so on rather than hardware or software failures per se. The system requires little manual intervention, so staffing requirements for dealing with technical problems were minimal (the system was run without any paid staff). Two problems we feared we might have with public terminals, theft and vandalism, never arose.

Ease of use is somewhat hard to measure, but a large number of people used the system with little or no help from us. Owing to limited resources, we put very little effort into training users, and yet the terminals stayed busy doing reasonable things a significant percentage of the time (the terminals were in use about 25% of the time they were available—about six hours of use per day).

Explicit user comments about the system ran the gamut from joy at "how easy it is to use, and I've never used a computer before" to long diatribes on how it ought to work some other way.

Although many people used the system successfully, it was apparent from examining session transcripts that most users got into occasional trouble, or were consistently confused about certain things. Also, we had no way to measure how many people saw the system but were inclined not to try it.

Our initial expectation was that with such a small system, not enough information would be collected to hold anyone's interest. Thus we anticipated having to be very active in feeding new information into the database, and encouraging other institutional information providers to do so. For better or for worse, this never happened, so the database reflected whatever happened to enter the minds of the users of the public terminals.

Since the system was not heavily publicized, most people were exposed to it by accident. Thus users generally had no clear idea of something they wanted to say or look for when using the system. As might be expected in these circumstances, a lot of people would just play, typing anything just to see the cursor move around. This caused a lot of nonsense messages to appear in the database.

All that being said, the level and types of use of the system were encouraging. Most of our basic expectations were met or exceeded by the first system. Most essentially, people were willing to contribute information even though receiving no immediate gain, and people used the database to search for information, and even entered questions into the database (for subsequent users to answer) if they couldn't find what they wanted.

Even with the small number of terminals, a wide variety of use patterns were exhibited. Besides typical classified ad activities like selling cars and looking for roommates, people published poetry, discussed politics and witchcraft, and found bicycling partners. Even with the small number of terminals, interesting conversations and interactions occurred.

Our policy of not editing or censoring information worked fairly well. We had only a very few instances (five out of over 10,000 messages) where we were asked to remove a message that someone perceived as damaging. In each of those cases the messages in question were clearly offensive, without redeeming content, and sources of harassment, so we had no reason not to comply with the requests. In each of those cases, we were able to correct the problem and reach an understanding with the person drawing the message to our attention.

The main problem with our policy of not filtering messages was not messages with offensive content, but messages with no content whatsoever. These resulted from people "trying out" the system without really having anything to say. These messages might consist of random characters, or unordered collections of sexually explicit words. The presence of these messages (which formed 10-20% of the database) created a negative impression among browsers as to the quality of the database, even though the majority of the messages had worthwhile, or at least entertaining, content.

DEVELOPMENT OF THE SECOND SYSTEM

Despite a confirmation of our basic ideas about the suitability of the technology to public settings, the use by people without computer experience, the variety of types of messages, and the low incidence of abuse, the first system revealed a number of problems that we wanted to correct.

Chief among these was our desire to provide more tools for organizing information. The first system provided a number of tools for searching for messages, but they were complex and hard to use. Furthermore, there was no good way for a user to save work done to track down relevant messages, or share the results of that work with other users. All our users shared a sense that the information on the system needed a much higher degree of organization to be really valuable. We needed to decrease the frustration of the person searching the database by reducing the amount of work required to do a search and the number of irrelevant messages encountered.

A related problem was that the user interface design we used in the first system wasn't readily expandable to support a large number of options. This meant we needed a more powerful paradigm to support the expanded set of organizing tools.

We wanted to test a larger system, which, in light of a limited budget, meant we needed to reduce the per-terminal cost. We also wanted to test the coin-operated terminal concept.

Finally, we wanted to try a much more hands-on approach than we had used the first time. We wanted to examine the effect of being actively involved in promoting the system, recruiting information providers, and putting information on-line.

Fortunately, technological advances made solutions to all these problems possible. The price of low-end IBM-PC compatible machines had dropped to the point where it was cost-effective to build one into each terminal. We adopted the concept of putting all user interface functions out at the terminal itself. This allowed us to provide a very high-quality user interface without worrying about limited communications bandwidth between the terminal and the central machine. Also, this intelligence could be used to run the coinbox mechanism. By limiting the central machine to database and administrative functions, many more terminals could be supported on a given piece of hardware. The increased capabilities of high-end PC class machines allowed us to move away from the proprietary, expensive central computer used in the first system. The combination of all these effects allowed us to put together a ten-terminal system (funded by the Telecommunications Education Trust, established by the California Public Utilities Commission), for approximately what the four-terminal system had cost four years earlier.

DESCRIPTION OF THE CURRENT SYSTEM

Community Memory sites are located in Berkeley at the main public library and three branches, a senior center, a neighborhood development corporation, an office building that houses nonprofit groups, a university dormitory and meeting center, and two laundromats. Because over half of the terminals are situated in institutions that serve the economically disadvantaged, participants include homeless people, seniors, low income people, and minority youth—constituencies who might otherwise be barred from participating in community dialogue and decision making.

Messages are the basic units of information on the network, and are grouped by topic in "forums." A message can be included in more than one forum. Since anyone may start a new forum, there are no restrictions on what subjects or topics people discuss. Anyone who starts a new forum becomes that forum's host, and gains the authority to purge messages from his or her forum, thus keeping it topical and pertinent. Forum hosts also establish recommended index words, although message authors may specify their own index words for the messages they write.

Messages may be added directly to any forums or attached to a specific message as a direct response to that message. The opportunity to "talk back" to any message gives rise to conversation-like interaction. A response gains a response and long branches of messages grow from a single root message.

Although the 1980s were marked by an enormous increase in the number of people who had access to computers and the type of information resources they can supply, we believed that in part this change simply reinforced the split between the information rich and poor. To encourage those with little access to technology we worked to make the Community Memory network nonintimidating. The appearance of the computer was downplayed by enclosing the hardware in blond wood cabinets that serve as freestanding kiosks. Modified keyboards featured color-coded basic keys: yellow, red, green, lilac, and blue. Easy-to-read documentation totaling only 150 words, colored to match the appropriate key, is mounted above the keyboard for quick reference.

Participants can also access a user tutorial that reviews the basic keys and the system's structure. An on-line Help system is also available. The Community Memory system operator also responds to questions and suggestions and provides technical help to confused users. Under our initial Telecommunications Education Trust grant we provided drop in training sessions, training 200 people in six months, including 87 who had never used a computer before. On the basis of our experience in these trainings, and through examining transcripts of use at public terminals, we fine-tuned the user interface to alleviate common problems.

The kiosk includes a coin slot similar to ones found on pay phones. Reading messages on-line remains free. However, writing a message costs a quarter. Once a message is written, the author may return to it at a later date and edit it for free since all messages are password protected. Moreover, a participant who writes four messages gets her fifth for free. The coin box serves two functions: it is an effective "nonsense" filter, and an attempt at making each terminal self-supporting. Eight new messages need to be added each day at a terminal in order to cover phone costs. However, no terminal yet is self-supporting. Although "meaningless" messages have been stifled, it's unclear how many more people would write if messages were free.

Initially we gathered information from local institutions including a community calendar, listings from the Berkeley Public Library's information, and referral catalogue other material to include in the database. Unfortunately, we probably didn't demand enough "buy in" from information providers and the Project itself ended up maintaining a number of forums we had hoped would be hosted institutionally. Nonetheless, individuals and groups continued to come forward with a broad range of information.

Within two years the number of forums exploded from an initial 20 to more than 90. Some forums are ongoing. Others are timebound—such as a forum about the war with Iraq—and eventually fade.

We retained the same basic policy as with the initial system. No registration is required and "drop-in" use is encouraged. All participants can remain anonymous and we encourage complete freedom of speech with the exception of a rare message that encourages harassment.

Low cost, durable, and easy to use, the network currently facilitates dialogue, information-sharing, and constituency-building. Two thousand people each month use Community Memory to share ideas and inspirations, exchange goods and services, meet, talk, gossip, debate and support each other. Over 200 small businesses and community groups have used use Community Memory to announce meetings, publicize events, promote services, recruit new members, find volunteers, advertise for staff, and assist in community organizing. Still the primary users of the Community Memory system are individuals who do not have computers at homes as a rule, do not make their living from the manipulation of language, use public transit, and generally are an atypical group of computer networkers.

Many participants use Community Memory as a bulletin board—to post messages about needing a roommate or selling a bicycle, finding a new employee or promoting child care, gardening or towing services. Others use Community Memory to track down information from local institutions—to scan the Berkeley City Council agenda, to find social service information for seniors or homeless people.

We developed a summer program for disadvantaged youth. Teenagers participated in ongoing discussions about issues that mattered to them as well as creating a Young People's Yellow Pages as part of Operation: In Effect!! Developed in partnership with local youth agencies, Operation: In Effect!! was structured to build leadership, provide mainstream language and computer skills, develop peer support, and create an ongoing source of local information for youth.

Participants developed other uses. Berkeley's cable TV consultant answered queries from cable subscribers as part of her community needs assessment. An Ecology Center board member fielded questions about recycling. A senior citizen decided that rather than listing local poetry readings (information easily available elsewhere), he would encourage local poets to publish their work on-line. In response to the troop build up before the war with Iraq, Country Joe MacDonald pulled together a group of veterans to create an interactive War Memorial. An out-of-work musician created a Musician's Exchange to share information about professional opportunities.

Active participants are rarely spokespeople or opinion makers. However, we often see people interacting with each other on-line who ordinarily rarely interact. A forum about the war in the Gulf included comments from both peace activists and marines. A forum about University development in Berkeley's controversial People's Park engaged both University of California students and homeless people.

Some of the most compelling messages are extremely intimate, encouraged by the network's policy allowing anonymity. One man who needed a reason to go on living was inundated by suggestions. Another man, who said he'd been avoiding relationships for years, claimed to have fallen in love as a result of confidence he gained using the net. A sex worker described her ambivalence about her job and eventually found other work.

CONCLUSION AND FUTURE

Since the Community Memory Project began testing the potential of community computer networks, there has been a growing interest in local networks. A few major institutions that can provide ongoing support and attract outside funds have started such systems. The City of Santa Monica's Public Electronic Network, Case Western Reserve's Cleveland FreeNet, as well as less interactive systems designed as municipal information systems such as the Public Technology Institute's 24 Hour City Hall, are all based on Community Memory's initial experiments.

Community Memory plays a unique role, however, because of our commitment to an open, public access network. Our experience has demonstrated that an open network provides the best opportunity for a broad range of people and institutions to create an on-line neighborhood.

As a small nonprofit leaning heavily on volunteers to survive, we are trying to work more closely with large local institutions such as the University of California and the city of Berkeley to provide ongoing support. We are also consulting with the city of Berkeley as they work to provide public access to their municipal computer network. We will be stepping up our ongoing commitment to advocating for access to technology in an attempt to bridge the chasm between the information haves and the have nots. Also we are interested in encouraging organizations that have greater resources than we do to test out the ideas and values we have pioneered for 20 years.

Across the nation many more individuals and groups could benefit from access to computer networks than currently participate online. We have found that when ordinary people have access to these tools, they see the value of them in a unique way. Ironically, many who see computers as mysterious, impersonal, and threatening may actually have the most to gain. A young single mother who finds a babysitter over Community Memory begins to see computer networks not as instruments for the benefit of big business or the IRS, but as tools that she can use to gain greater control of her life. Over the network, a homeless person can interact with other community members, not as a specimen of social turmoil, but as an equal participant in community life.

We believe that easy-to-use telecommunications can put diverse people in touch with their communities in new ways that revitalize links with neighbors and local institutions. The Community Memory Project proves that computer technology can enhance community life by providing pertinent, user-friendly tools that go far beyond word processing, Nintendo, or ATM machines. If knowledge is power, actively using that knowledge is empowering. The Community Memory Project creates a reassuring, replicable way for a broad cross-section of society to participate in community dialogue, debate, and discussion.

14

*The Rainbow Pages: Building Community With Voice Technology**

*Paul Resnick***

AT&T Bell Laboratories

Mel King

MIT Department of Urban Studies

INTRODUCTION

There is no such thing as a poor community. Even neighborhoods without much money have substantial human resources. Often, however, the human resources are not

* This chapter appeared in *Proceedings of DIAC-90: Directions and Implications of Advanced Computing.* Boston, MA, July 1990.

** The author received support from an NSF graduate Fellowship.

appreciated or utilized, partly because people do not have information about each other and about what their neighborhood has to offer. For example, a family whose oil heater is broken may go cold for lack of knowledge that someone just down the block knows how to fix it.

We are developing a voice bulletin board, which we call the Rainbow Pages, for the South End, a neighborhood in Boston. It will be accessible free of charge from any touchtone telephone. We hope that the Rainbow Pages will foster better *utilization* of human resources, which will create a material payoff. We also hope it will foster *an appreciation* of the resources available in the neighborhood, which will have a psychological payoff.

Bulletin boards of all kinds have great potential for building and maintaining communities. Universities put paper bulletin boards in corridors and lounges and the city of Cambridge, Massachusetts even has outdoor bulletin boards on main thoroughfares. The greatest asset of a bulletin board is that the person who posts a flyer does not need to know in advance all of the people who might be interested in reading it. Complementing that feature, if a bulletin board is sufficiently well organized and has social conventions governing its use, most people who are not interested in a flyer need never even look at it. As well as disseminating information efficiently, a paper bulletin board may be a location where conversations begin: Two people reading a flyer have a topic on which to begin a conversation.

A major problem with paper bulletin boards is accessibility. The people who are interested in a flyer have to pass by the bulletin board and have spare time right then to stop and read the message. Even if they read the flyer, they might forget important information unless they copy it down or take the flyer with them, which would preclude others from reading it.

In certain settings, electronic bulletin boards are an improvement over paper bulletin boards. First, the participants can be physically separated, sometimes by thousands of miles. Second, a user can choose to read messages whenever she has spare time, rather than having to read a flyer while rushing to somewhere else. Finally, a user can copy an electronic bulletin board message or print it out without removing it from the bulletin board.

Unfortunately, electronic bulletin boards have accessibility problems of their own: They require computers as front ends. In poorer communities few people have access to computers. Some groups that have set up public access electronic bulletin boards have simply restricted the set of potential users to people who already have access to computers (e.g., Cleveland Free-Net, USENET, PeaceNet). Other groups have put computers or terminals in public locations (e.g., Community Memory [Levy, 1984], New York Youth Network,[Chaiklin and Schrum, 1990] Santa Monica Public Electronic Network [Guthrie, Schmitiz, Ryu, Rogers, & Dutton, 1990; Antonoff, 1989).

A voice bulletin board, on the other hand, need not suffer from such accessibility problems, because it uses a touchtone telephone rather than a computer as a front-end. A person calls up, navigates through the recorded announcements by pressing buttons on the telephone keypad, and perhaps records a message of her own. That solves three accessibility problems. First, access is mostly not restricted by income, because, in this country, even a very poor family, so long as it has a home, is likely to have a telephone. Second, access is not restricted by time or location, since it is easy to find a public phone even when one is away from home. Third, many people are far more proficient at speaking and listening than at writing and reading: A voice bulletin board does not restrict access by literacy skills.

This chapter first describes the information sharing needs of Boston's South End and our design of the Rainbow Pages to meet those needs. Then, we discuss our user interface innovations for voice bulletin boards that, hopefully, will make it easy for callers to use the Rainbow Pages. We present results from a successful use of voice technology for a public information line about Nelson Mandela's visit to Boston in June, 1990. Finally, we discuss our phased introduction plan for the Rainbow Pages itself.

Community Needs

We begin with the dual goals of improving the material quality of life for residents of Boston's South End and of enhancing the sense of community. For example, if a resident finds someone to fix his washing machine at a reasonable price or learns about an interesting art exhibit to go to, that improves his quality of life. A sense of community is less tangible: It is largely a matter of self-definition. It occurs when people define themselves and their neighbors in ways that say they are deserving and have resources, when people stick together in hard times, when people have enough pride in their neighborhood that they choose to stay there, even if they have enough money to move elsewhere. We believe that a system that disseminates information about the skills of neighborhood residents, about community organizations and events, and about neighborhood struggles and achievements can help to accomplish both the material and community-building goals.

Boston's South End is a racially, ethnically, and economically mixed residential community, just a few blocks south of downtown. Its population of about 26,000 includes significant Black, Hispanic, Chinese, Lebanese, and Gay communities. Its housing stock ranges from public housing developments (some rundown, others well-maintained) to modest rental units to gentrified apartments and condominiums. Many residents take pride in the diversity of the South End.

The need for a community information center is best illustrated by an incident that occurred at a tenants' meeting of a public housing development. Mel King led a discussion around issues of community economic development, based on the argument that changes at the microeconomic level are the key to macrolevel improvements. He discussed the concepts of import and export of goods and services to and from the neighborhood, then brought up an alternative, trade within the neighborhood. One tenant volunteered that he could fix washing machines for other people in the neighborhood. Another tenant exclaimed that she had been trying to get her machine fixed for six months, but that repair companies had been unwilling to come to the housing development.

At that point, the energy level in the room jumped. Someone else needed a wedding dress for her daughter and found another person in the room not only to sew the dress but to bake the wedding cake as well. One person even offered his expertise at filling out tax forms. There was amazement around the room at how much the 20-25 people had to offer each other.

A community information center can be an electronic marketplace, helping neighborhood residents to make the same kinds of matches that were made at that tenants' meeting. In addition to their positive economic impact, such transactions help to build up the relationships with multiple roles that are a necessary ingredient in establishing a sense of community. If your barber is also in your church and serves on a PTA committee at the school where you are a teacher, as well as being a neighbor who you do handyman jobs for, then there is a chance for community.

Another function of a community information center is to provide information about church and community organizations. Those organizations provide important services in urban settings, including after school youth programs, job training, counseling, emergency food aid, and housing construction. Especially for someone who has just moved into a neighborhood, a listing of all the churches and community organizations, and the programs that they sponsor, would be of great value.

A third function of a community information center is to disseminate community news and opinion. The citywide news media cover only bad news in poorer neighborhoods, usually drugs and crime. Such coverage certainly does not create community pride. In order to get a balanced and informative self-portrait, poorer communities need to create their own news channels. Radio stations and community newspapers are probably the best way to do that, but a community information center can also help. One way is to publicize the school honor rolls, and interesting health care and housing statistics. Another way is to provide a public opinion forum for controversial issues, such as the Boston Police Department's current stop and search policy against youth in Black neighborhoods. An opinion forum could have a similar format to a radio talk show, but also allow for voting on issues that have clear sets of alternatives.

Organizations need a way to publicize events such as tenant meetings, school plays, and so on. Existing methods are adequate but leave much room for improvement. For example, posting flyers outside takes a long time. Sending in listings to newspapers and radio stations requires a lot of lead time. If it is not a big event, the announcement may not be aired at all.

Finally, a community information center can provide a forum for people to share their creativity with each other. The poetry corner is an especially popular feature of the New York Youth Network. Some people also have special talents as joke or story tellers that they can share. Group games, such as fictionary, in which people make up fake definitions for words, may also be appropriate.

Overall, a community information center can help people find events, organizations, community news, goods, and services. All of these functions are of immediate benefit to the people who use the information center. These functions also have the potential to improve the sense of community: They help people to meet each other, to get a sense that the neighborhood has human resources and is a place where "things are happening."

Application Design

With these community needs in mind, we have designed a community information center, Rainbow Pages, as shown in Figure 14-1. To illustrate how users would find and record information, consider two scenarios: A first-time caller exploring the system and an experienced user calling to record event announcements for an organization.

Consider a first-time caller who is told by a friend that a lot of useful services are available at low rates. He is given the phone number and goes home to try it. He calls and hears a welcoming announcement in five languages. He understands the English welcoming message with some difficulty but is relieved to hear (in Spanish) that he can press **3** to get the rest of the prompts in Spanish. He does so, and the system now recites the second layer menu in Spanish. The user presses **1** for Classified Ads, then **3** for Services Offered. At that point, other people's recorded offers of services are presented in the form of a list through which the user can skip forward and backward.[1]

This scenario, then, demands that a user, without the aid of any instruction or written materials, be able to access information. If the user's friend gives him some instruction, such as, "Press 3 as soon as you hear it start talking, so you can get everything in Spanish," then he can get started even more quickly. Similarly, if the user consults written materials that we will distribute widely in the community, he will have an easier time choosing the correct branches to take. Thus, with no aids, a novice user can follow the prompts to get started, but can do even better with spoken or written instructions.

Now consider the scenario of the experienced user who is making her biweekly call to record announcements for her community organization. As soon as the system answers her call, she presses **3-2-#-5-1-7-#-3**. The first two digits choose Spanish for the prompts and navigate her to the branch for the Directory of Community Organizations. **#** Initiates entry of the id number for her organization, which is 517, and the second **#** terminates entry of the id number. That skips her forward in the directory to her organization's listing. The final **3** indicates that she would like to add or change information associated with the organization. She is prompted to enter a password, then is allowed to record event announcements.

Each event announcement is a semistructured object (Malone, Grant, Lai, Rao, & Rosenblitt,1987; Schmandt & Arons, 1984). The user fills in an "auditory form" with entry blanks for the date, a short description (less than 10 seconds), a longer description, the sponsoring organization, the location, and a contact person and phone number. The user speaks the information for most of the entry blanks, keys in the date with touch tones, so that the Events Calendar can sort events by date. The sponsoring organization

---

[1] Over time, there might be enough offerings in a category to warrant splitting it into subcategories, It is better to add subcategories as needed than to create many empty subcategories initially.

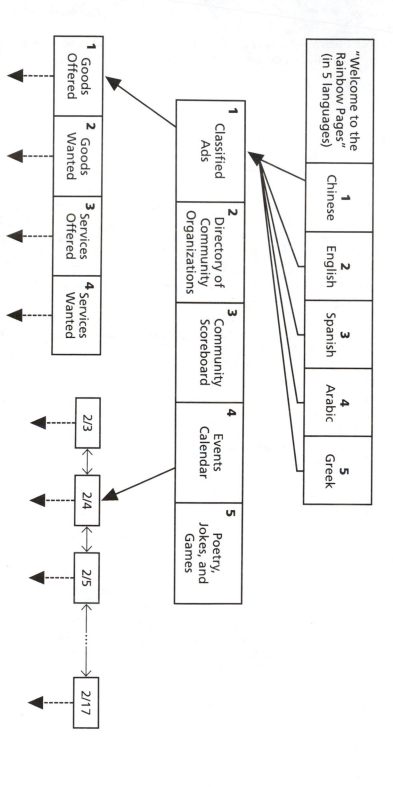

Figure 14-1. The layout of the Rainbow Pages Community Information Center as it would be presented to the user on February 4. (The Events Calendar changes each day.) Callers start at the top left, then press touch tone buttons to navigate to the information that interests them.

is filled in automatically, since she has already entered in the password for her organization. Her event announcements can then be accessed by future callers either from the Events Calendar for the appropriate date, or through the Directory of Community Organizations.

Overall, the Rainbow Pages is designed to be used by a beginner with no aids, but to gracefully allow users to learn more advanced features and take advantage of written instructions. The eventual goal is to have a two-page instruction manual, including one page for Figures 14-1 and 14-2, and a business card-sized summary.

USER INTERFACE INNOVATIONS

Although voice bulletin boards offer accessibility advantages over other electronic bulletin boards, it is harder to design a good interface for a voice bulletin board. With a visual interface, the user can see a whole screenful of text at once. For example, with a visual interface the user might see all of Figure 14-1 when making a choice at the top level. By contrast, existing audio interfaces are strictly serial, speaking one word at a time.[2] A second difficulty is that many people can read

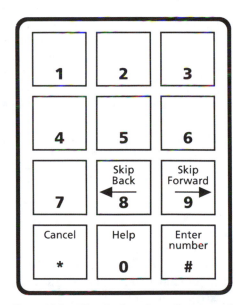

Figure 14-2. The telephone keypad commands,
Buttons 1 through 6 are reserved for numbered
menu opions.

---

[2] Note that this may not be an inherent limitation of audio interfaces. After all, people do manage to do at least some processing of mulitple conversations at cocktail parties.

a sentence silently much faster than it can be read aloud. Together, these two deficiencies amount to a bandwidth problem: It takes much longer to present the same amount of text through auditory than through visual channels. One final difficulty for telephone interfaces is that there are only twelve buttons available for the user to enter commands.

Some of these difficulties are readily apparent in the current generation of telephone-based interfaces, which use numbered menus. For example, a telephone banking system might recite: "Press one for account update, two for check update, three for account balances..." Such a menu can be effective if the options decompose nicely into distinct categories with short descriptions. Otherwise, the user needs to listen through the whole menu before deciding which option is appropriate. By then, she may have forgotten whether to press **1** or **2** for account update.

We have made improvements to purely menu-based interfaces that give the user more control and allow better use of the limited available bandwidth. Telephone keys **1** through **6** are still used for numbered menu choices. Keys **8** and **9**, respectively, are used to skip backward and forward by one message (Figure 14-2). ***** Allows the user to move back up to the previous menu. Our keypad layout follows many of the design guidelines in [Norman], such as using "natural mappings" (the skip back button is to the left of the skip forward button) and drawing on existing social conventions (dial the operator for help).

The reservation of **8** and **9** as arrow keys allows the use of lists and other structures besides menus. For example, structuring the event announcements for a given day as a list has several advantages over creating a menu with a number for each event. First, it matches the usual way of presenting events in newspapers and newsletters. Second, the user need not listen for the numbers associated with the event names, but can concentrate on the contents of the announcements instead. Third, the user chooses how much of each announcement to hear (**8** and **9** are available to interrupt boring announcements) instead of the designer choosing how long to make the menu prompts. Finally, using the list avoids the need for an additional layer in the tree structure of Figure 14-1, which should make it easier for users to keep track of where they are.

The use of audio forms for semistructured input has several advantages. First, the user is reminded separately of all the important pieces of information to record. Second, the system can change the order or the selection of which parts to play back, depending on the context. For example, in a list of events sponsored by an organization, the organizations's name need not be repeated each time, whereas it should be repeated when the announcements are accessed through the events calendar, where they are mixed in with events sponsored by other organizations. Third, by piecing together parts of different messages, it is possible to automatically provide a form of context-sensitive help. Finally, the symbolic input of some information, such as the date of an event, allows the system to sort the recorded announcements in appropriate ways, and even to take such actions as deleting old announcements.

COMMUNITY INTRODUCTION PLAN

We have developed a community introduction plan that we hope will improve the chances of gaining popular acceptance for the Rainbow Pages. The major goals of the introduction plan are to test and improve the user interface, revise the structure of the information center to more closely match community needs, and to gather sufficient postings so that the system will contain useful recordings when it is first widely publicized. A secondary goal of the introduction plan is to identify and train individuals to maintain the bulletin boards. Maintenance includes deleting obsolete and inappropriate messages and moderating-editing the news and opinion sections. The introduction plan attempts to draw on the existing resources of the South End.

The United South End/Lower Roxbury Community Development Corporation (UDC), has agreed to help with initial user interface testing. Through their contacts, they will find volunteers from the community. We will seed a restricted version of the Rainbow Pages with information and ask the volunteers to perform retrieval and recording tasks while we observe them. We will then revise the interface as needed.

We will attempt to involve other community organizations prior to a public announcement of the system. At a minimum, we would like to have a recorded directory of all of the organizations and the programs that they offer. We will also ask for feedback on the overall structure, as to whether it meets their perceptions of the community's needs. Finally, we will ask them to record announcements of events just after the official unveiling of the system.

Once we have built up a base of information in the system during the pilot testing phase, we will announce the system publicly. This will include press releases to local media, posting of flyers on the streets and in local businesses and community organizations, and speaking appearances any place that will have us. Following this initial publicity blitz, we will publicize statistics on system usage. Hopefully, the individuals and organizations who have recorded information will continue to do so if their recordings have been listened to frequently.

At least initially, we will maintain the system ourselves. During the introduction process, however, we will be looking for a group of people that can take over maintenance tasks on a longer-term basis. One idea is to recruit a youth group, either through a school, a community organization, or a church, to take on the responsibilities. For example, a communications class in a community college or high school could gain experience in reporting local news, in public speaking, and in using computer technology.

TECHNOLOGY AND SYSTEM STATUS

One of the exciting aspects of the Rainbow Pages is that the hardware and system software necessary for a voice bulletin board with space for 9 hours of recorded speech can be purchased for about $2000, and prices are coming down every month. The required hardware is an IBM AT-compatible PC with a large-capacity hard disk and a commercially available voice card. A telephone line plugs into the voice card, which performs such functions as detecting touchtones and digitizing speech that comes in over the telephone line so that it can be stored on the computer's hard disk. The software for the Rainbow Pages is written in C.

If the Rainbow Pages is successful in Boston's South End, we hope to replicate it in other neighborhoods. People in other communities will be able to call up the South End bulletin board to explore the possibilities it offers, which should facilitate the spread of the technology. The low price tag should help, too.

CONCLUSION

The chorus of calls for community-based computing initiatives is a three-part harmony. One voice calls for community-based organizations to be effective users of computers, in the form of database, spreadsheet, and desktop publishing technology. Another voice sounds that people in disadvantaged communities should not be just users, but should learn computer skills so that they can get the good jobs that, increasingly, are available only to the computer literate. The third voice claims that people in disadvantaged communities should have access as users to the benefits of computer technology, such as communication networks, news services, and databases of toxic waste locations. This paper falls in the last camp. In particular, we are trying to bring the benefits of a communication network, in the form of a voice bulletin board, to a neighborhood in Boston, using the existing technology base of touchtone telephones.

In the book *Chain of Change*, King (1981) charted the stages of the struggles for Black Community Development in Boston, from the service stage, to the organizing stage, to the institution building stage. He argues that the next stage requires a struggle for minds as well as for material resources. When a community *believes* that it has skills and internal resources, it will be able to lobby for its share of external resources and make effective use of the resources it acquires.

The Rainbow Pages will help people to find out about each other and about their neighborhood. Such information can improve the quality of life for the individuals who get the information, and increase the self-sufficiency of the neighborhood. We also believe that such information is one key in the struggle for minds that enables a neighborhood to become an empowered community. The experiment is just beginning: Stay tuned.

EPILOGUE

A full-fledged community information center is still on the horizon. In the past three and a half years, however, I developed, tested, and refined many simpler applications such as event calendars and issue discussions that could be components of such a system.

The first successful application provided information about Nelson Mandela's visit to Boston on June 23, 1990. The system answered nearly 1400 calls in the 10 days before Mandela's visit, dispensing information about the schedule of events and allowing callers to leave their names and addresses if they wanted to volunteer. More than 200 did so.

The Boston Peace and Justice Events Hotline has been in continuous operation since January 1990. Unlike the Mandela information line, anyone can add a new event announcement, using a telephone form. During the Gulf War, the system handled nearly 2000 calls and approximately 30 different people posted announcements. The emcee at one citywide rally hailed it as the best source of up to date information about peace activities. A short sound clip even appeared in a National Public Radio story. Usage waned after the Gulf War, but then stabilized at 10–15 calls per day. The phone number, as of December 1993, is 617-787-6809.

Several other applications, including information sharing systems for elementary school teachers and MIT students, had mixed success. (See Resnick, 1993 for details.)

Preparation for the field trials led to the development of a software toolkit (Resnick, 1993). The toolkit makes it easy to create new event calendar and issue discussion bulletin boards. A version that handles one call at a time is available free for noncommercial uses. A commercial version that handles many simultaneous phone calls may eventually be available.

A wildly optimistic vision can provide sustenance in times of doubt or unexpected setbacks. This paper served that role for me, keeping a dream alive, somewhere over the rainbow. Now it is time to update the dream, at least the technology part of it. Text- and voice-based electronic bulletin boards should merge: Telephones, fax machines, and computers should all provide access to the same collection of information.

REFERENCES

Antonoff, M. (1989). "Fighting city hall at 2400 baud. *Personal Computing 13*:170–172.

Chaiklin, S., & Schrum. Community-based telecommunications. Presented at the *Third Guelph Symposium on Computer Mediated Communication*, University of Guelph, Ontario, Canada, May 15–17, 1990.

Guthrie, K., Schmitiz, J., Ryu, D., Rogers, E., & Dutton, W. (1990). Communication technology and democratic participation: The PEN system in Santa Monica, Presented at the *ACM Conference on Computers and the Quality of Life*. Washington, DC.

King, M. (1981). *Chain of change: Struggles for black community development*. Boston: End Press.

Levy, S. (1984). *Hackers: heroes of the computer revolution*. New York: Bantam Doubleday Dell.

Malone, T. W., Grant, K. R., Lai, K. Y., Rao, R., & Rosenblitt, D. (1987). Semi-structured messages are surprisingly useful for computer-supported cooperative work. *ACM Transactions on Office Information Systems* 5(2):115–131.

Norman, D. (1988). *The psychology of everyday things*. New York: Basic Books.

Resnick, P. (1993). Phone-based CSCW:Tools and trials. *ACM Transactions on Information Systems.*

Schmandt, C., & Arons, B. (1984). A conversational telephone messaging system. *IEEE Transactions on Consumer Electronics,* CE-30.

15

*Building Community Networks**

Philip E. Agre
University of California, San Diego

The community networking movement has grown rapidly over the last several years from a few pioneering projects such as Berkeley Community Memory (Levy, 1984) and Big Sky Telegraph (Odasz, 1991) to a full-blown social movement (cf. Kling & Iacono, 1988). This movement includes computer people, librarians, educators, government employees, and ordinary citizens who believe in the democratic values of open access to information. Some reports on community networking movements, mostly circulated informally or over the Internet, have been written from the point of view of designers (Cisler, 1993; Schuler, 1994). In providing a service to the general computer-using public, these designers must face a broad range of technical and social issues, and the papers that synthesize their experiences have been valuable as professional contributions and cultural documents alike. Others have been written by foundations seeking to

*This chapter is an edited transcript of a speech I contributed to the British Columbia Information Policy Conference. I would like to thank Brian Campbell for his role in organizing this conference. Another version of this transcript appeared in *The Network Observer 1* (12), December, 1994.

develop a rational strategy for funding community networking projects as part of a larger program of community development (Civille, Fidelman, & Altobello, 1993; Morino, 1994).

My own goal here is different. I propose to place the social movement of community networking in the context of the social organization of knowledge in communities. To this end, let us distinguish between two valid perspectives on community networking, the aerial view and the ground view.

When taking the ground view one asks, how can I best go about building my community network? It is a normative question, oriented to action in concrete circumstances.

When taking the aerial view, by contrast, one asks, how do communities take hold of computing and networking? It is an empirical question, oriented to developing concepts and making certain kinds of social maps, and it posits "the community" as an active agent of a collective sort. It is a problematic question, of course, because it presupposes some analysis of what a community is, what it means to speak of a community taking hold of something, how to maintain a consciousness simultaneously of the unitary action of a community and its often deeply divided daily reality, and so forth. Nonetheless, I would like to sketch some of the issues that arise in any attempt to adopt an aerial view on community networking. Communities differ, of course, and the analysis presented here has been shaped by my own experiences in urban settings in the United States. The point of this type of inquiry is not to make generalizations, although it is hard to avoid making generalizations, but rather to offer some potentially useful concepts—a handy reference card or checklist that one might take into an analysis of any particular setting. The utility of these concepts will be tested in attempts to apply them to a variety of settings.

THE DEMOCRATIC TECHNOLOGY MOVEMENT

One context for an aerial-view analysis of computer networking is what might be called the democratic technology movement: an increasingly global, politically diverse, loosely organized, heavily networked movement of grassroots activists who wish simultaneously to employ computer networking to support a range of democratic projects *and* to contest the future architectural and institutional development of the global information infrastructure in order to ensure that opportunities for this kind of technologically mediated democratic organizing are preserved and expanded in the future. This movement might be analyzed on three levels.

On the first level is the concept, widespread both in the media and in the thinking of a remarkably broad range of social activists outside the computer-and-information world, of "equity of access to the information superhighway." Although the widespread consciousness of this idea has contributed to unprecedented levels of public involvement in technology policy issues, the notion of "access" has important limitations. "Access" presupposes that the technology and its architecture are givens, that "access" to that commodity is scarce, and that the issue is one of an equitable distribution of that commodity. These assumptions are at least arguable in the case of past technologies such as Plain Old Telephone Service, but they do not accurately describe the situation with emerging digital technologies. Many urgent issues concern the future shape of network architectures, and the notion of "access" does not do justice to the possibility and necessity of acting on these issues. Bandwidth is rapidly getting cheaper, but concern is widespread that a poor architecture or the erosion of common carrier and universal service principles might lock large segments of the population out of full participation in society.

On the second level are specific movements, such as the largely libertarian on-line community that is concerned with cryptography and other privacy issues, and the largely progressive and communitarian local and regional movements for community networking, educational networking, preservation and expansion of the social role of libraries, among others. These movements are the focus of my analysis here.

At the same time, it is worth distinguishing a third level of the democratic technology movement, namely the participatory design movement that began with a collaboration of labor unions and academics in Scandinavia (Greenbaum & Kyng, 1990), and that has spread to North America through work by industrial researchers and activists (Schuler & Namioka, 1993). Participatory design focuses not just on choices about technologies but also on the process through which technologies are designed, with an emphasis on involving all stakeholders in the design process in a democratic fashion. This focus on process comes naturally to the community networking movement, given the considerable reflection and creativity involved in reaching out to various stakeholders and getting them on board, and participatory design would encourage a deepening and systematization of this reflection on process.

COMPUTING AS COLLECTIVE ACTIVITY

The democratic technology movement challenges us to conceptualize computing as a collective activity—as something that communities and groups and networks of people do, not just individuals. This challenge in turn directs attention to the many ideological constructions of computing as an individual activity. These begin with the stereotype of the asocial computer nerd, but they extend much further. They are also found in certain visions of the "information superhighway," in which new technologies permit people to shop, work, and vote at home. This kind of vision is the antithesis of community and democracy, particularly when "interactivity" is conceived wholly as button-pushing to purchase commodities, gamble, or participate in plebiscites.

Individualistic conceptions of computing are found in even subtler places as well. Although training and good user interfaces are certainly important, in my experience many arguments for these things are really, underneath, arguments for a one-person-one-computer view of computing. In real life, however, computing is almost always, as a matter of necessity, something that people do as part of extended social networks. It is true that people often use computers while sitting alone in front of a terminal. But this does not change the complex facts of individuals' embeddings in larger social networks. Recent research has demonstrated the enormous role of the associational structure of social networks in both political and economic life (Granovetter, 1995; Putnam, 1993), and it seems likely that participation in computer networking should reflect this structure in some way. To understand this larger context from an aerial view, it is necessary to ask the much more difficult question of how communities take hold of computing and networking.

To begin with, any given community will most likely have several nuclei of interest in computer networking. These nuclei might be computer professionals, business owners, teachers, librarians, retired people keeping in touch with their families—anybody who has been exposed to the benefits of networking and wishes to take some initiative to secure these benefits for themselves or their group. These people probably will have a diversity of understandings of themselves, their communities, their goals, and the technology itself, and they will not automatically encounter one another or necessarily see themselves as having anything in common as a group.

The technology, however, does its best to disrupt this picture of scattered participation. Computers, after all, are complex and delicate machines. Although some people assert that mass participation in computing requires that computers be stripped down and idiot-proofed, another perspective is that the complexity of computers, or that complexity that is necessary and not just bad design, is a positive force for bringing people together into user groups, a form of collective action that has been little written about despite the dozens or hundreds of such groups to be found in most cities in North America and in many other places as well. Many Macintosh user groups, for example, have hundreds or thousands of members. These groups bring people together through a complex pattern of interests, including users seeking information and software for their own use, consultants maintaining their referral networks, other computer professionals keeping their knowledge up-to-date, vendors selling their wares, volunteer system operators trying to build communities on their bulletin boards, and so forth. Underneath, though, the fuel that drives these groups is the immense rate of change in the technology. People must band together to keep up with the changes and to anticipate where things are going in the future, and the result is a complex sociology of knowledge that warrants our attention on several grounds.

COMPUTING KNOWLEDGE AS COMMUNITY PROPERTY

The aerial view of computing suggests taking this analysis further by considering the distribution of computer knowledge through a community. Consider an analogy between knowledge about computers and knowledge about cars. Knowledge about cars really is community property. Various degrees of automotive expertise are widely distributed in most communities, and this is fortunate since expert knowledge is by its nature hard to evaluate and best obtained within a web of relationships of family or neighborhood or reputation. This expert knowledge, of course, is not distributed equally. As a cultural matter automotive knowledge, like computer knowledge, is heavily marked as a masculine domain, and the group settings within which this knowledge circulates—auto clubs or computer clubs—strongly tend to be homosocial in nature.

Access to reliable auto knowledge is also conditioned by the structure of an individual's social network, so that, as a rough generalization, working people whose social networks are structured by family and geography will tend to have better access to automotive knowledge than middle-class people whose social networks are structured more vocationally.

The point here is that the growth of computer networking, like any other social movement, is going to be shaped by the existing structures of social networks in a community. The civil rights movement in the United States grew largely out of churches, as has the conservative evangelical movement more recently. The Sierra Club's environmental activism grew out of that organization's nature hikes for families and singles. And groups like Amnesty International operate heavily through paper mail, with many small local chapters, since their base is not otherwise organized by community or vocational ties.

But computer networks also afford the creation of new forms of social connection among people, and I would suggest viewing a wide variety of network-based activities in terms of their immersion in these networks of interrelationship. Access to government information, for example, is usually of limited utility to isolated individuals unless those individuals are strongly motivated by a specific goal. Interest groups may thus retain an important role as intermediaries. The general point is that computer networks extend and transform existing social networks, becoming integral parts of them rather than replacing them. When the participants in a computer bulletin board decide to get their families together for a picnic, the result is a restoration of the normal order of things, namely computer networks as merely one among the many media through which people conduct their relationships.

Computer networks have a tremendous capacity, then, to bring people together by extending the already diverse and complex ties that people have among themselves. But the broad and diverse applicability of computer technology simultaneously makes it hard to help people incorporate the new technology into their lives. The functionality of computers is defined in very broad, abstract terms—"communication," "information," and so forth. But most people do not routinely think of themselves as communicating or using information. Rather they think of themselves as organizing social events, looking for work, persuading the city council to pass an ordinance, settling the kids' fights, getting dinner on the table, and so forth—activities bound up in a dense fabric of relationships and practical dilemmas, all of them defined more concretely than "communication" and "information."

If an individual or group is going to incorporate new computing technologies into their lives—assuming of course that this would actually be a beneficial thing for them to do—then they are going to have to travel a long cognitive path. Specifically, they are going to have to reconceptualize their own activities in terms that are commensurable with the concepts that underlie the technologies. They will have to see "looking for a job" as a matter of communication and information, and not just abstractly, but in terms of a real, practicable involvement in a system of human relationships—computer clubs, next-door computer gurus, kids' school activities, professional networks, and so forth. (For the analogous point in workplaces see Kling (1987); Nardi & Miller (1991).) Once they *do* make this transition, they are in a position to recognize some important commonalities with an enormous variety of other people who have come to place a personal importance on the future of computing and networking. But this will not happen automatically.

MESSAGES ABOUT COMPUTING

How, then, do people learn about computing and networking—that is to say, how do they become involved in the social organization of computing and networking? What routes do they take? No doubt many of them start with a general awareness of the discourses of information superhighways and equity of access. They might also hear stories about people using computers and networks through their participation in various kinds of groups (computer-related or not). They might hear the tales of computing and networking that their kids bring home from school, assuming that their kids' schools can afford such things, or their children's education might provide the impetus for a more active investigation of the issues. The fact is, little is known about the stories people hear about computing and networking—the messages that shape their understandings of the roles that these technologies might play in their own lives. Do these messages provide models for active and creative use of the technology, or do they point toward exciting but essentially passive processes of consumption? Do these messages portray computing as a collective activity or a solitary one? As something associated with particular social groups or social values? As settled and inevitable or as wide open to shaping by movements of ordinary people? No doubt the messages will not be univocal; nor will they all be received with equal attention or simple credulity.

An increasingly significant source of messages about networking is the advertising and public relations of commercial access providers such as America Online. These access providers have long cultivated the press, for example, by providing free accounts to journalists, and many television and newspaper stories exhibit a close alignment with the providers' marketing message, which essentially is that networking is something for ordinary people, and that ordinary people are having a good time right now talking about immediately accessible and interesting topics within the discussion groups of these services. As media messages about technology go, this type of message is an improvement on many other genres of technology tales (mad scientists, gee-whiz counterintuitive gizmos, apocalyptic disaster, the inevitable march of progress, so complicated that only Einstein can figure it out, and so on. But we should pay attention to the subtexts of these stories nonetheless, and we should also tell some others of our own.

This is one point at which the aerial view of community networking suggests strategies for work on the ground. A community networking project must build and maintain computers, but it must also help people to get involved with networking. Central to the process are stories. Talk to people in your community who are using computer networking. Ask them how they got involved. Listen to their stories. Ask permission to tell their stories to others. Take their stories apart into pieces—what messages about networking did they receive where? What other messages might they have received? Collect stories. Collect stories that fit under particular headings—stories about people who managed to get help with their computer problems, stories about people who reinvigorated their nonprofit organizations through the use of a bulletin board system, stories about people who brought their neighborhood closer together with networking, stories about people who called out for help on a network and got it, people who broke out of social isolation through networking, people who got involved in politics through networking, people who joined in a user group, people who served as networking evangelists in their particular social world, and people who made a difference in the technology itself through the force of their vision about how technology could be usefully brought into the lives of real people and real groups. It is important to categorize the stories—to name them in ways that help you to recognize when they are relevant, how they compare and contrast to other stories, what types of stories you have not been hearing, what messages about networking and people the stories really convey, and what difference it makes to tell them. Almost any categorization will suffice, so long as it directs attention to the forms and uses of stories about networking.

Telling the stories, of course, is the point. Tell the stories to journalists and city council members. Volunteer to speak in front of every organization and club in your community— tell them the stories and invite them to get involved in community networking. Keep telling the stories to like-minded people, and gather up their stories as well, since story sharing is very much a collective activity. Tell your stories on the net, and ask the people on the net to tell their own stories. Ask the people on the net if they have any stories of a specific type. ("We want to convince the city council to allocate a little money to get our bulletin board going, but they want to hear stories about what this has to do with their priority, namely regional economic development. Does anybody have any stories about this?")

Tell the stories in press releases. Create newsworthy events that focus attention on information issues in your community. Hold a panel discussion on the topic, ideally in a meeting room at your local public library. Get on the phone and find out who has ideas on the subject, and ideally who is doing something about them. Include the major community groups and the chamber of commerce. Send out a press release about the event to every publication within two hundred miles, especially the smaller newspapers.

At one level this advice is common sense—everybody knows that telling stories is a powerful way to communicate a vision. When done professionally, though, these activities of structured collecting and retelling of stories are much of the substance of public relations. Public relations has a poor reputation and sometimes this reputation is deserved. However, in my view, a revival of democracy is going to require citizens to reappropriate the tools of public relations—of consciously structured story telling—for democratic ends. The goal of these stories is to provide people with a certain kind of opening—an intelligible, attractive path into the community activities of computer networking, thereby making shared involvements with technology the basis for recognizing shared interests of a deeper and wider sort.

REFERENCES

Cisler, S. (1993). *Community computer networks: Building electronic greenbelts.* Cupertino, CA: Apple Computer.

Civille, R., Fidelman, M., & Altobello, J. (1993). *A national strategy for civic networking: A vision of change.* Cambridge, MA: Center for Civic Networking.

Granovetter, M. (1995). *Getting a job: A study of contacts and careers.* 2Nd ed., Chicago: University of Chicago Press.

Greenbaum, J., & Kyng, M. (Eds.). (1990). *Design at work: Cooperative design of computer systems.* Hillsdale, NJ: Erlbaum.

Kling, R., & Iacono, S. (1988). The mobilization of support for computerization: The role of computerization movements. *Social Problems 35*(3). 226–243.

Kling, R. (1989). Defining the boundaries of computing across complex organizations, in Boland, Jr., R. J. & Hirschheim, R. A. (Eds.). *Critical Issues in Information Systems Research.* Chichester, UK: Wiley.

Levy, S. (1984). *Hackers: Heroes of the computer revolution.* New York: Dell.

Morino, M. (1994). Assessment and evolution of community networking, presented at the Apple Conference on Building Community Computing Networks.

Nardi, B. A., & Miller, J. R. (1991). Twinkling lights and nested loops: Distributed problem solving and spreadsheet development, in (Greenberg, S., Ed.). *Computer-supported cooperative work and groupware.* London: Academic Press.

Odasz, F. (1991). Big Sky Telegraph. *Whole Earth Review 71*, 32–35.

Putnam, R. D. (1993). *Making democracy work: Civic traditions in modern Italy.* Princeton: Princeton University Press.

Schuler, D. (1994). Community networks: Building a new participatory medium. *Communications of the ACM 37*(1), 38–51.

Schuler, D., & Namioka, A. (Eds.). (1993). *Participatory design: Principles and practices.* Hillsdale, NJ: Erlbaum.

16

Affectionate Technology

David Durlach
TechnoFrolics

MY OWN WORK

I am currently in the process of designing and engineering 3-dimensional computer-controlled kinetic sculptures that have enough flexibility in their motions, and/or physical appearance, that one can reasonably think of composing for them. Thus, one could think of them as visual analogs for musical instruments. Alternatively, one could think of them as nonhuman dance troupes that can be choreographed. (One of the images I enjoy thinking about is that of a stage filled with all different flavors of visual instruments; thus one could have a visual symphony—perhaps performed by the deaf.)

I got into this whole area for two reasons. First, most of the high-tech art I had seen tended to be either technically sophisticated but artistically naive, or artistically sophisticated but technically naive. Since it seemed obvious to me that a better balance between these two extremes would naturally lead to wonderful "living sculptures," I was excited by the opportunities I saw in this area.

Second, I was miserable at always having to *choose* between entering environments that were technically sophisticated, innovative, and alive, but emotionally and relationally naive, or entering environments that were emotionally and relationally sophisticated, innovative, and alive, but technically naive—it seemed impossible to find work that was deeply rewarding in both these areas simultaneously. Designing and building "living sculptures" has given me one of the few opportunities I have ever had in my life where my understanding of physics, electronics, and computer systems, and my understanding of human emotional dynamics each contributed equally to the success of the final "product."

It has been meaningful and touching to see that artworks that incorporate many of the pieces of life I value, appeal so broadly to other people of all ages and all professions—ranging from professors of computer science, to street kids who dance, to art therapists. Exhibiting my work has also provided an occasion for computer scientists, street dancers, and artists to talk with one another—an occurrence that in itself is highly valuable. The whole project has been very exciting, and has reinforced my feeling that the world could use more bridges between art and engineering.

THE AFFECTIONATE SIDE OF TECHNOLOGY

In this part of the chapter I will highlight certain biases I see present in the way technology is currently viewed, biases that greatly inhibit technology's integration with the arts and humanities. Essentially, the point is that technology can be a medium of emotional expression just like painting, dance, theater, or writing; that technology need not be used only for making tools and for extending our intellectual capabilities, but can be used equally well for extending our empathy and compassion, increasing our emotional understanding of ourselves, and generally adding a richness and physical beauty to our lives. In other words, that technology is a true art form.

I further wish to show that the extent to which our current technology is cold and emotionally sterile is attributable more to our cultural biases than to anything intrinsic to the technology itself.

To begin, I would like to discuss some technological devices that are available now, that are almost exclusively being used for emotionally sterile purposes, but that with a slight change in orientation could be central elements in an emotionally and visually rich artwork.

First, let us consider robots. Frequently in robot design, high speed repeatable motions, accurate to within (say) 1/1000 of an inch, are considered highly desirable and part of the aesthetic that defines success. This is reasonable because these robots are used to assemble objects where exact positioning and speed of assembly is critical. What the robots are not frequently engineered for is grace of motion—no one funds *grace.*

We have the necessary skills, right now, to build extremely graceful robots; all we would have to do is change the perspective. The problem is that very few people engineering robots have grace of motion as the governing aesthetic (particularly since there tends to be a tradeoff between achieving repeatability and achieving grace). Thus, we have lots of robots around that can repeat their motions accurately, but are clunky and not graceful to watch.

I would like to highlight how, in a certain sense, the aesthetic governing robot design is "inhuman." Consider the sentence "I fell in love with her/his grace." It is a plausible sentence that sounds reasonable to the ear; on the other hand, the sentence "I fell in love with her/his repeatability" is ludicrous—no one cares.

The point I'm trying to make here is that the aesthetic that defines a "good" robot is not a human, emotional, rational aesthetic and if we merely changed our aesthetic, we could be surrounded with "robot art" whose grace was *stunning.*

Second, let us consider computers. There exist chess programs now that can beat all but the best human players; there also exist what are called Expert Systems that assist in diagnosing certain diseases. These things are important. Chess programs are intellectually rich and diagnostic. Expert Systems may save your life. However, neither of these structures is *emotionally* rich. Why, for example, have we chosen to write programs that evidence a "human-like" skill at playing chess, but not programs that evidence a "human-like" desire to play chess in the first place? Why are we not surrounded by programs that are lousy at playing chess, but that (seem to) care about playing a great deal, and express extreme distress if they don't get a chance to play?[1]

Computers are rarely programmed to behave in a playful fashion, or in fact in any fashion that would cause you to enjoy their company and emotionally bond with them. Again, emotional issues such as these are not generally the primary goal of the programmers. Why, I wonder, do we not have operating systems whose *primary* design goal is to convey to the user the collective sense of humor of the software engineers who implemented it, with issues like speed of response, device independence, and so on, rendered secondary?

On a humorous, but nevertheless significant note: A friend of mine created a computer "character" that you could converse with in written English. One of the things he found that was crucial to making it seem human was that it not listen to you very carefully. It had its own agenda and invariably it would bring the conversation back around to, say, its sick grandmother living in Arkansas. No matter what you talked about, eventually the grandmother that lived in Arkansas came up. It is rare that computer scientists have not-listening as a design goal—but it is a *human* characteristic.

To give a contrast to the typical state of affairs—when my sculpture *Dancing Trees* was reviewed in the *Boston Globe* magazine, the reviewer, Mopsy Strange Kennedy, wrote, "The iron clumps, with amazing anthropomorphic aplomb, begin to shiver, to plump up narcissistically, to swoon toward one another, to receive the computerized wind like gracefully moving wheat."

Now, the reason I'm bringing this in is that this is not a typical review of a new high-

---

[1] I suggest, if you think this a wild example, to consider the purpose and the tasks involved in creating fictitious but richly evocative characters in novels, theater, or dance.

tech development. It is not typical simply because few high-tech objects were designed to "plump narcissistically." Mine *was* designed to plump narcissistically. I don't mean that literally, but rather, I mean that it was designed to "plump narcissistically" as well as "plump aggressively" as well as "swish petulantly," and so on. That is, it was designed to be emotionally evocative. That was its design goal; when a particular implementation failed at that, I threw it out and tried something else.

Now, if our technological society chose "plumping narcissistically" as its *general* design goal, then we would have all kinds of high-tech devices plumping away—your toaster might burn the toast, but damn if it didn't plump! Similarly, your word processor might not do such a great a job at checking the spelling, but it would sure as hell convey the image of plumping. It's all a matter of priority.

If we, *as a culture*, chose, we could be surrounded by relationally rich and visually fascinating high-tech artworks, spanning a wide range of visual appearance and *personality*.

We have the technology, right now, to implement a device that would be sensitive (and potentially responsive) to one's mood. The very same pattern recognition technology that is *currently* used to identify characters on a printed page could be modified to detect sadness, joy, or anger in the human face; the same acoustic recognition technology that the military uses to identify submarines and aircraft by the sounds of their engine could be used to detect these selfsame emotional states from tonal qualities of the human voice.

One fact that tends to impede progress in this area is that the computer science and artificial intelligence community tends to focus on extending the head, the intellect down, as opposed to extending the heart, or loins up. It's a question of where you start. Eventually we may get *emotionally interesting* objects by making them smarter and smarter and smarter and smarter, but it's a damn long path, and we already have the ability to make things that are truly emotionally rich right now; we don't have to wait until it happens by a roundabout path.

I would like, for contrast to the intellect extending paradigm, to bring in dogs. I grew up with golden retrievers. Now, golden retrievers can't play chess very well, nor are they very good at diagnosing diseases. However, they are playful, responsive to your moods, beautiful to watch, and I consider them works of art and important additions to our world.

In addition, dogs know (at least the golden retrievers I grew up with knew) when a joke has been told. The way that they know a joke has been told is *not* by analyzing the words for meaning (as some members of the Artificial Intelligence community focus on)—they know because they pick up the laughter and the body language and the exuberance of the people in the room who have heard the joke.

We have all the technology to do that very same thing as I just mentioned that a golden retriever does. Thus, *at least*, we could have a high-tech art object that knew when a joke was told, and that alone would be an interesting thing to play around with!

There is one more perspective I would like to introduce before concluding this section. I begin by recalling to you my friend's conversational program *Racter*, and noting that its strikingly lifelike quality was a direct consequence of its *having its own agenda.* This brings me to a very important point, and that is, that our technology has almost exclusively been used for tool building.

The consequences of this cannot be stressed enough, for tools are by their very nature passive. They are designed to do nothing but what they are directed to do by the user. That is, they are designed to be extensions of our autonomy. (You do not want a hammer that refuses to hit the nail because it doesn't *want* to; you want a hammer that just hits the nail.) It is not surprising, therefore, that it is of no interest to "get to know" a tool—there is nothing there to get to know; no sense of autonomy, no hopes, dreams, fear, and so on.

I think this period of history provides us with a unique opportunity, through the advent of computers, to create devices with enough flexibility (including the potential for self-modification and learning), that the label "tool" is at best incomplete. I sincerely hope that computers do not continue to be used to predominantly for implementing intellectual tools, for if they continue to be so used, they will remain, in certain profound ways, emotionally lifeless, cold and sterile, which I think will be very sad.[2] It's time we free computers to act as central elements in creations who, like us, are both beautiful and playful—I think people are one of the highest art forms around, and really neat.

To conclude, in this section I have introduced an image of a world in which the high-tech objects in our environment are visually striking, radiate emotional accessibility, and contribute to a general feeling of warmth. I also hope to have made clear that the changes I envision do not require advances in technology so much as an alteration in people's orientation—in other words, what I am presenting might be *emotional* and *social* fiction, but is *not science* fiction.

WHY ALL OF THIS IS IMPORTANT

The first image that comes to my mind when I think of why all this is important is that of a human face expressing enchantment, calm, and satisfaction. In other words, the real reason why all this is important is because of the effect it has on people.

I have shown my work around the world, and have had the privilege to watch people's faces as they experience my piece and others. The expressions people have watching *Dancing Trees* sometimes remind me of that parents have watching their child walk for the first time; it is a combination of joy, satisfaction, and mild incredulity. More interactive pieces (created by other high-tech artists) tend to engender

---

[2] One explanation, I believe, for the current state of affairs is that the scientific tradition has given high-tech development environments a legacy in which navigation via emotional reaction is *explicitly* relegated to second place behind navigation via formal analysis. Adhering to this navigational directive is, in my opinion, gaining our culture incredible and advancements in science and technology while simultaneously crippling our ability to decide what aspects of this very same science and technology are meaningful to us.

expressions that initially consist of caution and exploration, and then rapidly extend to include wonder and joy.

Bringing audiences great joy is reason enough, I think, to pursue this area.[3] However, there are other reasons to support this work aside from audience enjoyment—reasons directly related to the concerns of computer professionals, and in particular, computer professionals worried about the directions computing and other technologies are heading.

I previously described my despair at finding environments (and tasks) that were simultaneously technically and emotionally rewarding. Unfortunately, having spoken to many, many people, I have found myself far from alone in this despair. Generally, the people who care deeply about both technical research and emotional exploration either are unhappy or have managed to split their lives into two relatively distinct parts: one that satisfies their emotional and relational needs, and another that satisfies their intellectual and analytical needs.

There are many people who understandably find this type of split lifestyle both unpleasant and rather difficult to arrange in practice.[4] Therefore, engaging in activities that naturally form bridges between the different worlds is likely to positively impact the lives of these people. Creating high-tech art is one particularly effective activity in this regard (more on this later), and thus it is not only the audience that benefits from high-tech art, but also the computer programmers and engineers who spend their lives developing it.

Let us focus next on some more subtle consequences of the mentioned split, particularly as it impacts the very content itself of high-tech research. In order to do this, I feel the need to reiterate how really pronounced is this split. It is so extreme that it is a frequent occurrence for people to think I am slightly crazy (or at least a romantic dreamer) for even *trying* to combine, in one activity, technological research and emotional exploration![5] Our society, for some reason, views these activities as mutually exclusive. Unfortunately, because of this (in my opinion completely unfounded) point of view, people who highly value and enjoy emotional exploration tend to avoid working in areas such as computer science.

The consequences of this cannot be overstressed. To begin with, the situation is

---

[3] We are discussing an art medium that is rich almost beyond dream, for it will permit joining, in a single creation, the relational sophistication of a novel, the emotional richness of a symphony, the physical beauty of a sculpture, and the immediacy, playfulness, and audience responsiveness of a street performer.

[4] The problem has some similarity to that of finding a mate: Getting involved simultaneously with two people, one emotionally warm but intellectually uninteresting, and the other intellectually challenging but emotionally cold is a solution neither satisfactory nor straightforward to navigate.

[5] It is interesting to notice that people I speak with generally fall into one of two rather distinct groups: The "artists" who readily accept the importance of emotional expression, but who don't believe technology is well suited for this; and the "technocrats" who readily grant that technology could implement the creations I envision, but don't really see the point.

dangerously self-perpetuating. What I mean by this is that the more emotionally sterile and intellectually focused high-tech development environments become, the more the devices engineered (programmed) therein will be intellectually sophisticated and emotionally simplistic. The proliferation of such devices throughout our society will then contribute to the already rampant belief that technology is suitable only for addressing the "physical," "practical," and "computational" needs of people, and is virtually useless for addressing their emotional needs. This will then lead to high-tech development environments attracting only those people who rate the practical–physical significantly above the emotional–relational, and so on.

The negative consequences of this self-reinforcing and unhealthy rift between technical research–sensitivity and emotional exploration–sensitivity are already clearly visible in areas both concrete and abstract. To give a concrete example: In contrast to the astronomical amount of money and research put into developing high-tech medical equipment engineered to keep people *physically* healthy—artificial hearts, dialysis machines, and so on, virtually no one has built sophisticated high-tech devices to address the feelings of fear, isolation, and simple boredom that frequently accompany a hospital stay.

On a more subtle note: I occasionally encounter people who react negatively or with reservation to the idea of developing creations with extremely lifelike qualities and onto which human beings would undoubtedly project. This reaction seems to imply that these people feel such creations are not already prevalent (and highly valued) in our culture. I find this quite interesting.

Let us consider novels for a moment: Perhaps the highest praise one can give a novel is to say that the characters "seemed real" and "came alive." The whole purpose of a novel is to take one into a fictitious world, in comparison to which the real world recedes into the background. Yet few people actively debate whether it is ethical or prudent to have novels loose in our culture. Puppet shows and stage dramas are similarly engineered to create, by simulating human behavior, an "illusion" onto which people strongly project emotionally, and yet such art forms are all tacitly accepted as healthy and important.

Because of the omnipresent association of the technological with the cerebral and artistic with the emotional, debates over whether it is desirable or prudent to create objects which simulate lifelike behavior are not even being held in the right arena. We *already* are creating objects and structures which simulate lifelike behavior. The significant thing to notice is that technocrats tend to create objects–structures that simulate people's cerebral and computational aspects and artists tend to create objects–structures that simulate people's emotional and relational aspects—and that is the primary thesis of the chapter.

Now, all that we have been talking about might not be so important if we were discussing, say, building sand castles. First, there is only a small fraction of our population regularly involved in building sand castles, and so if the working conditions are not ideal—well that might not be so terrible. However, in the case of creating technological devices–computer programs, a significant fraction of our culture *is* involved in their design and implementation (and an even larger fraction is directly impacted by their use).

Second, creating sand castles does not give the builder access to the kind of power that can, on the one side, greatly enrich our lives or, on the other side, wipe life off the face of this planet. So, if it turns out that the environments in which sand castles are built are a bit particular, and this particularity results in the creation of a rather narrow genre of sand castles—well, so what. However, in the case of creating high-tech devices–systems, the builders do get access to just such power.

To conclude this section: In my opinion, unless we start building objects that embody a more even balance between emotional–relational sophistication and intellectual–computational sophistication, we will head further and further down the road toward the creation of amoral juggernauts.

WHY DEVELOPING HIGH-TECH ART MIGHT HELP

I believe the high-tech art development process itself to be very healthy, for it engages, in a necessarily integrated way, the emotional sensitivity and technical expertise of the human designer.

In addition, I project that the presence of high-tech artworks in our society will help counteract the current tendency of people who choose to devote their life to emotional exploration and developing relationships, to avoid entering research areas such as computer science. This would be good.

I would like to articulate and explain further these two perspectives, both of which come in part out of my own personal experience. Let me begin by describing my own high-tech art development process.

When I work either on designing physical systems or on choreographing (programming) these systems to enact dances and dramas, I hold in my mind a human face. I then imagine what expressions I would like to elicit on that face, and what emotions would need to be evoked to prompt such expressions. I then fantasize various high-tech art mediums whose visual appearance and personality might elicit such an emotion. Then, while holding the image of this as yet unbuilt high-tech art medium clearly in front of me, I carefully examine my *own* emotional response to this fantasy creation as it runs through dramas in my mind. If I like what I *feel*, and the art medium seems sufficiently rich and flexible, I then start *intellectually* examining concrete implementation issues, such as the state of artificial intelligence, the availability of large sensor arrays, the construction time, the cooling requirements, the overall cost, and so on. If, after all this, things appear practical, I then build a small test model—a process which invariable involves solving many concrete technical problems. I then examine my emotional response to this concrete embodiment, hoping for the best.

One significant and rather unusual feature of this high-tech design cycle is that human emotional response is *never* put into the background—it is intimately coupled to the design process; all the hundreds of thought–feeling experiments act to integrate the analytic and the emotional. I contrast this explicitly to many computer programming projects where, although there usually *is* an intimate bond formed between the computer programmer and the computer, the governing aesthetic is often determined more by the relationship between the programmer's intellect, the computer hardware, and design goal of (say) speed, than by the human feelings of play, sensuality, and compassion.

I would like to focus next on the effect that seeing such high-tech artworks has on the general public.

One feature, and in my opinion a very wonderful one, of good high-tech art, is that the feeling (if not always all the thought) that went into it is as immediately comprehensible to a child as to an adult, and as meaningful to an art therapist as to a computer scientist. Thus, one's work naturally acts as a common bond between diverse groups, for it is something to which they can both immediately relate. Furthermore, since a high-tech art development project benefits equally from the skills of computer programmer and those of a psychotherapist, it is one of those rare and wonderful situations where two such different types of people are each given the opportunity to feel competent and be active contributors toward a jointly valued goal.

Another feature of this type of art is that it portrays technology being used in an emotionally rich and accessible manner. Thus, young people (and others), who are *particularly* focused on emotional issues and relationships, will not be given such a stark message that a career in technology mandates putting into the background their central concerns.[6] I would hope, therefore, that exhibiting high-tech art would induce more emotional and relationally focused people to enter careers in engineering.

One more reason to support high-tech art: A common path taken by engineers who feel alienated by their experience in engineering environments, is to step back and become policy makers, science advisors–writers, and so on. I think this is a good solution for some to adopt, but we also need such people to remain involved in the day-to-day technical tasks as will, in order that they may change the very essence of what constitutes hard engineering. Developing high-tech art presents many real problems in hard engineering, yet is an activity that might nevertheless appeal to such people. This would be good.

And finally, on a related note, if we can succeed in changing the values surround-

---

[6] Unfortunately, our educational institutions (along with the rest of the world) frequently *do* give the message, if only implicitly, that a career in engineering does require a lessening of focus on these emotional dynamics: Why, for example, are there not more engineering classes where the professor begins the lecture with a sentence something like "*Today, we are going discuss technologies well suited for conveying sadness?*" (Imagine how much poorer our world would be if writing courses restricted their discussion to the shear-strength of book bindings.)

ing high-tech development "from the bottom up—from the inside out," as the integration I have been suggesting would lead to, then we may reduce the need to pass formal legislation restricting technology's use. This would be good, for it would alleviate the resentment people invariably feel whenever laws restrict their possible range of actions (as well as help avoid all kinds of lengthy legal battles).

THE HAPPY ENDING

I would like to end this chapter with some hopeful notes. First, developing high-tech art presents, in my opinion, one of the relatively few engineering opportunities where the resultant devices can compete in sparkle and flash with devices developed by the military. This is good.

Second, because relatively little time and money has been devoted toward the serious development of high-tech art, one can make significant contributions in this area if one can remove from one's perspective certain profound biases.

Third, we are right at the forefront of an exciting revolution in microengineering. This revolution will make possible and economical the creation of sculptures with hundreds of thousands of (computer-controlled) moving elements.[7] Thus, we will (soon?) be able to have full computer control of the texture, color, light reflectivity properties, and overall shape of three-dimensional sculptures.

And finally, for the process of evaluating our high-tech art creations, I am pleased to note that each and every one of us is integrally equipped with the finest and most sophisticated testing and quality control feedback system in the world—that of our own emotional responses.

There is so much to talk about and to build—let us begin.[8]

---

[7] They have already made electric motors so small that something like 60,000 of them fit on a 1 square inch piece of material, and research in this area is proceeding forward at a furious pace.

[8] There are four books I would like to suggest whose subjects, when combined, can lead to a vision of a whole new world:

The Engines of Creation by K. Eric Drexler (Anchor Press/Doubleday), which is a comprehensive summary on the potential for what I was referring to as "micro-engineering."

Vehicles by Valentino Braitenberg (The MIT Press): He is a neuroanatomist who has conceptualized a variety of simple mechanical "vehicles" that exhibit strikingly life-like behavior.

Reflections on Gender and Science by Evelyn Fox Keller (Yale University Press), which discusses possible gender biases inherent in the manner in which we view and practice science (and thus, engineering). This book also contrasts, explicitly, cultural stereotypes of artists "vs" engineers. (It might be appropriate to note here that I consider myself a *Feminist Engineer,* and my business card lists my title as such."

You Just Don't Understand by Deborah Tannen (Ballantine Books, New York), which discusses gender differences, in both the language and intended purpose in speaking at all, of men and women engaged in dialogues within intimate couple relationships.

Author Index

Subject Index